YANKEE BOOKSELLER

The Compleat Angler ON PARADE
(From the collection of the author)

YANKEE
BOOKSELLER

BEING THE REMINISCENCES OF

CHARLES E. GOODSPEED

With Many Illustrations

GREENWOOD PRESS, PUBLISHERS
WESTPORT, CONNECTICUT

Library of Congress Cataloging in Publication Data

Goodspeed, Charles Eliot, 1867–
    Yankee bookseller.

    Reprint of the ed. published by Houghton
Mifflin, Boston.
    1. Goodspeed, Charles Eliot, 1867–
2. Booksellers and bookselling—United States—
Correspondence, reminiscences, etc. I. Title.
Z473.G57 1974   658.8'09'0705730924 [B]   73-15401
ISBN 0-8371-7173-3

Originally published in 1937 by Houghton Mifflin Company,
Boston

Reprinted with the permission of Houghton Mifflin Company

Reprinted in 1974 by Greenwood Press,
a division of Williamhouse-Regency Inc.

Library of Congress Catalogue Card Number 73-15401

ISBN 0-8371-7173-3

Printed in the United States of America

TO

MY WIFE

ACKNOWLEDGMENT

I T WOULD be a poor return for the advice and correction received by me while writing this book to mention by name those from whom the assistance came, for it might embarrass them to be associated with a work of so many imperfections. I therefore trust that this acknowledgment will be accepted by these friends as evidence of my gratitude.

I must, however, record in a more personal way my indebtedness to the work of the late Sir James Murray, his associates and abridgers, for without the companionship of *The Shorter Oxford English Dictionary* at a time of retirement in a region where that book is somewhat rare, the defects in the following pages would have been multiplied. To the manuals of the Messrs. Fowler my thanks are due to the extent that I have benefited by them. I regret my limited familiarity with these aids to authors, as I am sure that my readers would travel a smoother road with me if I had a better acquaintance with *Modern English Usage* and *The King's English*.

C. E. G.

CONTENTS

ILLUSTRATIONS

(*Ghost.*) *But soft! methinks I scent the morning air. Brief let me be.*

I. MORNING HOURS

IN AN old book not much read today there is the injunction — 'Never be ashamed of thy birth, or thy parents, or thy trade, or thy present employment, for the meanness or poverty of any of them' — an admonition which I shall cheerfully heed in these pages. For while an unbroken residence in one village for three hundred years is the only noteworthy fact in the family annals, I know of nothing in the records of the town in which my ancestors lived for that long time which requires explanation or apology.

Roger Goodspeed, sire of the line in America, came over on the second wave of English emigration. The seat of John Hampden, whose impassioned speeches against the ship-tax imposed by Charles I on his subjects were largely responsible for this movement, was in close neighborhood to the home of the Goodspeeds who lived in the parish of Wingrave in Buckinghamshire. In *The History of the Goodspeed Family* the compiler writes, 'A thorough examination of the English books on peerage fails to reveal the name of Goodspeed. To those of our great family who will regard this as a serious social blow, the author of this volume extends his profound pity, sympathy and commiseration.' In common with many people, I look on the right to bear coat-armor as a proper matter for gratification, but I am one with the family annalist in his estimation of its importance in American life. And as for the assumption of arms to which the only claim is identity of name, such an action would give me no more satisfaction than I should get from cheating myself at golf. However, there could be

no such temptation in this case: there are no Goodspeed family
arms. Roger Goodspeed was a yeoman, and the place of a
substantial yeoman in the English social order is fairly well
established. We cannot all be Stanleys or Howards; neither
can we all possess copies of the First Folio edition of Shakespeare.
There are not enough Caxtons to supply every book-collector,
but of the minor treasures of literature there is a supply sufficient to satisfy the taste and the resources of everyone. It is
not always the greatest things which bring us the most pleasure.
How precious to Jeremy Taylor must have been the jewelled
trinkets which his royal master, Charles the First, gave to him
before his death! Would the good bishop in his turbulent
diocese of Down have valued more highly the See of Canter-
bury from the hands of Charles's son?

As to my trade, the traffic in old books does indeed suggest
a certain association not wholly pleasant as when, for example,
there appeared on the steps of our old shop on Park Street in
Boston a man with a Byronesque turn to his open-shirted collar
and a rich brogue in his throat. His fist closed tightly on the
door-knob for support and his head swung slowly from side to
side like that of a huge turtle as he demanded, 'Have ye a burrd
cage? — No? — Ah I see it's only books ye have. I thought ye
had all kinds of junk!'

The disesteem in which the trading class generally has been
held for centuries is even more unpleasant than such poor-
relationships of commerce, and for this reason I am grateful to
Jeremy Taylor for my introductory text. Taylor was no demo-
crat, but as a devout Christian he may have remembered that
among the apostles there were some fishermen and a tent-
maker and that if Demetrius is a name of reproach there was,
also, a certain woman named Lydia ——

The earliest years of my childhood present a few pictures to
the recollection: the small cottage and the pond bordered by
arching willows which cast depths of quiet shade where huge
pickerel (at least they seemed huge then) poised in motionless
expectancy; the pond itself on which I fished and acquired
some skill in the use of oars in a green-painted and finely

modelled rowboat — an exercise which I have enjoyed through life — the wooded slope on the far shore with its priceless treasures of spring flowers — anemone, columbine, and, above all, the delicate blossoms of the hepatica pushing through the dry oak leaves. To this day the sight of no flower moves me as does this blue gem of the woods. At the top of the hill beyond was a house of which I recall little save that the owners were hospitable to a very small boy who, curled up on a sofa, there made his first acquaintance with adventure in the pages of Gordon-Cumming's book on lion hunting in Africa and, out-of-doors, revelled in the deliciously tart-sweet fruit of a near-by tree of Bartlett pears. Although memory does not identify these kind friends of long ago, my gratitude is as deep as it would be if I could recall their faces.

An experience which came to me a little earlier, when I was perhaps three or four years of age, I relate because it is so vivid in my memory of childhood days. With the coming of night I was often subject to a peculiar terror. It usually came with the first sleep and recurred for many years, gradually fading away as I grew older and, although brief, the effect was so awful and overpowering that I can recall it perfectly after more than sixty-five years. To express what I felt on those occasions is not so easy. It was as though the whole material universe, of which I was a part, had suddenly been exploded by a cataclysmal event which at the same time left me in ago-nizing consciousness of the terrific destruction of the whole creation.

The first school to which I was sent was near that part of the town of Needham locally known as 'Dog Corners.' It was divided in two grades, primary and grammar. I remember but one teacher. Frequently her pupils were asked to repeat some piece 'in concert.' The word had but one association to me at the time, the periodical 'Sunday School Concert' of the. church which my parents attended. Miss Hoffses belonged to a different sect and I mentally resented the intrusion of school-practice for her concerts. This matter interested me particu-larly as I had, unluckily, the ability to memorize, a talent which

I was often called upon to exercise for the entertainment of my elders, notwithstanding frequent rebellions. I can see myself now as I was at the age of five or six, clad in a plaid skirt, seated on the red ingrain-carpeted 'parlor' floor, industriously absorbing lines which began —

Go forth to the battle of life, my boy.

Of the brightly colored illuminated Bible texts given in reward for worthy efforts at memorizing, I can now call to mind but one. The Psalmist's 'When my father and my mother forsake me, then the Lord will take me up' sticks in my memory, perhaps because it puzzled me to understand why my father or my mother should ever forsake me. As I never passed that point of mystery, the consolatory assurance which ends the verse failed, with me, of its purpose. Curiously enough I remember but one book in our house — *Songs for the Little Ones at Home*. This collection was published by The American Tract Society and may be remembered by others of my generation. Verses like the following are doubtless familiar to many people:

I love little pussy, her coat is so warm,
And if I don't hurt her she'll do me no harm.

Or the pastoral:

THE COW

Thank you, pretty cow, that made
  Pleasant milk to soak my bread,
Every day and every night,
  Warm and fresh, and sweet and white.

Do not chew the hemlock rank,
  Growing on the weedy bank,
But the yellow cowslip eat
  That will make it very sweet.

Where the purple violet grows,
  Where the bubbling water flows,
Where the grass is fresh and fine,
  Pretty cow, go there and dine.

When I was ten years old my parents removed to Newton Centre, a nearer suburb of Boston. There, handicapped by the more limited school facilities of the earlier grades at Needham, I spent the four remaining years of my school life and was graduated from the grammar school at the age of fourteen. As it was decided that I should then go to work, it fortunately (I think it was then so regarded) happened that through the assistance of a friend I secured employment as office-boy in a stationery store. Comparing notes recently with Richard Lichtenstein, proprietor of Burnham's Antique Book Store and the dean of the Boston book trade, he told me he entered Burnham's Book Store in 1858 at the age of eleven. 'Well,' I remarked, 'I am sure you got paid more for your first year's work than I did.' 'You're wrong,' he replied, 'I got just two dollars a week.' I laughed, 'I can score on that point. We each were employed at one hundred dollars a year, but you had a liberal employer who gave you eight cents a week more than you were entitled to; our bookkeeper counted the pennies and my Saturday envelope contained just the amount for which my services were contracted — one dollar and ninety-two cents!'

An undergrown boy without much physical stamina, I was, nevertheless, contented and happy in my work. To clean the windows and sweep the floor or to polish up the handle of the big front door is not in the tradition of the American office-boy. His duties embrace errands to post-office and bank with minor clerical employments. In my case, they included taking down daybook charge-entries from dictation by floor-salesmen lounging against the office-window counter where they sometimes made humorous comments on my errors. I remember that they were greatly amused when I wrote 'Corks, Young & Gardner' for 'Cox,' etc. Taking press copies of the day's bills and correspondence was my most important task. This delicate operation called for the use of an iron screw press, a tissue-leaved copy-book and sheets of wet blotting paper backed by oiled pressboard. If the blotters were too wet or the press screwed unduly, the batch came out blurred, and that part of the day's work was ruined. Typewriters and carbon papers had not come into general use. Lunch was taken at Wyman's (the original Wyman's Sandwich Depot in Water Street) where a large roll enclosing a liberal slice of mustard-smeared ham, three doughnuts and cheese, plus a liberal schooner of milk made a satisfying meal at a cost of fifteen cents. I was fortunate in making friends of the clerks in the stationery store, a fine group of men and women, about fifteen in number. Leland T. Powers, one of these associates, developed, while in the stationery store, a talent of elocution which later brought him success in his career both as an entertainer and as the founder of a school of expression. My first independent business venture was undertaken when I employed Powers and the Lotus Glee Club to give an evening's performance and concert in the school hall of the village where I lived. Powers gave his often-repeated monologue 'David Garrick' and the music by the popular local quartette was sung acceptably, but a boy of sixteen who undertakes the duties of impresario, press-agent, and ticket-seller is handicapped; yet although the enterprise resulted in a profit of only fifteen dollars, even that amount was a welcome addition to my meagre earnings. Today, my work in the stationery store would be rated as child-labor, and if such employment had been permitted at all in the historic days of the Blue Eagle, would receive the minimum wage of fourteen dollars a week with a half-day allowed off for school attendance. It never occurred to me, nor to anyone interested in me, that there was any hardship in my lot, neither did I then realize that I suffered any loss by leaving school so young. The understanding of what advantage I might have gained by more schooling came much later when it dawned upon me that I had missed not only the training which is so important an asset in one's work, but also the acquaintance with languages other than English of which I have so often felt the lack. For while a boy or a man may pick up in rough-and-tumble experiences with the world enough information to carry him along, nothing is likely to compensate him for the loss of early studies and their cultural influence.

I first went to the theatre to see *Romeo and Juliet.* Margaret Mather was the star acting at the Boston Theatre, and the next morning I paid fifteen cents to a Water Street cobbler for the gaudy balcony-scene poster which adorned his window. But for several reasons the theatre never got hold of me. Although the amusement was not forbidden me, I was not encouraged to go, and my pay was so completely absorbed by household necessities that there was little left for such pleasures. Then there was the inconvenience of suburban life which, adding to a late hour the fatigue of the homeward journey, dampened the enjoyment of the stage performance, never to me of the absorbing interest which it is to most youth. There were some exceptions.

My budding activities at the time reached towards journalism. Somehow I managed to attach myself to a local newspaper as Boston correspondent. Either because I had the nerve to ask the editor to share with me the books sent him for review (in lieu of pay) or, which is more likely, because the boy's stuff which I sent him was too bad for even the country paper of the day, my efforts in journalism lasted only a fortnight. However, in that brief time I was puffed up by the possession of a press-card which gave me free admittance to the theatres. The only occasion on which I used it was at the Hollis Street, and the performance was *The Mikado.* I shall never forget the thrill which I felt as I walked down the orchestra aisle and as I sat eye and ear entranced by that bright and tuneful opera. Over and over again I saw *The Mikado* and other Gilbert and Sullivan productions — *Pinafore, The Gondoliers, Ruddigore,* and the rest. I have never tired of them nor of another old-time favorite — the colorful *Erminie* — with delightful Francis Wilson exciting uproarious laughter as he slid down the inn banisters, cutting off slices of a French loaf with a wicked-looking knife. It is in entertainment received from pieces like these and from the polite conversation comedy of the last generation that, with rare exceptions, I have found most pleasure. Melodrama always made me feel like laughing at the crucial moment, and I had not enough acquaintance with the fine art of the drama to appreciate tragedy. Any theatrical performance, serious or comic, was always followed by depression when I stepped from the lighted foyer to the chill darkness of the street.

After three years in the stationer's, I entered the employment of a company which manufactured agricultural implements. The fourteen years which followed brought me in touch with country life in the eastern provinces of Canada and the northern parts of New England and New York. Over-busy in the summer, working eighteen hours of the twenty-four at times, there was little to do for the rest of the year save in the winter, when journeying for orders brought me to the most rural parts of the territory covered by our office. Although often tedious, the long drives to remote villages, sometimes as much as twenty miles from the railroad, had, nevertheless, a pleasure of their own. As I sat within a buffalo-skin coat impenetrable to the cold dry air, companioned by a livery-stable driver, riding over roads bordered by thickets of spruce and hemlock, the winding panorama of rolling country slowly unfolded itself to the eye. Save the monotonous jingle of the sleighbells, all sounds were muffled by the deep snow, dazzlingly white in the sunshine. Occasionally a farmhouse would appear with, rarely, a solitary figure at the door, but for the most part of the way we saw no life except scattered birds flying across the road, or a cat sitting in the window of a house. On these trips, I sometimes spent the night at a farmhouse in which I gained an intimate acquaintance with the hospitable home-life of the backbone of New England. I was particularly impressed by the cheerfulness of these country people and the general comfort of their lives. It took hard labor to clear and maintain their rugged acres, of which every field bore its division walls of grey stone in memorial. Doubtless the lot of their owners was humdrum, but happiness rather than pleasure was their life's aim, and they were not made miserable by lack of so many of our necessities simply because those particular comforts and enjoyments did not exist then and, in the main, what made life endurable for one was attainable by all.

Sometimes I went to less distant places, and on a trip to Cape Cod an incident took place which will serve to introduce a word about my birthplace. The story concerns an order which I had taken at Hyannis in the hardware store of Cash and Bradford. Mr. Cash, the county sheriff, was the buyer, but was out of the store at the time. As a salesman my persuasive powers never reached par, but on this occasion I persuaded the junior partner to order a few lawnmowers and then hurried to get out before Mr. Cash should return. In this fortune did not serve as Cash appeared before I could take my departure. Learning what his partner had done, Cash shook his head and protested that it was 'too far ahead' to place orders for spring delivery. As I was anxiously considering the situation, the thought came that perhaps my name might help, so I handed him my business card. I watched him finger it listlessly. Then the bait caught his eye. He remarked, 'Goodspeed! That's a Cape name.' 'Yes,' I replied, 'I was born in Cotuit' (about twelve miles distant). 'Is that so! Ye don't happen to be Eliott Goodspeed's boy, be ye?' I answered that he was my father. '*By gosh!*' he exclaimed, '*the fust May-basket I ever hung was to your Aunt Phoebe!*' The order was saved!

Cotuit, the home of coastwise seamen, boat-builders, fishermen, and cranberry growers, is one of the southerly villages in Barnstable, a town extending across the Cape from the southern part of Massachusetts Bay to the northern shore of Vineyard Sound. In this little village I was born seventy years ago.

Strictly speaking, Cotuit is not a typical Cape village in its physical features, as it lacks the wind-swept sand-dunes and the long stretches of surf-washed shore which mark the landscape farther to the east. It is, happily, still several miles from either railway or main highway. Its principal street, entering from the older part of the village to the north, skirts a neat harbor, follows an exposed bluff to the west, and loses itself in a wood-road leading towards Popponessett Bay. Something less than a mile from the shore there is an island of considerable size, now called Oyster Harbors but in my boyhood days more picturesquely known as Hannah Screechum's Island from the legend that it was haunted by the spirit of an unfortunate wife of the pirate Kidd whom he murdered for her curiosity. Her ghost was said to flit by night through the scrubby oak and pine grove into which she had followed the freebooter when he buried his treasure thereabouts. In my time the island, now meliorated by seasonal sojourners, was uninhabited except by fiddler-crabs, land-tortoises, wood-ticks, mosquitoes, gulls, and screech-owls whose doleful hootings perhaps gave rise to this bit of folklore. In the sheltered waters between the island and the mainland are grown the oysters whose delicious flavor is so well known. Each year seed oysters are brought from Long Island Sound in small sailing craft of the place and 'planted' in the various areas known as 'grants' assigned by the town selectmen. Other local conditions may contribute to the superior quality of Cotuit oysters, but their perfection is principally due to the entrance of small streams of pure fresh water and the absence of any defilement of the harbor. These oysters, with the scallops, clams, quahaugs, and eels abounding in Cotuit waters, make generous contributions to the tables of local epicures.

Cape Cod life has been liberally exploited in literature, but the intimate nature of the social relationships found there may not be as familiar to outsiders as are the quaint characters described in popular fiction. Palfrey, the historian of New England, once made a comment on the homogeneousness of New England life. In that remark he declared that in this section a purer strain of English blood would be found than in any English county. What he said of New England, generally, is even more true of Cape Cod. Its geographical situation has served to preserve to a remarkable degree that peculiarity which attracted Palfrey's attention.

Of local characters, with whom Cape Cod is generously peopled, Cotuit has produced several. Reuben Crocker, the village bell-ringer and wood-sawyer, was the chief of them. As he travelled from door to door cutting up the winter wood-piles, his gift of rhyming improvisation furnished endless entertainment. Two girls, Ella and Celia, each munching an apple,

COTUIT OUTER HARBOR

greeted him — 'Hey, Uncle Reuben, give us a rhyme.' Promptly came the response — 'Ella, yer apple's meller. Cely, yer apple's mealy.' Mr. John Coolidge, always looking for an opportunity to help someone, accosted him one day with — 'Uncle Reuben, I have a good suit of clothes which would just fit you. You may have it on one condition. Make a rhyme for hippopotami!' 'Hoh!' replied Reuben, 'it takes such folks as you an' I to rhyme the word hippopotami.' A local greenback politician had vociferously supported the Democratic ticket in the Butler-Long governorship campaign. On hearing of the result of the election Uncle Reuben broke out with — 'Mr. Sargent, was very argent, that Butler should be elected. But they voted so strong, for Mr. Long, that Butler was rejected.' Uncle Reuben was a good man and an exemplary Christian. Peace be unto him.

In this village, where my forbears have lived since the year 1639, I was born, and although my parents moved away when I was a child it was here that I spent most of my summer vacations. When I was a boy Cotuit had not become a resort for alien people. It is true that a few Boston families had established summer homes there years before, but these — the Hoopers, Coolidges, Lowells, Perkinses, Codmans, and Morses — people of insight and sympathy, cordial, kindly, and helpful, had become as much a part of the life of the community as the native folk themselves. Happy in the hospitality of my father's relatives, I passed the time in fishing for scup and flounders and spearing eels, gathering beach-plums while rambling along the island shore, or sailing toy boats which my great-uncle whittled beautifully from soft pine and rigged with marvellous skill.

The social life of a community whose members are nearly all descended from the remote original settlers presents problems of kinship and tradition which are of exceeding interest, and within it the inhabitants of any generation are bound by ties more significant than those of the ordinary New England village. The nearest approach to wealth in Cotuit of those days was found in a small group of the more successful shipmasters.

At the other extreme there was lack of possessions but little destitution. If fire destroyed a cottage or its contents, if someone broke an arm or leg, if, through peril of the sea, there were widows and orphans, the needs of the distressed were relieved by the neighbors less in a spirit of charity than in the feeling that the sufferer was one of the family. A refusal to respond on such occasions would have been unthinkable. So close was the community life that to lock one's door at night would have been thought an affront to the rest of the village.

From the hours spent in this environment I call to mind an incident which is an excellent example of the fascinating subject of coincidence. Always given to hobbies, my chief interest then was in the collection of 'minerals.' One hot summer noon as I walked along the sandy cart-path beneath scrub pines which led to Popponessett Bay, there came to me a sentence from some book I had read (probably an English work applying to a different geological situation) — 'Amethysts are often found by the sea-shore.' As this quotation passed through my mind, I said to myself with some petulance, 'I don't see why I never can find any' — quite an irrational idea as quartz in any form is not geologically native to Cape Cod. Nevertheless the next instant my eye caught sight of something bluish in the wagon-rut. Stooping down, I picked up two small attached crystals of amethyst! They were pale in color and the facets were worn by friction with the sand, but they were really amethysts, doubtless deposited there on the melting of the glacier by which the land was once covered.

To these brief notes of early life which I have set down to show some of the formative influences of youth, a word should be added concerning my first interest in reading. Possibly it was because of an inferiority of physique which did not allow me the proficiency in sports which other boys enjoyed that I turned to books. Mr. Dooley might have had a case like mine in mind when he said, 'Books is for them that can't enjoy themselves in any other way.' My very first reading of fiction was fortunately of a good sort. The pioneer stories written by the Reverend Elijah Kellogg, *Lion Ben of Elm Island* and the

rest,[1] were of absorbing interest to me. On the other hand
(sound juvenile judgment!) I disliked the priggish characters
of the popular 'Oliver Optic' books. The Waverley Novels
which I read a few years later were then as they have been
ever since my favorite works of fiction. Contrariwise (excepting,
of course, *The Posthumous Papers of the Pickwick Club*), Dickens
has long since ceased to interest me. Although it takes some
courage to confess it, I do not like the children of Dickens.
'What! Not like Little Nell or Tiny Tim or Oliver Twist!' I
hear someone exclaim. Yes, in honesty I must say that I find the
pathos of these characters so exaggerated that it makes them
painful. As Barrie puts it, Dickens 'introduces children into his
stories that he may kill them to slow music.' This element of
pathos, overworked and unrelieved by healthy qualities of normal childhood, leaves me unsympathetic, but on the other hand
when Dickens pictures such an engaging young imp as Master
Bardell, I find the glimpse he allows us all too brief. If I were
voting with the Dickens Fellowship, my favorites would surely
fail of election as I should like to have at least one ballot counted
for that out-and-out reprobate, Sally Brass, and another for
that picaresque character, Alfred Jingle. I am sure Dickens
himself must have loved Jingle! (How came it that the favorite
of Marjorie Fleming gave us no children to love? Did Scott
find that children are no easier to manage in literature than
they are in life?)

With this feeling towards Dickens, it now seems strange
that with adolescence there came to me a dangerous tendency
towards sentimentality. I read Keats, whom I admired ex-
travagantly, committing to memory many pages of *Endymion*
and, to better purpose, the wonderful odes and sonnets. And
then I came upon Ruskin whose eloquence and moral fervor
cast on me a spell which, although the years have tempered my
uncritical enthusiasm, I have never shaken off.

My earliest purchases of books were from a New York publisher of cheap editions put out for a few pennies per volume,

---

[1] Yet they are 'lifeless and wooden' according to *The Flowering of New England.*
I wonder if Mr. Brooks read the Kellogg books when he was a boy!

but it was not long before my taste in bookmaking improved, and one day a salesman in Estes and Lauriat's, to whom I confided my interest in Ruskin, went to a safe and brought out a large octavo volume in a chocolate-colored binding stamped with an allegorical design, showing it to me as a special favor. It was a first edition of *The Seven Lamps of Architecture* and was valued at seventy-five dollars!

From that time I became a haunter of bookshops and auction rooms, a searcher of junk-shops and odd-corners. The embryo bookseller was there. It was a good while before I came to the door of the bookshop, but I was on the road.

In all the official references of the thirteenth and fourteenth centuries to the book-dealers, the ground is taken that they formed a class apart from mechanics or from traders in ordinary merchandise. They were considered to be engaged in an intellectual pursuit, and were treated as members of a profession. . . .
GEORGE HAVEN PUTNAM.

II. OLD-TIME BOOKMEN

I MAY perhaps be expected to say a word here about my introduction to the occupation of bookselling. To those older readers who recall the depression of 1893 and the years immediately following, it is quite unnecessary to explain how I found myself without a job in the fall of 1898. The silver lining in that cloud was the opportunity of fulfilling a long cherished desire. Now, I said, I can do what I always wished to do; I can try bookselling. The love of books had become a passion with me. I cared for them not only for their contents; I was keenly, if not too intelligently, interested in editions and publishers and the harmony of paper, type, illustrations, and binding, which leads towards perfection in bookmaking. The last three years of my employment in the agricultural implement business had been spent in lower New York, and Ann Street became a convenient and seductive noontime resort. So, when a change of business was forced upon me, I went to Isaac Mendoza, who still occupies the store at No. 15 which I most frequented at the time, and said, 'Mr. Mendoza, I have lost my position here in New York. I am going back to Boston and in these times there are no new jobs to get. I am planning to go into the secondhand book business. What do you think of my chances?'

I got my first encouragement from his reply, 'I never knew but one man who failed in it; that was Tom——, and he drank rum and played the races.' Stimulated by this assurance I invested my savings of a few hundred dollars in miscellaneous purchases at Bangs's Auction Rooms and some 'remainders' which I bought from Mendoza. The latter included a lot of books from the bankrupt stock of Stone and Kimball, of which Mendoza had been a large buyer. Coming to Boston I called at Libbie's Auction Rooms. 'Mr. Libbie,' I said, 'you have known me for a number of years' (as a buyer of little things with small profit to him, I fear!) 'and I am thinking of opening a secondhand bookstore. What do you think of my prospects?' 'Mr. Goodspeed,' he replied, 'if you can get a job at twenty dollars a week, don't think of going into the secondhand book business.' I was leaving a salary of twenty-seven hundred dollars a year, and twenty dollars a week seemed a meagre sum on which to support a family. But the die was cast. Like others in similar circumstances, I was not looking for advice but for encouragement. Although Mr. Libbie failed me in that, he proved a good and helpful friend during the whole period of our acquaintance which terminated with his death in 1904.

Back in Boston with my few boxes of books I had next to find a store or 'shop' as I called it. (Most book-dealers had 'Book Stores' in those days. I liked 'Book Shop' better and so I adopted that word.) Thinking that the most direct way of securing a location was to go to a real estate office, I went into Whittier's agency where I was politely received. The first question asked was how much rent I wished to pay for the small premises I needed, the clerk at the same time pulling out a card index. I replied, 'Not over fifty dollars a month.' Bang closed the drawer! Driven to look for myself, I wandered about the streets finally fixing on the vicinity of Boston Common as a desirable neighborhood. Walking up Park Street, I saw about half the way to Beacon Street a low basement window with the sign 'To Let.' The rent was fifty-five dollars which I thought I could manage and I took the place immediately. Pessimists told me I should fail because all previous occupants had been unsuccessful; when it appeared that my venture was not to miscarry, the same critics credited the result to the superior location.

Nothing in my previous business experience seemed of such

importance as that exciting first week. Christmas was at hand. The beautifully printed books of Stone and Kimball, not distinguished in contents, but attractively bound, were offered at twenty-five cents each, suggesting something between a Christmas card and a gift. The ladies of Beacon Hill and the Back Bay were appreciative of the opportunity to buy Christmas gifts for so little and they sold quickly. Odd volumes of Poe in the Stone and Kimball edition of which I had bought a quantity were sold at fifty cents, and my personal collections of Ruskin and of Doctor Thomas William Parsons, the translator of Dante, whose books I had collected for several years, gave a slightly superior flavor to the stock. My furniture was a chair and a wooden box covered with denim which, when stood on end, served for a desk. A shelf nailed inside the box held the three volumes of *American Book Prices Current* (all that were then published) and these comprised my reference library. The cash receipts of the first week were one hundred and forty-four dollars. At that time (this was in the days before accounting practices had come to be dictated by a government-partnership) I reckoned no transaction in my sales until the books had been paid for.

I was once called on for counsel by a lady whose son wished to open a bookstore in another city. He asked for several thousand dollars for himself and the friend who was to share the enterprise with him. Would I advise her to give him the money? I answered 'No,' but added that if the boys had a love for books and some knowledge of business, I would approve their starting on a smaller amount provided they would keep half of it in cash for working capital.

In my own case I used all of the money I had, about six hundred dollars, for the purchase of books; I should not, however, advise another to enter business so handicapped. Yet the control of too much money is liable to result in extravagant purchases of stock. At one time I was asked by a customer if I would accept from him twenty thousand dollars to be invested in the business, an offer which was wisely declined. The investor would naturally expect a larger return on the loan than the bank rate of interest; this would be an added expense and there was no prospect that the business could be increased sufficiently to justify it.

When the bookseller's means are limited, he is prudent and exercises judgment in making selections. The ever-present opportunities of private buying, the insidious auction room where purchases are always made in haste and sometimes regretted as quickly — these are the efficient solvents of a fat bank account. It was on such points that I found the value of previous business training. Mowing-machines and rare books have nothing in common, but as merchandise they are subject to the same principles of economics by which those trading in them must be governed. The bookseller must temper the enthusiasm of the collector with the reserve of a banker. He should have no difficulty in doing this. It is only necessary for him to obtain the views of his banker on the value of first editions as merchandise. Regardless of what speculative propositions in other lines of business may have received his favorable consideration, I am of the opinion that if the average banker were rash enough to advance, say, ten thousand dollars on a Shakespeare quarto, he would enjoy little sleep until that loan was repaid.

One of the very earliest customers to discover the new Park Street bookshop was the Reverend Monsignor Arthur T. Connolly. Father Connolly was an outstanding priest of the Boston diocese. He made a fine collection of Americana and American first editions which he gave to Saint Charles College, Baltimore, Maryland, before his death. Another early buyer was the Reverend Harlan P. Amen, principal of Phillips Exeter Academy. He bought my Ruskin books and they are now in the Academy library. Other buyers found the shop and, having made its bow to the public, Goodspeed's took a place in the book trade of Boston.

Fancying myself possessed of some ability at advertising, after much laborious thought I adopted the motto 'Anything that's a book,' meaning by this that I intended to cater to all classes of buyers. That little phrase, although not bad for a motto, has been a source of embarrassment at times, being quoted against us by would-be sellers disappointed when we have had to decline their offers of unsalable books. A motto should have a trade-mark to bear it. The Heintzemann Press suggested a bookish design featuring a tonsured monk absorbed in the reading of his office as he made 'goodspeed.' The facsimile given here is from the first rough drawing before the motto was given its final form.

At the conclusion of his first few weeks in business the young dealer will find some difficulty in replenishing his shelves. A considerable part of his receipts has already gone to pay his personal and business expenses. Some of his sales have been on credit. His contacts with sellers of books are yet to be made. Faced with this problem, I was for a while driven to the device of shifting the stock. Monday morning the contents of the rear shelves would be moved to the front, the top shelves to the middle, the middle to the bottom, and so on, so that even the most frequent visitor remarked on the changes, not realizing that he was looking at the same books in different positions.

My relations with the Boston booksellers were from the start, as they always have been, most cordial. Prominent among them was George Emery Littlefield, at the time dean of the Boston secondhand book trade. Mr. Littlefield was a Harvard graduate and had a decided bent towards historical research. He specialized in Americana, particularly in genealogy. I found him a good friend, always most helpful, and in return for his good-will I made no effort to enter the field of genealogical books in which the profit was meagre enough even for one. This amity reminds me of a story told recently by my bookselling colleague and neighbor, Andrew McCance, when introducing me to a customer. 'You see,' he said, 'Mr. Goodspeed and I have an understanding between us by which he sends to me people having Christian Science literature to sell and I send the sellers of Americana to him. Like Tony, who had a sidewalk permit for his fruitstand from the bank. A friend asked him for a loan of ten dollars. Tony was sorry but, "I have agree with da Bank. They no let me." "What you mean, they no let you?" "Well, when I come here they say, 'Tony, we no sell da banan, you no loana da mon.'"'

Cornhill, a short street descending the lower slope of Beacon Hill easterly from Scollay Square, was at the time of which I write, even as it is now, distinguished by the old-book shops on either side. The aspect of Littlefield's establishment at No. 67 was rather unattractive. Its walls were lined by shelves built to the ceiling. These and a central stack contained a miscellaneous lot of books in which the proprietor appeared to take little interest. His desk, surrounded by rows of Americana and buttressed by dusty piles of pamphlets, was on a raised platform in the rear. Here he sat and wrote or entertained his cronies who, although not numerous, included most of the Boston collectors of the time. The Hollingsworths (Amor L., Sumner R., and Zachary T.), William G. Shillaber, John P. Woodbury, Alfred Bowditch, Frederick L. Gay, Doctor David Hunt, Charles E. Stratton, James F. Hunnewell, Henry F. Tapley, John W. Farwell, and Doctor Samuel A. Green, to mention only those not now living, were the customers with whom he had the most intimate relations. He was brusque in manner and intolerant of casual visitors. When I was in his store one day a woman called with a bundle of books to sell — trash, of course. 'Don't want them,' was the curt comment. The owner was persistent — 'What's the matter with them?' 'They are not old enough.' 'Not old enough? Here's one printed almost a hundred years ago.' 'I want books more than a hundred years old.' Exit, with the indignant retort, 'Huh! They didn't print books that old!'

Opposite Littlefield's was the shop of W. G. Colesworthy. Colesworthy was a genial soul who conducted a business inherited from his father. On Monday mornings — the parsons' 'blue-Monday' — a gathering of ministers mostly of the Methodist persuasion would be found in Colesworthy's. A few steps below, the venturesome book-prowler might wander into Bird's, only to be repelled by a mysterious atmosphere of secrecy and suspicion which would cause him to make a hasty retreat. This peculiarity for some incomprehensible reason often marked such places in the old days, how much to their disadvantage it is not necessary to say.

Overshadowing these and the other neighboring shops in importance and, as if conscious of its superior attractions, at a little distance below them towards the end of the street near Adams Square, was Bartlett's. N. J. Bartlett and Company, a concern dealing primarily in new theological works, was the centre of interest to the bookish Episcopal clergy, as Colesworthy's in a lesser degree attracted those of other denominations. The real interest in this place, however, lay in its excellent stock of the best books to be obtained in the London market. Here would be found Aldines, Elzevirs, Baskervilles, Bodonis, Bulmers, Pickerings — all that the world has esteemed as models of typographical excellence. English literature of the seventeenth and eighteenth centuries would be well represented and the visitor would be greeted by an array of sets of the English classics, *Spectators*, *Tatlers*, editions of Pope, Swift, Fielding, Richardson, and their contemporaries, rich in warm tones of shining calf. There also might be a few first editions — Goldsmith's *Vicar*, *A Sentimental Journey*, Boswell, Johnson's *Dictionary*, or an early *Robinson Crusoe* or *Gulliver*. All of these were then to be had for moderate prices. The memorialists and historians from the Georgian to the Victorian period were by no means neglected, neither were those books with the beautiful colored aquatint plates which illustrated so many English works in popular favor in the first quarter of the nineteenth century lacking. In short there would be found in Bartlett's all the volumes which Bostonians bought fifty years ago when the ambition to acquire a general library of fine books was more common than it is now.

Of Bartlett's principal salesman, William H. Chase (in after life a partner in the firm), I shall have something to say farther on. The senior Bartlett with whom I had only a slight acquaintance had at that time become less active. I remember him as a grey-bearded, silent figure seated near the door greeting his acquaintances with a nod as they passed on to the rear of the store where Mr. Chase, perhaps engaged in stroking the back of a favorite cat, was ready with a quick, twinkling smile. Chase was the genius of the place. Mr. Bartlett's son Ned, when he first came into his father's store after graduation from Harvard, was given the morning floor-sweeping as one of his duties. At the time I first knew him he was taking his place in the store management, but had not yet begun to alternate with Mr. Chase in the latter's semi-annual trips to London for the purchase of stock. Ned Bartlett never equalled Chase in book-knowledge and lacked the enthusiasm of the older salesman. He had, nevertheless, an engaging personality and when, at a later time, he and I spent a few days together in London, I found him an agreeable companion. On that occasion we had forgotten the bank-holiday which follows Whit-Sunday, and as we were debating how the idle time should be spent Holland was suggested. Over the Channel we went and wandered around the streets of Amsterdam. I recall our lunch in that city where, in the vast restaurant of Krasnapolsky's in the Warmoesstraat, we two helpless Anglo-Saxons conned the interminable menu presented by the waiter, noted the

N. J. BARTLETT
From an etching by Sidney L. Smith

seventeen (or was it twenty-seven?) varieties of omelettes followed by several pages of dishes unknown to either of us and
called for — mutton chops! As for drinking our habits were
similar, for, while I was a total abstainer, Bartlett was also
abstemious and seldom accepted alcoholic drinks. In Holland
I was, therefore, mildly shocked when Ned ordered a glass
of gin,[1] a beverage which had not attained its modern quasi-
respectability, its consumption at that time being, as I supposed, generally restricted to the lowest orders of the London
slums. It was on this London trip that Bartlett introduced
me to a typical British bachelor hostelry — the Tavistock
in Covent Garden. Here the late diner was served from a
buffet where the joints were exhibited for his selection, and
here also the American, new to the mysteries of English customs, might be initiated into some of those unfamiliar ways
of London life which could be studied by him to his advantage.
That bumptiousness too frequently exhibited by our countrymen when abroad is often due as much to ignorance as to bad
manners. Some London-domiciled American could do his
compatriots a real service by compiling a manual of foreign
customs and conventions, subjects upon which the ordinary
travel book touches casually, if at all. Such a work would
smooth the path of the tourist and make his travels of more
pleasure to himself and of greater credit to his country.[2] Simply
bad manners, however, are responsible for such incidents as this:
I was waiting in a London picture-card shop while the elderly
proprietor was showing some Swiss photographs to a stout
American matron. When he called her attention to some un-
usually fine Alpine scenery she remarked with contempt, 'Well!
We've got lots of bigger mountains than those in our country!'
When she had gone I tried to offer a modest apology for her
rudeness, to which the Englishman replied, 'Oh! I don't mind
it now. I have been listening to that sort of person for forty
years!'

[1] It is said that gin was, in Colonial days, reckoned to be fit only for slaves.
[2] Two chapters of Mary Ellen Chase's recently published *This England* seem to
answer this need for the traveller in that country.

The ground floor of the Tavistock was a part of the Market. Here the early morning scene displayed a medley of green-groceries, flowers, and fruits, with country-grower attendants, hucksters, and city buyers, all so novel in aspect as to tempt the American guest to an early rising. It has been several years since I was last in London, but I understand that the old Tavistock has gone its way, unable to resist the innovations of progress.

Somewhat along the same lines as Bartlett's was the stock of Little and Brown, then located on Washington Street near the Boston Globe building. In those days it was not the great publishing house into which it has grown since, although it did a notable business in the publication and sale of law books. One side of the deep and high-studded store was filled with long rows of red-labelled sheep-bound sets of Massachusetts Supreme Court Reports and other legal works. The opposite wall was set apart for the display of choice English literature. There were sets of Pickering's edition of the British poets in the traditional polished calf bindings of Zaehnsdorf; collections of Napoleonic memoirs in Rivière's best half-levant morocco, and the usual nine-volume set of Ruskin (*The Seven Lamps of Architecture, Modern Painters,* and the *Stones of Venice*), which were then never lacking from a stock of the better English books. There, too, were collected sets of the best editions of Thackeray, Dickens, Scott, and Trollope, to mention but a few of the standard works, all finely bound in leathers of prismatic colors — books for the gentleman's library.

That neither of these firms carried in stock the more expensive books which were to be found on the shelves of some dealers in New York City should not be attributed to a lack of enterprise. Not more than a few drops of the golden shower which irrigated the metropolis in normal times or dazzled the streets with its plenitude in days of super-prosperity ever fell in Boston. When, at a later time, Little and Brown were about to move to Beacon Street, Hulings Brown said to me, 'I want to have a fine book-parlor up there. I should like to stock it with books that are really rare and valuable. I want to make it the

George D. Smith bookshop of Boston.' I told him that, in my opinion, he could not make it pay. Heavy local taxes, interest on the investment, depreciation, and other overhead charges would be too heavy a burden. There has never been a volume trade of rare books in Boston sufficient to make profitable such a stock which, in value, might amount to half a million or more of dollars.

If both Bartlett and Little and Brown catered to a somewhat limited range of interests, the firm of Estes and Lauriat (soon to become Charles E. Lauriat Company) was on the lookout for a wider clientèle. They also aimed to supply the private buyer of choice editions, but much of their trade was in books which had come from old English estates and bore the armorial insignia of noble families — works of English topography, illustrated books of bygone days, sets like *Lodge's Portrait Gallery*, *Vanity Fair* with its clever portrait-cartoons, London *Punch*, publications of the English learned societies. Of course there was the usual assemblage of books with plates by that greatest of English illustrators, George Cruikshank. Their stock abounded in such publications as these, and as they also dealt extensively in new books, their sales at retail must have exceeded those of either of their principal competitors.

Readers may wonder that no mention has been made of Boston's oldest book establishment, the famous Old Corner Book Store. At the time of which I am writing, it still occupied the original building at the corner of School and Washington Streets from which it took its name, one of the few surviving examples of early Boston architecture. I was not in business, however, in the palmy days when Oliver Wendell Holmes and his famous contemporaries made a meeting-place of this shop. It is, moreover, my intention to consider only those establishments which specialized in old and rare books, so I will pass on to some others of this class.

I first knew Burnham's Antique Book Store, the oldest institution of its kind now doing business in Boston, while Burnham was alive. He occupied a part of the basement of the Old South Meeting House, in which one of Goodspeed's shops

is now located. The basement, before its renovation and
further excavation, was a dark labyrinth of alleys, to be visited only by the light of a candle. Many of the books were
covered with the dust of years which made a general examination of the shelves impossible and, indeed, the visitor was not
expected to attempt it. If he came with a definite want he
would be served, as there was some arrangement of the stock
which was familiar to the attendants. At Burnham's death
the business was taken over by two of his old assistants, one of
whom, Mr. Richard Lichtenstein, who continues on Cornhill,
has the preëminence of conducting now the oldest old-book
shop in the city. Of smaller dealers, besides those on Cornhill
already mentioned, there were many to whom book-hunters
from the country over resorted when in Boston. Men like
Francis Wilson, John F. Hurst, F. M. Bristol, J. DeWitt Miller,
and others of even greater prominence were familiar figures in
these shops. On the dusty shelves of Cornhill and Bromfield
and Brattle Streets many a treasure was to be found. The
Johnsonian form of DeWitt Miller — coatless, perched precariously at the top of a ladder in Smith and McCance's —
was a scene of which I should now like to have something better
than a mental picture. Miller was a great collector and a little
vain, I believe, of his fancied likeness to Doctor Johnson. He
assembled a vast library of books which was sold a few years
ago. Miller, Wilson, Eugene Field, Doctor Gunsaulus, and
Bishop Bristol formed a remarkable group of book-collecting
friends who, with the exception of Field and Gunsaulus, were
regularly seen in Boston.

The firm of DeWolfe, Fiske and Company, now as a corporation located in a fine building on Park Street, occupied in 1898
a store which they called 'The Archway' on the west side of
Washington Street near its Bromfield Street corner. Before
buying the 'Archway' business of Lovering, a bookseller who before my day had moved to New York — and perhaps out of this life
— DeWolfe and Fiske were salesmen for the house of D. Lothrop
and Company, publishers of children's books. Following, I suppose, along the lines of these concerns, the new firm cultivated a

new-book trade with public libraries, more profitable then than now, and, being a time when small-town booksellers existed, they wholesaled extensively the sort of books — juveniles, standard reprints, etc. — which were in most demand through the country districts. With these activities to occupy their principal attention it is not strange that the trade of this firm in secondhand books, although vigorously conducted, did not progress beyond the simple merchandising of them. Consequently, it followed that the counters of 'The Archway' (containing the secondhand department of the store), which was entered from the sidewalk without hindrance of wall or door, were particularly watched by bargain-hunters. On the rumor of a fresh lot of books at 'The Archway' this group would come scurrying down the street as early-rising boys in my youth would scamper to the chestnut-grove on a frosty morning. Lined up along the counters the eager-eyed collector would hastily turn over the volumes heaped before him, jealously watching the while to see what prizes were being grasped by his neighbor. Stories of 'Archway' bargains are still occasionally recited by veterans amongst the local collectors.

Smith and McCance were then located on Bromfield Street. Smith was a dapper little fellow whose qualities in no respect matched those of his modest partner. I have known Andrew McCance more intimately than I have known any other Boston bookseller, and to none of them am I under so many obligations of courtesy and friendship; a friendship once expressed by an unsolicited loan of five hundred dollars for the purchasing of a library. Andrew's fund of anecdote is inexhaustible and, what is more important, through some mysterious ability he can always produce a story to fit the occasion. There was once a woman whose purchases of books were confined to the sidewalk cases, and she had the bad habit of boasting to other dealers of the bargains which she found. One day finding Mr. McCance in an unresponsive mood she exclaimed, 'I just bought *Sartor Resartus* in Mr. Goodspeed's ten-cent box. Now wasn't *that* a bargain?' To which he replied, 'Did I ever tell you about Michael Murphy? Well, I will.

Michael Murphy was long suspected of illegal liquor-selling, but the police were unsuccessful in their search for evidence. One day they arrested Michael, although all that could be offered against him was the possession of a pint of whiskey. Tom Gargan, his lawyer, offered no defense, but just before the case went to the jury he got up and addressed Murphy's bleary face with "Michael Murphy, stand up! Look at the jury! Gentlemen of the jury, look at Michael Murphy! Now, gentlemen, I want you, after seeing my client, to tell his honor the judge if on your solemn oath you can say that you believe that if Michael Murphy had a pint of whiskey he would *sell* it?"'

As some of the shops in Cornhill attracted congenially minded people, so McCance's was the meeting-place of friends. People dropped in there because they liked the proprietor and were entertained by his stories, or often because he was notoriously easy to touch by the unfortunate. Another anecdote tempts me, the appeal of a poor old school-teacher. 'Mr. McCance, I left my purse at home this morning and have only five cents in my pocket. Can you lend me twenty cents to get some lunch?' Pulling his hand full of change from his pocket he thrust it before her. 'Twenty cents won't buy you a lunch. Here, take what you need.' 'Do you *really* mean it!' she exclaimed, tears rising in her eyes. 'Oh, Mr. McCance, are you *Irish?* I *always* thought you were Scotch!'

Even the briefest sketch of the book trade of Boston would be incomplete should it fail to mention a specialist who has become known all over the land as the pioneer in American first-edition bibliography. Wherever there is interest in the collecting of first editions, the name of P. K. Foley is known. Librarians and students as well as collectors are indebted to him for his intimate acquaintance with American literature. Foley generously shared his knowledge with all who came to him for information in his field of research, and many important collections are indebted to him for the interest which he took in their development. Anyone who visited Foley in his office where, surrounded by the implements of his profession, he sat in retired dignity, or who came upon him in a quiet corner

P. K. FOLEY

of McCance's where he was always to be found between six and eight of the evening, was impressed by the meeting of an unusual personality. And those who knew him only through correspondence have long since learned to prize his remarkable epistolary talents. No collector will ever destroy Foley's letters to him, for they are an asset to any collection.

The auction business of C. F. Libbie and Company, at the time when I first knew it, was conducted in a large, well-appointed room, the walls lined with portable bookshelves on which the books were carefully arranged in catalogue order. The auctioneer was seated before a desk mounted on a large table to which the books were brought from the shelves in small lots as the sale progressed. This arrangement made it possible to examine any volume up to the last second before the fall of the hammer. Libbie sat at the rear of the room, his left hand resting upon the catalogue where mail orders were recorded. At his right was the sales record. He executed with uplifted left hand the bids entrusted to him and with the other recorded the sales on sheets which were sent to the book-keeper as soon as they were filled. The bills made from these sheets were all finished and the books ready for delivery by the time the sale was ended. It was partly owing to a perfect system of which this was a detail, but more to Mr. Libbie's integrity, that the business prospered.

To this enticing resort I gravitated while yet with the agricultural implement company, whose place of business was on South Market Street. Too often, I fear, I stole an hour which ought to have been employed in making sales-lists of rural customers for plowshares or mowing-machine knives to indulge in the excitement of a book sale. Often from a rear seat I would venture a timid bid when the book on the desk appeared to be going at a bargain. This was usually sufficient to revive the bidding and leave me behind the running. An occasional success would tear me with fear that I had overbid the value. Perhaps there was a defect in the book overlooked by me but detected by the underbidder. George D. Morse, who sold for Libbie, was an entirely competent auctioneer. His attitude was not obsequious. He was alert, confident, aggressive. The instant he got started the race was on, slow at first, but as the bidding quickened he increased the pace and urged the sale as a jockey pushes his mount. When the book was knocked down, he would pause to recover his wind before taking up the next volume before him. Stan V. Henkels of Philadelphia and George D. Morse were the two most competent men in America in their line. Although they differed from each other in every other respect, both were good judges of their audiences: Morse had a dry wit, but Henkels's gift was of satire, often sharp in its thrust. Morse was a shrewd Yankee; Henkels, although a Philadelphian by birth, having lived when young in Virginia, assumed the attitude of an unreconstructed Southern fire-eater and also dressed the part. He professed to hate the memory of 'Abe Lincoln!' but he worshipped even the relics of Washington. One day Morse invited himself to lunch with me and, in return, offered some helpful suggestions in regard to the book business. One of these I remember with amusement. 'When you get out your Americana catalogue, be sure and put in a set of *The New England Genealogical Register*.' 'But I haven't a set,' I replied innocently. 'Makes no difference,' he said, 'Littlefield always has one, and if you get an order he will have to give you a dealer's commission.' This was about the time I had begun to issue monthly catalogues. When the first of them was ready, Libbie, partly to encourage a new customer but also as an expression of his own friendly spirit, contributed the use of his mailing list.

The sale of books at vendue has been practised not only abroad but in this country from early times. Whether in the average case this is the best means for the disposal of libraries is an open question, much depending upon the kind of books, their value, and the circumstances under which the sale may be conducted. In London and New York such sales are a regular feature of the book trade; in Philadelphia they are held with less frequency and, since Libbie's day, in Boston sporadically. To serve the public to its advantage, the auction-house must have a skilled, highly efficient organization. It

LITTLEFIELD'S, ON CORNHILL

offers at times great speculative advantages for unique items and it also presents the danger of loss, especially when failing the liberal support of dealers. Unscrupulous practices on the part of consignees or even bidders have not been infrequent in the past and, being difficult to check, they sometimes bring this method of sale into disrepute. On the one hand collusion of buyers to depress the values of books sold at auction has been known, while on the other side we find owners seeking to establish fictitious values by self-bidding. In the latter instance the volume knocked down to the owner at a high price would afterwards be offered by him to an unsuspecting buyer for a smaller amount upon the representation of what 'another' copy had just brought at auction! These artifices are fairly well known and they are fortunately practised less frequently than in past days.

In Bagford and Oldys's *Notes on London Libraries*, there is this interesting eighteenth-century comment on book-auctions in London.

> The booksellers abroad may be more learned and make better judgment of their books than ours, but I believe few are better stored. I have known several of them mark at auctions in their catalogues the prices that books go off at, and so settle a value of their own to persons conformably, which is a most erroneous valuation, to make a general rule of a particular inclination or necessity. I have given, myself, twenty shillings for a thing that is worth to no other man, I believe, a tenth part of that money, nor to me after I had some little circumstance out of it. The atheistical book of Giordano Bruno sold at Paul's Coffee house for 30 *l.* in 1709; it has scarcely sold for so many pence since. And a complete Holinshead rose there some years after to 80 *l.*; it has never sold again for so many shillings. The value of it was thought to lie in its being complete, but now the castrated sheets are reprinted you may have many of the books complete, yet they will bear no extravagant valuation; therefore, the value arose neither from a desire of knowledge which the scarce part would communicate, neither from its intrinsic remarkableness or instruction, nor even from any use to be made of it, but merely from the empty

property of singularity, and being, as the contending purchasers erroneously thought, no where to be found. If there were no foolish bidders, there would be no extortionate sellers of books.

No less interesting is the following extract from a famous book of a hundred years later describing Doctor Syntax at a book auction.

At length the solemn auctioneer
Did in his hand a tome uprear,
All gilt, and in morocco green,
Fit for the boudoir of a queen;
I know not why so very fine,
Thought Syntax, for the work is mine:
But now I shall most surely know
What to fair truth the work doth owe,
And public fancy may bestow;
For here its value I shall see,
Without a spice of flattery.
Its value was most warmly stated,
Its Author's talents celebrated,
Its humour, verse and moral powers
Suited to grave and laughing hours,
And deck'd by nature and by fun,
With the gay skill of ROWLANDSON.
Syntax delighted beyond measure
Nodded to express his pleasure,
But started when the auctioneer
Told him he was the purchaser.

AUCTIONEER

The book's knock'd down at two pounds two,
The money to be paid by you.

SYNTAX

This sure is reas'ning most absurd,
Why, Sir, I never spoke a word.
I might have nodded twice or thrice,
To see the book fetch such a price:
With secret pride I was complying,
But that had nought to do with buying.

AUCTIONEER

Nodding is bidding, Sir, well known
In ev'ry auction-room in town,
And now the book, Sir, is your own.

SYNTAX

I know 'tis mine — because I wrote it,
But you will never say I bought it.
Nay that would be a scurvy trick,
Enough to make the Author sick.
If my nods bought it, as you say,
Why nods should be the coin to pay.
For this same book I could not bid,
A fool I must be if I did.
Besides I safely may express,
That he who doth the work possess,
Were I at any time to try
His honest liberality,
Would give me copies half a score,
Did I demand them, aye and more.

The Doctor now engross'd the eye
Of the surrounding company,
Nor was his person sooner known
Than ev'ry mark'd respect was shown:
Nay, as he did the case explain,
The Volume was put up again;
While on its page 'twas made a claim,
That he would just inscribe his name,
When this same autograph was found
To raise the price another pound,
And Syntax felt an added glee
When 'twas knock'd down for three pounds three.

One auction episode records a pleasant experience of which
an English woman was the principal beneficiary. In the early
summer of 1913, the librarian of the New England Historic
Genealogical Society brought to me a letter which he had
received from London describing four autograph letters of
John Eliot, the 'apostle' to the Indians. The letters, the
property of the widow of a clergyman of the Church of England,

were written in 1652–1657 to an English correspondent and had reference to a generous gift of cloths and other material for use in Eliot's missionary labors. In this correspondence Eliot described the church which he had established amongst the natives of Massachusetts and listed the commodities which would be most useful to him. Suspecting that other institutions had heard of these autographs, I found on inquiry of the Massachusetts Historical Society that their librarian had received a copy of the London letter and that Worthington C. Ford, who had just gone abroad, had taken it with him. On my writing to Mr. Ford at London, he replied that he had seen the letters, that they were fine specimens, and that he had recommended me to the owner with whom, in due course, I came to an agreement. As the value of John Eliot's letters was uncertain, I suggested taking them for sale at a commission of fifteen per cent. I had not then seen the correspondence, but from what was said of it I thought the letters ought to bring at least five hundred dollars. This being satisfactory, they were sent over. When they arrived, I found with them a manuscript bill of lading covering a shipment of cloth, etc., to Eliot by the *Mayflower* (whether the original Pilgrim ship or one of her namesakes, I never ascertained).

Finding them more interesting than I had expected, I decided to price the lot at twelve hundred and fifty dollars and printed a description of the letters on the back page of Goodspeed's catalogue No. 101, the largest autograph catalogue I had then issued, comprising one hundred and thirty pages. The result was disappointing for no order came for the Eliot letters. It was about this time that rare books and autographs began to rise in value. George D. Smith, then the leading American dealer, was active in this movement. The Anderson Auction Company was preparing a sale of some importance and solicited a consignment from me. I suggested these Eliot letters, but added that, as they were not my property, I should have to stipulate a reserve of a thousand dollars. With this agreed to, they went into the sale and to my surprise brought twenty-six hundred and ninety-five dollars. The lucky owner, therefore, realized something over four hundred pounds for them — four times the amount she expected.

I have already mentioned two of the customers who made purchases in the first week of my Park Street shop. Another was Doctor Charles E. Clark of Lynn, a physician although not in practice. He was one of a group who were keenly interested in book-plates (*ex-libris*) and the work of the early American engravers. Frank Marshall of Philadelphia, William E. Baillie of New Haven, James Terry of Hartford, and John P. Woodbury of Boston all belonged to this fraternity. Bookplates were of chief concern to most of these men, but they were all to some extent attracted to the general subject of early American engraving. Doctor Clark collected the delicate plates engraved on steel by John Cheney for *The Token*, *The Gift*, and other annuals. Others of the group bought examples of the stippled engravings by David Edwin, the crude line engravings by Doolittle, or the work of their contemporaries.

Trivial or foolish, these remote interests? Not so. No subject is so insignificant that a really valuable collection may not be made of it. Think of the lowly golf tee! That little wooden peg, mute witness of so many tragedies of temper, so many burnings of heart! I have a friend, a contemner of collectors until he happened upon an unusual variety of this innocent trifle. He was bitten! Now, strung upon ten feet of copper wire, he proudly exhibits (at this hour of writing) five hundred and forty-three specimens, in each of which he can show you a point of difference. He also has the very first one, the daddy of all, the *editio princeps* of golf tees!

Of these collectors Doctor Clark was my best customer. He was a liberal buyer, a very generous man, and an indefatigable hunter. He haunted bookshops, auction rooms, secondhand furniture dealers, and was not averse to contact with junk-shops, where wonderful finds were sometimes made. One day, I showed him the small five-, or it may have been seven-volume Boston edition of Josephus which had copperplate frontispieces engraved by Amos Doolittle. 'Doctor,' I said, 'I think you asked for Doolittle engravings and here are some.'

'No,' he replied, 'it must have been James Terry of Hartford.'
'You are wrong,' I said. 'If you were not the one, it was——'
'Oh,' he exclaimed, '—— wants them, does he? Well, he can't
have them. Charge them to me!' and he dropped the set
into his bag. The collectors' feud between the two men,
occasioned by a personal quarrel which I do not need to
relate, reminds me of a similar tale of George D. Smith.

The story goes that one of Smith's clerks was at an unimportant auction sale when his employer dropped in. Smith paid
little attention to the proceedings until a volume of no importance, but of some rarity, was put up. To everybody's
surprise the bidding for the book which started at a few cents
was carried to something over a hundred dollars before Smith
became the owner. Later in the afternoon his assistant said
to him, 'What did you want of the book that you bought at
Anderson's? Is it worth anything?' 'No,' Smith replied, 'and
I didn't want it, but So-and-So [mentioning a collector with
whom Smith was at odds] did want it; here it goes.' With that
he tore the volume into several pieces and tossed them into
the wastebasket.

At another time I offered Doctor Clark a copy of a rare
juvenile, *The Youth's Keepsake* (1828). This little book has on
the title-page a charming lithographed vignette showing a child
with a dog in its arms crossing a brook. The drawing on
stone was made by Cheney. 'I have this already,' he said,
'but I am glad to get it for my friend Koehler.' S. R. Koehler
was then curator of prints at the Museum of Fine Arts and the
compiler of a check-list of Cheney's prints. The next morning,
Doctor Clark was in early, as usual. 'Look here!' he exclaimed,
as he held two open volumes before me. 'This is the *Youth's
Keepsake* you sold me yesterday and here is the copy I had
before. Do you see the vignettes? They are different! One faces
to the right, and the other to the left. The first stone must
have been broken before the edition was completed and
Cheney made a second drawing in which he reversed the
scene. It's not a duplicate. Koehler can't have it! I need it in
my business!'

DOCTOR CHARLES E. CLARK
From a sketch made in Libbie's auction room

More important than this collecting of small book engravings and *ex-libris* was the interest displayed by my customers in views, historical scenes, and portraits of the colonial and Revolutionary periods. Peter Pelham, James Turner, Thomas Johnston, Henry Dawkins, Bernard Romans, Paul Revere, Amos Doolittle, Charles Willson Peale, and John Norman, are the engravers whose work was, and still is, most highly prized.[1] Excepting the mezzotints of Pelham and of Peale, none of the plates of these men have artistic value. They are as badly drawn as they are poorly engraved, but with all their crudities they are absorbingly interesting and of value historically. Unfortunately the subject of colonial engraving has not received the assistance of a selective check-list which would serve to concentrate the attention of collectors.

Bibliographical works stimulate buying. People like to read in print descriptions of things in which they are interested. This explains why persons often ignore quotations by mail but immediately order the same articles when seen in a catalogue. The catalogue of Washington engravings compiled by W. S. Baker once answered the need of collectors in that field, and fifty years ago the collecting of Washington portraiture attained considerable importance along with the more general subject of American engraving referred to above. The group of men who found recreation in the pursuit of this hobby during the pressure of business or professional life included James T. Mitchell and Hampton L. Carson of Philadelphia, W. F. Havemeyer, Charles S. McAlpin, Edwin B. Holden, R. T. H. Halsey, and Grenville Kane of New York, and in Boston, Z. T. Hollingsworth, George R. Barrett and Frederick L. Gay. I may have omitted some names which should be included in this list, but these come first to my mind.

With Baker's catalogue as a check-list, it was the aim of these men to make their collections of Washingtoniana complete. So eagerly did they compete for the rarer prints that high prices prevailed and when the printseller was offered an engraving the questions, 'Is it in Baker?' or 'Has Mr. So-and-So

[1] Edward Savage, a more skilled engraver than any of these, was of later date.

got it?' or 'What did Judge Mitchell pay for his copy?' became of considerable importance. If the print was 'not in Baker' it was presumed to be a great rarity and was priced accordingly. Fortunately for me the art dealers generally did not discover for a considerable time that a lucrative business in this line was escaping them; at least in Boston I found no competition from them. Robert Fridenberg and Joseph Sabin with a few of the general print dealers in New York were, however, alive to the profitable opportunity which the sale of American prints offered, and it was sometimes in coöperation with them that I found a welcome addition to the profits of my growing business. It was not long after I made my entry in the book trade that Charles Henry Hart of Philadelphia recognized that the old catalogue of Washington engravings compiled by Baker had been made obsolete by the discovery of many important prints previously unknown. Hart's new list, published in a handsome quarto volume by The Grolier Club of New York, presented a new objective to the collecting fraternity. (Stan V. Henkels, at whose rooms in Philadelphia several of the great Washington collections were eventually sold, for some reason refused to recognize the new list and kept to the old Baker numbers in his sale catalogues.)

Soon after Hart's *Catalogue of the Engraved Portraits of Washington* appeared, I made one of my earliest purchases of American prints, the excessively rare mezzotint engravings of George and Martha Washington described under No. 1 in Hart's *Catalogue*. When I bought these prints I knew little, if anything, about engravings or their makers, but their antiquarian value was apparent and I became very much interested in them. I tried to buy them from the dealer in antique furniture who brought them to me, but he explained that he would not have title to them for a fortnight. He could not be induced to leave them with me for safe-keeping and I had to let him go out with the package under his arm. Quaint in design, printed in rich tones of mezzotint and in the original crude black frames, these contemporary portraits bearing the simple letterings 'His Excellency General Washington' and 'Lady Washington' were

MEZZOTINT ENGRAVINGS OF GEORGE AND MARTHA WASHINGTON

From the collection of Mr. Amor Hollingsworth

irresistibly appealing to the eye. Of their origin, history, or value, I knew nothing; indeed, as I have said, I was then quite ignorant concerning prints in general, although I was making rapid progress in this part of my education! A fortnight passed and I began to think that I had missed the purchase, but the next day the vendor returned, only to tell me that he was about to send the engravings to New York. 'But,' I remonstrated, 'I thought you were going to let me have them.' 'Yes, I know I said so,' he replied; 'and you can have them, but I don't believe you will want to pay my price. You see, I have heard of a concern in New York named Kennedy which sells prints and I think they will pay me a lot for them so I am going to send them on to them. I think that's a concern that you ought to know; you might do business with them some time.' He then named his price, an amount which, although more than I expected, I thought a fair risk and I therefore bought them.

That night I took them home. My wife had been dropping quiet suggestions that a piano was becoming a necessity in our little family. When I showed her these crude old pictures I remarked with an assumed nonchalance — 'Well, my dear, this is where your piano is coming from.' She was interested — but sceptical. The next day they were put into the show window at Park Street without price or comment.

The interim between my first sight of the pair and the day of their purchase had given me time to attempt an investigation of their origin and probable value, but as neither the engraver nor the publisher of the prints had contributed his name, his address, or a date, there was nothing to go by. Hart in his *Catalogue* expressed the opinion that they were by Charles Willson Peale, basing this judgment on the evidence of certain records quoted by him. As Peale, besides being a painter, was an engraver in the mezzotint manner, Hart's idea was tenable, but, presumptuous as it might appear, I had the temerity to differ with him. Since that day the only information concerning the origin of these engravings which has been adduced is the one fact that all of the known examples came from Essex County, Massachusetts, and this counts somewhat against Mr. Hart's attribution.

The price was next to be determined. How much should I ask for them? Could I get enough out of their sale to buy a piano? Not unless I had courage.

Still undecided how much to ask for these curious-looking prints which ninety-nine people out of a hundred would not give ten dollars for, I displayed them, as I have said, in my window. While the matter was in this state a passer-by stepped in to inquire concerning them. He asked the price. I was not ready to make it. At this he took offence and I could not blame him. I then and there resolved that this was the last time that any merchandise would be shown by me before it was priced. However I promised to give this inquirer the first opportunity to purchase when the price was fixed. After some mental trial essays I decided to ask a thousand dollars for the two prints. When I named this amount to the prospective buyer he declared that the price was excessive, absurd. I answered, 'I have been told that you have two prints of Washington and Mrs. Washington engraved by John Norman which you wish to sell for fifteen hundred dollars. Are those prints of yours of more interest than these? Are not mine much scarcer?' I thought I had him there. But no, for he replied, 'That is all very well, but you are in business; I am not. I can ask what I like for my property without just criticism. You as a dealer are bound to put a reasonable valuation on your goods.' He was right in this, although in his estimate of the value of my prints, he was wrong.

The next inquirer was Frederick L. Gay. Mr. Gay was a prominent member of the Colonial Society of Massachusetts and contributed historical monographs to their publications. He owned a library of important Americana and had made a remarkable collection of Pelham's portrait-engravings in mezzotint. I shall digress from the subject of Washington prints to record a trifling anecdote of him.

The *A.L.A. Index to Portraits* published by the Library of Congress had been out but a short time and a copy was on Mr.

Gay's desk when he received a note from an acquaintance asking where certain portraits might be found, either in books or magazines. Mr. Gay in telling this story to me said: 'I sat down and copied two solid pages from the *A.L.A. Index* and sent it to him. He acknowledged the information in these words — "Gay, some of your friends told me that you were right up on these things; I didn't believe them, but I take off my hat to you now. You are a wizard!" '

Getting back to my own narrative, Mr. Gay asked me the price of my mezzotints of George and Martha. 'A thousand dollars!' he exclaimed, 'I am afraid that is beyond me, but I wish to say that this is the best find of rare American prints which I have seen for many a day.' With another envious look he reluctantly laid them down and went out. That evening he telephoned, 'How near would five hundred dollars come towards buying those prints?' 'I am sorry,' I replied, 'but I can't let them go for anything like that figure.' (There had to be something left after buying the piano!)

Next I decided to take them to New York, as I wanted to turn them into cash. However the day before I planned to go someone gave me the name of Z. T. Hollingsworth and suggested I write to him about them. I did so and received a call from him the next morning. He was very much interested. When I told him the price he said: 'No, I won't pay it. Were I sure that I should never have another chance to get those prints I would pay your price gladly, but I have been collecting Washington prints since I was twenty-five years old; I am now fifty-three, and in all that time I have never seen so many rare Washington prints come into the market as within the last five years. At the price you ask I think I will wait and take my chance that others will turn up.' More conversation followed and I reduced the price to nine hundred dollars. Mr. Hollingsworth advanced his first offer of seven hundred and fifty dollars to eight hundred and there we parted. Before leaving he said, 'Are you willing to let me think the matter over until tomorrow?' Of course I acquiesced and eagerly looked for him the next forenoon. The morning came without word from Hollingsworth, but about two o'clock a messenger brought a note, the wording of which I well remember: 'Dear Mr. Goodspeed, if you feel inclined to take fifty dollars less than the price you named yesterday for the prints, the bearer will hand you a check for the amount. *If not, I trust you will bear me in mind when any other good things in my line come your way.*' To emphasize the magnanimous quality exhibited by this last sentence, I have put it in italics. The prints went to Mr. Hollingsworth. Mrs. Goodspeed got her piano.

As I look back over the pages which I have written, I see that they lack the chronological sequence which some readers may have looked for. Instead of an orderly *table d'hôte* which they may have expected me to prepare, they will discover that I am about to offer them a New England boiled dinner, corned beef and vegetables cooked in the pot together and served on one platter. Anticipating criticism on this point and disquieted by the task of supplying a matter-of-fact account of the growth of my bookselling business, I recall an ancient example of autobiographical narrative. How neatly the old patriarch Jacob condensed his story of twenty years of active life when he appeared before the Lord in Mahanaim! Did *he* recite in a tedious narrative how his flocks increased day by day? Did he even confess his crafty contrivance against Uncle Laban? Not he! Sixteen words sufficed him to present the irksome record:

> For with my staff I passed over this Jordan, and now I am become two bands.

Like Jacob I started in Park Street with little more than a staff. To relate how, in thirty-nine years, the business has grown from one person to two bands — or what the modern equivalent of two bands may be — is a task which I do not find in me to make of real interest. From 1898, the year of Manila Bay and Klondike gold, to the commencement of the Great War, there are sixteen long years to be accounted for. What happened in them? Nothing which I recall of importance in itself except the taking of a partner towards the end of that period. In 1911 it became apparent that to meet the needs of a growing concern I must have a salesman. It was no longer possible for me to attend customers, go out to buy books, answer letters, and perform other tasks incidental to the daily round without more assistance. Furthermore, I felt that proper salesmanship demanded a detachment from other duties. I experienced difficulty in the search for a suitable person until I thought of Frank H. Valentine, then employed by DeWolfe and Fiske as manager of their secondhand book department. He, like myself, had started to work at an early age, serving eight years under Estes and Lauriat before entering the employment of DeWolfe and Fiske. I found Mr. Valentine unwilling to accept another subordinate position and, therefore, came to a partnership agreement with him. This began an association which lasted for more than a quarter of a century to our mutual satisfaction. This partner, at the time of his recent death Vice-President of the Goodspeed corporation, proved an entirely loyal friend and a co-worker of great assistance in developing the sales department of the business.

Since the days of the War, which at the start brought a sudden paralysis of trade followed by quick recovery, the annals of Goodspeed's show little more than the daily round of commonplace affairs. Buying and selling, hiring assistants, examining new equipment devices, studying modern methods of administration, testing plans of advertising, wrestling with problems of finance, of personnel, of the adaptation of the business to city and government regulations — these are the subjects which have engrossed the attention of our management from the day when all of these duties then existing were performed by one individual to the present when they require the coöperative attention of forty-odd persons. All that I can offer in the pages which follow is a narration of what seems to me the more interesting incidents of the years with, here and there, reflections on the sequence of events and the influences, either of persons, books, or of things in general, which have been factors of importance in my own life. I am entirely conscious that these incidents and my own personality are of small moment in themselves. Such apology for offering them to the public as may seem appropriate I therefore offer, at the same time submitting the opinion that lives, in themselves most insignificant, when presented with candor and in some detail, exhibit a microcosm which may be of a real, although quite impersonal, value.

Accordingly I shall omit a detailed account of our various changes of location as of no particular interest in this book. The two buildings in Ashburton Place which we occupied, one for ten and the other for fifteen years, were exchanged in 1936 for new and better located quarters at 18 Beacon Street and the lease of the basement store of the Old South Meeting House followed our abandonment of the Park Street shop. All of these changes were dictated by the needs of the business and the advantages which the new premises offered at the time. The Park Street location was given up with the greatest reluctance for reasons of sentiment, but after we had taken the Ashburton Place buildings and removed the larger part of our stock there, the business at Park Street proved disappointing so that when the opportunity of securing large quarters in Milk Street, which had been used by others as a bookstore for forty-seven years, presented itself, we decided to leave. On February 27, 1930, thirty-two years after I first opened the store, Goodspeed's at Park Street was closed.

I was not present to witness the scenes of the closing day at Park Street for which I had made the plans. Had I anticipated their remarkable success and the interest which they created, I am sure that my departure for a Southern trip on the previous day would have been delayed that I might have enjoyed the sight. For a few weeks before this we had conducted clearing-out sales, starting with a twenty-five per cent reduction which was increased progressively as the days passed and the stock became depleted. Finally the residuum was offered at a flat price of ten cents a volume. Even this left several thousand volumes unsold. Should we reduce the price to five cents? Should we dispose of the lot to some other dealer for a nominal amount? Should we discard the books altogether? Only three days were left. I decided that they must all go the next day. In the afternoon I had a conspicuous sign painted and put in the windows at closing time. It read —

FREE! HELP YOURSELF!!

EVERY BOOK IN THIS STORE GIVEN AWAY. NO DEALERS.

LIMIT TEN VOLUMES OR ONE SET TO A PERSON.

NO BOOKS WRAPPED.

According to the newspapers, several of which carried stories with photographs, there was a queue of one hundred persons on the sidewalk awaiting the morning opening.

Extracts from the press:

> 5000 volumes given away.... For a bread line, the customers assembled outside Goodspeed's basement shop at 5 Park Street between eight and eight-thirty in the morning were extremely well dressed.... One noted a shelf of American Year Books, Transactions of the American Institute, 1848, Ure's Dictionary of Arts.... U.S. Geological Survey, *Revue des Deux Mondes*, a copy of George Sand.... Ministers were there and social workers. It was a booky assembly... One dignified matron emerged from the shuffle shortly before nine and handed her ten books to a waiting chauffeur.... One ambitious man telephoned the store shortly before the gift-giving began and asked if ten books would be reserved for him.... While these picked and chose, a line continued to form outside waiting admission.... The customers were individualists, working swiftly, silently....

Did the books go? At eleven o'clock the shelves were bare.

In the law there is a court rule of evidence which forbids an attorney to impeach the veracity of his own witness. May an author be permitted to burlesque his own work? As I re-read the last few pages wherein I have tried to condense thirty-nine years, there comes irresistibly to mind an old statistical broadsheet which we once owned — the *tour de force* of an American printing office of nearly a century ago. At the top was a hand-colored woodcut wherein three figures, with their backs to the spectator, stand on the banks of the Hudson, surveying in amazement a four-by-eight-inch panorama of forest, river, prairie and mountain, reaching to a placid ocean on the western horizon. The central figure is Brother Jonathan, with his tall hat tipped jauntily on his head and his left arm concealed beneath his long coat-tails while the right arm, extended showman-fashion, indigitates to the crowned figures of Victoria and Louis Philippe the wonders of the American continent.

Will blushed, looked round the room, and with a forced laugh, 'Faith, gentlemen,' said he, 'I do not know what makes you look so grave, it was an admirable story when I heard it.' STEELE.

III. MOSTLY ANECDOTE

A N' NOW, so it please you, we shall reopen the Park Street door in which the key has but this moment been turned. We shall look up the old calendar, set back the clock, conjure old faces from the past. We are going to be young again!

Let us take a glance about the premises where our growing concern was established. The building was an old residence, formerly occupied by the Quincy family. It faced on Boston Common. A few rods to the north the scene is dominated by the Bulfinch-fronted State House on an elevated situation at the top of Beacon Hill. The lower end of Park Street is distinguished by a monument to an English architect's genius, the graceful spire of the Park Street Church which, in lofty tranquillity, stands sentry over the crumbling stones of the Granary Burying Ground. Looking from the bookshop towards the southeast, through the unending traffic flowing up and down Tremont Street, one may catch a glimpse of the portico of the Cathedral of Saint Paul, and at the close of a winter's day the crimson sunset flames to the west through the bare trees of the Common.

In entering the Park Street store, the visitor descended granite steps to a door which opened onto a small landing from which two more steps led him to the low narrow basement room. This was lighted by a window which extended along the front to a height of about four feet from the street level. A shelf inside the window served to display to the attention of street-passers such allurements as the shop had to present from time to time. There was no heat in the room excepting that furnished by quite inadequate radiation from a furnace pipe passing along the ceiling. When the weather became cold we relied on a large open fireplace for warmth. This fireplace was supplied with cordwood cut once, and stored in a small yard in the rear from whence it was brought in and piled upon the hearth as high as we dared. Once or twice the roaring blaze nearly brought disaster. At the best, it was difficult to make the room liveable in the winter, and on mornings when the cold was severe, several hours might pass before our benumbed hands could do any work. A small built-in safe originally used for silver (or perhaps as a wine closet) and secured by an imposing iron key served as a repository of records, money, and books of particular value. Below the room there was a sub-basement, vaulted by brick arches designed for structural support, whose unlighted depths of dungeon-like atmosphere never failed to excite the interest of visitors.

When I first entered on my occupancy of this Park Street shop, I had only the front half of the floor. The rear, separated by a thin partition, was used for a workroom by the fashionable tailor who did business on the floor above. When increase of our business made it necessary to secure more space in which to house the accumulation of stock and to supply room for a book-keeper and other assistants, we leased the third story. The building had never been remodelled and, sorely as this store-room was needed, its usefulness was diminished by the long tedious stairways which led to it. The quaint basement, how-ever, answered my needs excellently for many years. In that room the kitchen-hearth of the Quincys was now dedicated to the *Lares* of the bookshop.

Surrounded by these sympathetic deities we will mark a few incidents in the routine of a day. The postman enters and tosses the morning's mail on top of a small desk which now replaced the primitive box first used for that purpose. Here is a letter addressed to 'Any Good Secondhand Bookstore, Boston, Massachusetts.' On this envelope the postal clerk has pencilled a bit of unconscious satire — '*Try Goodspeed's 5A Park Street.*'

We may alphabetize the morning correspondence in this

INTERIOR OF GOODSPEED'S OLD PARK STREET SHOP

fashion: A, asks for catalogues. B, sends his bill. C, can't pay yours. D, declines your offer. E, (dear man!) encloses check. F, (ditto!) forwards an order. G, gathers autographs. H, has books to sell. I, inquires about genealogies. J, is a job-hunter. And so on. Letters from half-wits are occasionally received. One (quoted verbatim) reads: 'Please answer me about Boston Tell me prices of Map, pictorial Book photo postals of Bldgs at Boston Mass — yellow satin Irish ribbon glossy 10 × 12 in. sheets and tablets. I want you to send me a list of photo $3\frac{1}{4}$ × $5\frac{1}{2}$ postals of Bldgs. Where can I buy postals colored of Bldgs at Berlin & Europe's cities — Has Boston any Fruit market Busy Bee Confectionery, Armory, Interurban Depot? Tell me address of Tourist Bureaus — Where can I get Germany & Europe facts magazines very quickly. List of 5 Best theatres — 5 branches libraries, 10 Best hospitals, 4 Hotels.'

Orders come by mail from every state in the Union and, occasionally, from foreign parts. A New Zealander asks for old editions of Cook's Voyages. Baldwin's *Flush Times in Alabama* is wanted by a Southern correspondent. An order for a primer published in Monaghan, Ireland, comes from a Dublin collector who has made a bibliography of Monaghan imprints and now finds this little chap-book advertised in a catalogue from overseas Boston, reminding us that there is a collector somewhere for nearly everything, however unusual the subject. Often a laggard buyer has exclaimed in disappointment, 'Why, I never dreamed that there was another person in the world who was interested in that book,' when in fact he was not even first in the number of those whose orders for it came too late.

As the morning progresses we notice various types of people pausing on the sidewalk to examine the miscellany which the cheap case offers. Look at this individual who has left the group and is about to enter the door. Observe his wild-eyed frenzy and his bristling mustache of a week's growth. Also view the curious costume which he wears — odd coat, corduroy knicker-bockers, nondescript hat, and the preposterous purple cambric bag bulging beneath his right arm — the ensemble suggesting a dandified Barnaby Rudge! Holding a volume aloft in his left hand he advances into the room, takes the floor, and strikes an attitude. 'Sir!!!' he declaims in a voice of tragedy, 'I have here a book! It came from your case! It is priced at ten cents! May I have it for three?'

Another original of a different kind, well, although not favorably, known to the book trade, was familiarly designated as 'Old Man P——.' A generation ago he was a reputable bookseller. Now, old, deaf, and bent in body, he hobbles about in search of a living. See him peering in at the door-window. He fails to see us where we stand, and believing himself un-noticed starts down the street with a book stolen from the case, which he intends to sell to someone else. Turning back on feel-ing a restraining hand on his shoulder he follows without protest into the shop, offers no apology for his lawless conduct, and slowly searches his pocket for the dime which, however, he fails to produce.

Ejaculating, 'Gimme a pencil!' he opens the cover of the book and finds the price mark '10.' Painstakingly he adds to this figure a period and two ciphers. Next he draws with trembling hand an unsteady line through the new price-mark of $10.00 and completes the operation by pencilling below it '$1.75.' Returning the pencil to its owner, he now holds up his revision of the price for our inspection saying, with a grin of satisfaction on his wrinkled face, 'Otter git it, hadn't I?' When reminded of the forgotten dime, he exclaims in assumed surprise, 'Haint I paid ye?'

Once the proprietor of a neighboring store thought he saw him slide a seventy-five-cent magazine under his coat as he went out, but not being sure, did not stop him. On checking up the stock, however, he found his suspicions correct. Next day the culprit came in. Not wishing to shout an accusation, the dealer wrote on a piece of paper, 'Bring back that magazine you took yesterday!' Upon which P—— exclaimed in a loud voice, 'I never took a magazine here in my life!' 'Yes, you did,' was the pencilled reply. 'Who says so?' was the old man's response. The dealer hastily scribbled, 'That man there — he saw you.' P—— looked up and seeing the figure of a stalwart six-foot visitor looming menacingly in the back of the store promptly replied, 'All right! I'll bring it back t'morrer!'

Some of the odd characters who haunted the bookshop were good customers. Father K——, a small likeable old priest, was such an one. He had the unusual habit of demanding a duster when he had decided on the purchase of a book subjecting the volume to a brisk whisking before giving the order to wrap it up. A singularity of his person lay in the remarkable resemblance of his profile to the popular representations of *Punch*.

That famous collector Bishop John F. Hurst was also a character. The bishop, a learned scholar with bibliographical attainments and a national figure in the Methodist Church, was withal a great collector of books. The catalogue of his library as it appeared in the auction rooms in 1904–05 is rich in many classes of Americana. I must resist the temptation to enlarge on the features of especial importance in the Hurst collection, but the second part of the sale, which includes works on the native languages of America, the writings of the Mathers, and various editions of the *New England Primer*, is worthy of the careful attention of any students of those subjects. Hurst's collection of New England Primers was very extensive; the sale catalogue lists over one hundred specimens of this famous book.

I cannot identify in this list a particular edition of the *Primer* which Hurst bought of me in my early Park Street days, but it was one of the half-dozen dated about the year 1790 in his collection. The bishop had a native shrewdness and an instinct for canny bargaining which prevented his concealed enthusiasms from leading him to extravagance. When, therefore, I offered this old primer to him on a morning which found me sadly in need of money, I was compelled, through necessity, to accept an amount much below the value of the book. The conclusion of the transaction happened about noontime. Looking at his watch, the bishop noted the hour and asked to be directed to a grocery store. I may have taken a malicious satisfaction in sending him around the corner to a concern which specialized in the more expensive food supplies. In a few minutes he returned with a paper bag in his hand requesting permission to eat his lunch in the shop. After he had finished the frugal meal of crackers and cheese, I placed before him the remaining books he had selected and we proceeded with the bargaining.

In a biographical note found in the first part of Anderson's sale catalogue of the Hurst library there is a happy description of the bishop's book-collecting written in words which in part would have fitted another famous and scholarly divine of an earlier day — the Reverend George W. Bethune — a learned man and a collector of books on angling. The Reverend Albert Osborne in the catalogue mentioned above says of Bishop Hurst:

> Book-hunting was his choice recreation, though a close second was travel on foot. His happiest and most successful vacations were those in which these rivals were yoked together. A walk that promised punctuation by a chance at the drawers and corners and upper shelves of some book-stall had no superior as a spur to his striding pace. A book-shop three or four miles distant from his lodgings drew him more strongly than one near at hand — the enchantment lent to it not being due to mere distance, but rather to the opportunity to step it off in lively and tonic fashion. His daily and voluminous correspondence, entailing a great variety of cares and burdens, was lighted up and lightened by the ever-present bibliographic message. Booksellers were by no means the only ones to whom he wrote, when the emergency did not suggest the telegraph, but soldiers and sailors, consuls and missionaries, or whoever might be in touch with specimens of literature, ordinarily inaccessible, in any part of the postal world, were on his address list. His journeys by car and steamer and stage were often relieved of monotony by the study and butchery of the 'cats' which had accumulated on his desk since his last trip. His favorite method of search was of the mousing kind, especially where the deposits had outgrown the primal plan of the shop and found their overflow into every sort of cranny or angle, or even invaded the most private precincts of the dealer's *sanctum sanctorum*. He was usually present by proxy at the leading book sales in New York, Boston, and Philadelphia, and was as eager to learn the results of the bidding and the destination of particular items as the angler is to know where the shining sides of the largest trout have been latest seen, since the wary prize slipped from his own hook.

THE PARK STREET FRONT

As these customers come and go we may find it of interest to contrast their appearance or their occupations with the kind of books which they select. Detective stories are said to comprise the chief reading of one of the foremost librarians of the country, as also of several college heads, of most of the recent Presidents of the United States, and the late King George of England, but, in contrast, I have often known persons with quite unintellectual backgrounds whose literary tastes were above their vocations or the ordinary associations of their lives.

Standing in imagination, as we now do, in the old Park Street bookshop, suppose that we look across the street where, beside the iron fence of the Common, a short man of studious face is standing beside his herdic. (The herdic, by the way, unknown at present even by name, was a link in the rapid evolution of urban transportation during recent years. Now, following its predecessor the hansom, Peter Herdic's four-wheel underslung cab has departed to the limbo of transitory vehicles.) Mr. Sullivan, the driver of this particular herdic, is a buyer of books whose bent is well known. At this moment no fare is in sight and he seems about to cross the street to spend a few minutes with us.

What do you think he will find to interest him? It may be Lecky's *Map of Life* or Mill's *Autobiography*; or possibly Leslie Stephen's *Essays* or a volume of Symonds. Whatever his selection, the book will be of worth and the buyer will read it diligently. I had almost written that he would undoubtedly buy 'a worth-while book' but I dislike that pretentious expression. Once, when asked to talk to a group of theological students, I chose the subject 'Books that are not worth while,' suggesting that there were times when such books could be read to advantage. The idea came to me when, appealed to at the Christmas season for a suggestion, I asked the inquirer what kind of book he had in mind. Musing afterwards on his reply — 'Oh! anything as long as it is worth while' — I wondered, 'Is there no profit to be gained from diversion? Are we under no debt to Soapey Sponge, to General Ople and Lady Camper, to the protean curate of the Birmingham stories, to Helen of the High Hand, to Jeeves, or Alfred Peasemarch — not to mention others of that choice band?' Our herdic driver would not have enjoyed such sprightly company, but he had nothing of the precisian in him. Some men are unfitted by temperament to associate with high spirits.

The motives of buyers are numerous. Some people want books for general information; others collect first editions. This one buys only an occasional book; another is interested in all books on a given subject. The most profitable of old-time customers were those who bought omnivorously, their acquisitions covering a wide range of reading and only ceasing when space limits were reached.

Frank Smith of Roxbury was a customer of this sort. He made frequent visits and bought in such amounts that his account was valuable. The dialogues between Smith and a favored salesman who was given to badinage were highly amusing to bystanders. One day, examining the pile of books laid by for his inspection, Smith came upon a ten-volume set 'How to Succeed in Life.' 'Why, Mr. Tenney,' he protested to the salesman, 'why did you put these books aside for me. You know that I am out of business. What do I want of them?' 'Yes, Mr. Smith,' the salesman hastily replied, 'I know that very well, but this is what I thought. Some day a young fellow may come to you and say, "Mr. Smith, you are a successful man. You have had a long career and you have made money. Won't you tell me how you did it?" And then instead of wasting on him half an hour of your valuable time, you will say, "Here, take these books. They'll answer your question. I present them to you." ' Tenney, glancing at his customer's face to see how that ingenious argument was received, then added, 'And, Mr. Smith, they will cost you only seven dollars.' This was the sort of half-jesting which Smith enjoyed and he responded with a hearty laugh, 'All right. I'll take them. Put them in.'

Mr. Smith's purchases were not only satisfactory in their amount in dollars; the moving of books in bulk was an important consideration. Such sales are of especial consequence to the dealer whose space is small, as without them his stock would accumulate so fast that he would have to discontinue buying for lack of room.

Another buyer of large lots was that genial, strapping, New York club-man and benefactor of Harvard College Library — Evert Jansen Wendell. His interest lay in a single field, the drama. It was useless to offer Wendell a few items, priced at their individual values. He wanted quantity. No lot was too large to be of interest. In fact the size of the lot was an attractive feature to him and increased the chances of a sale. Buying in this way, he gathered a vast collection of plays, play-bills, prints, autographs, books, and other matter relating to the stage. On his Boston visits the bins containing stuff reserved for him by the booksellers would be brought out for examination. Many a battle was fought by dealer and collector before a bargain was struck.

Typical of these encounters is one described by Andrew McCance. On this particular afternoon Wendell professed a wish to dispense with the usual jockeying. 'Andrew,' he said, 'I am going back to New York tonight and it is getting late. Let's cut out all the trading this time. You just name your lowest price at the start and we will call it a deal.' 'All right, Mr. Wendell,' McCance replied, 'that will suit me fine. Have you got your check-book with you?' 'Yes,' Wendell replied. 'Then write me a check for a hundred and fifty dollars and I will send the lot on to you tomorrow,' said McCance. 'That will be fair to us both.' Wendell roared a 'Ha! Ha! Andrew! I see you will have your little joke! Come down to business. I will give you ten dollars for the lot. What do you say?' With this preliminary skirmish, the duel began. McCance reduced his price to one hundred and twenty-five dollars and Wendell advanced his offer to twenty-five.

After further concessions on either side, a truce was called and the contestants adjourned for supper. The meal disposed of, the fight was taken up. When, after half an hour, Wendell's final offer of forty-five dollars had been accepted and the check written, he said, 'Well, Andrew, now that it's all over, and we're good friends, tell me, what was the very lowest amount you would have taken for the lot?' 'Why, Mr. Wendell,' was the reply, 'I don't know that I can answer that question better than by saying that when you made your first offer of ten dollars, *I had more than half a mind to take it for fear that you might back down.*'

Buyers of Wendell's type were not, however, customers for a bookseller like P. K. Foley who dealt exclusively in rare books. While the two were on friendly terms, Wendell's methods of buying did not recommend him to Foley, whose stock was small and selective. On the occasion of one visit Wendell walked to the shelves where the dramatic books were usually kept, only to find nothing there. 'Where have your dramatic books gone, Mr. Foley?' 'I am not carrying dramatic books any longer,' Foley responded. 'Why not? What's the matter?' 'Well, Mr. Wendell,' came the reply in Foley's deep rounded voice, 'I have been handling dramatic books for a long time, but the trade in them has steadily fallen off; and when at last I found that only paupers were buying, I decided to quit.'

Thirty years ago Boston dealers in rare books were to some extent dependent (as they have been since) upon scouts for supplying their stock. Book scouts as intermediaries between the bookseller's stock and casual or out-of-the-way sources of supply have flourished beside the trade for many years. Walter Scott's description of Snuffy Davy 'the very prince of scouts' will come to mind, 'searching blind alleys, cellars and stalls for rare volumes' with the 'scent of a slow-hound, sir, and the snap of the bull-dog. He would detect you an old black-letter ballad among the leaves of a law paper, and find an *editio princeps* under the mask of a school Corderius.' None of Davy's descendants today are likely to duplicate his purchase of Caxton's *The Game and Playe of the Chesse* for two-pence. Opportunities are less, nor do any of the present-day breed of scouts rival Davy in his wide knowledge of literary *desiderata*.

The Boston scouts were of varying degrees of intelligence and reliability. On some of them absolute reliance might be placed, but in dealing with others — *caveat emptor*. A few of them displayed traits of roguery ranging from venial offences to more serious deviations from rectitude. One of the scouts, a jolly, roly-poly fellow, had the amiable fault of romancing; amiable at least when it was clear that he *was* romancing — and consequently amusing — but when the stories of his pretended discoveries became too convincing and were acted on, with barren results, then this attribute became very reprehensible.

The following will describe a typical interview with this man: 'Mr. Goodspeed' (it may be that this should begin 'Mr. Foley,' as I am not sure whether this incident happened in his office or mine, but as the name does not matter I let it stand) — 'Mr. Goodspeed, you know that old house out on the Wilmington Road near Billerica? It's a long, clapboarded, story-and-a-half building that used to be a tavern way back in the Revolutionary days. Well, that building has been closed for fifty years. When the man who owned it died he had two sons and they had a row over the estate. They couldn't agree and the building has been closed all these years. Now both brothers are dead and the heirs asked me to go out and look over the stuff. Up in the second story there is a room which is just filled with broadsides and almanacs and primers and old school-books and Revolutionary pamphlets and old pictures, and — well, you never saw anything like it in your life.' This was pure imagination.

On a Monday morning this scout came in with — 'Oh, Mr. Goodspeed, I went out to church last night. I don't go to church very often, but my wife got me to go to the Congregational Church with her, and when the minister got up he said, "I am not going to take my text tonight from the Bible, but I am going to talk about something that was suggested to me by the motto that Mr. Goodspeed has over that shop of his in Boston, 'Anything that's a book,'" and my wife nudged me and whispered, "How much do you suppose Goodspeed paid him for that?"' Fiction once more.

At another time he made me the victim of a hoax, although I was myself responsible for its going farther than the author intended. We had been talking about a certain rare engraving of Washington. He said, 'Why, I know where there's one of those.' It is probable that he thought the matter would end there, but in my eagerness I pressed him for the name of the place. 'Plaistow, New Hampshire,' was his answer. On further questioning he supplied additional information, described the house, the street, the location of the building, and named the owner. Of course it was my own fault that I should have made two trips of forty miles each (the second following an elucidation of the imaginary locality after my first failure to find the place), only to discover what I might have known at the start. I had been chasing a 'ghost' print.

This man, however, did make some real finds. The very rare portrait of Washington surrounded by the arms of the thirteen states of the Union engraved by Amos Doolittle which he found pasted on the inside of an old trunk-cover was one of them.

There is a copper-plate engraving by Abel Bowen of the U.S. Frigate *Constitution* which is rare and much sought for by collectors of naval prints. A scout by the name of Forehand brought one in. Forehand was a stutterer. 'I won't t-t-t-take a cent less th-th-than twe-twe-twenty dollars for it. It's n-n-no use for you to of-f-fer me any l-l-less,' he stammered. As he was notoriously hard in his dealings with others I had no compunction in accepting this offer, but the alacrity with which it was taken made the scout suspicious. He took the check, walked meditatively towards the door, and then turning said, 'G-g-good' (the abbreviation by which he always addressed me) — 'G-good, I know I g-g-gave you a big b-b-bargain, but d-d-d-don't l-l-laff!'

This Forehand, who came from Worcester, was a character. He had a sour wit, a shrewdness that was generally overreaching, and a more complete knowledge of book prices than most scouts possessed. He owned a large collection of book catalogues, including a complete set of Goodspeed's which he had bound in red morocco. But his practice of deceiving his customers brought him occasional retribution, and on one occasion a trick was played on him not unlike that from which I suffered at Plaistow. Some Worcester wag on whom a game had been

THE 'CONSTITUTION'

After the line engraving by Bowen

played by Forehand decided that he would get back at him. To a travelling friend he gave a letter for mailing to Forehand from a northern Vermont town. It purported to have been written by a destitute woman of that place who wished to sell some old books which she had found in her attic. The three-page list of titles crudely scrawled in pencil contained *The Whole Book of Psalms*, Cambridge, 1640, Roger Williams's *Key into the Language of America*, the Eliot Indian Bible, and *Tamerlane*, interspersed with a number of sermons and institutional reports and other junk. Forehand immediately started for Vermont and after a day's journey to the town found that the address given for the woman's house was a vacant lot. By that time the last train had gone for the day and he had to spend the night there, returning the next day to Worcester, wiser but very angry.

The confines of the book trade in Boston used to range narrowly from the Common to Brattle Street. This limitation of area resulted in considerable intimacy between the various shops where, fertilized by regular visits of scouts and the daily round of bargain-hunting customers, a spice of gossip flourished which relieved any monotony in the routine of trade without diminishing the prevailing spirit of good-fellowship. In fact such competition as might be found in the trade was more in purchasing than in selling. Within this fraternity an occasional prank was played, the instance which I shall relate involving a scout, a dealer, and a private buyer.

Before the metropolitan sewerage system now serving greater Boston had been constructed, the unpleasant though necessary task of removing fecal matter was performed by carts operating from the suburb called Brighton. It was on account of this local housing of the night-soil carts that boys sometimes gave them the canting description of the 'Brighton Artillery.' One day a scout named Rickards called at the office of a man who, because he is living and is also my friend, I shall designate as a fictitious Mr. Smith. The book offered by the scout was a ponderous four-volume history of the Ancient and Honourable Artillery Company of Massachusetts. 'Don't want it! Take it away!' was Smith's reception of the proffer. Rickards was aggrieved. 'Mr. Smith, why don't you ever buy anything from me? Swazey, old man Bradford, and the rest sell you books, but you always turn me down.' 'You never have what I want,' came the quick response. 'But I don't know what you want,' Rickards answered. 'Tell me a book you are looking for and I'll get it.'

Instantly came the rejoinder. 'You've brought in this Ancient and Honourable Artillery book. I haven't the slightest use for it, but you get me the history of the *Brighton* Artillery and I'll give you ten dollars.' 'All right,' was the confident reply, 'I'll get it.'

Off went the scout, not knowing what the 'Brighton Artillery' was and ignorant of the fact that no 'history' of it existed. Most of the booksellers whose stock he searched were equally uninformed. However, after a while one man was found who knew. Thinking it some kind of joke, the proprietor of the shop was about to make a suitable reply to Rickards's request for a ghost-book when it dawned upon him that after all the man was in earnest. Probing for the reason for the inquiry he demanded the name of the buyer. The scout, a secretive fellow, demurred; he had no intention of giving his customer's name to a bookseller. 'Very well, then, if you won't tell me you can go without the book; when you tell me who it's for, though, I will supply it.' Thus pressed, the customer's name was given and the scout left with a promise that he should have the book in a week. In the meantime the dealer, appreciating the humor of the situation, prepared a quiet joke on Mr. Smith.

On the bookseller's shelves were some old sheep-bound medical books. Amongst them was a treatise on dysentery published a century ago. From this the bookseller removed the title-page and the blank end-leaf. The latter he sent to a printer. When Rickards returned he found his book ready, with this title, printed in antique type, 'A History of the Brighton Artillery,' etc., and the imprint — 'Printed for *John Smith*, 1826.' Not noticing this name, the scout paid three dollars for the book and hastened down the street.

Entering the customer's office he said, 'Here is your book, Mr. Smith.' 'What book do you mean?' 'The book you ordered from me.' 'The book I ordered from you? I haven't ordered any book from you!' 'Yes, you have, Mr. Smith, you offered me ten dollars for the history of the Brighton Artillery.' 'Let me see it!' Smith demanded. He opened the volume, read the title-page, and glanced at its contents. Then he roared with laughter and handed the scout a ten-dollar bill. Mystified by this strange reception but well-satisfied with the sale, Rickards slowly pocketed the money and departed.

Much of the scouting I did myself, and as soon as I had an assistant whom I could leave in charge of the shop, I made various excursions, some to near-by, others to distant places. One expedition took me to New Bedford where I found a venerable, long-bearded, eccentric shopman whose room was divided — the front half for callers, the rear a *sanctum sanctorum* from which the public was excluded. I never knew just why he happened to admit me, but after a little talk I was allowed to enter the reserved room from which I brought away a bundle of very satisfactory purchases. The most interesting of them was an anonymous *History of the British Dominions in North America*, printed in London in 1773. This was formerly owned by Josiah Quincy and contained, besides his book-plate, the following note in his hand on the flyleaf: 'Purchased in Philadelphia out of the library of Benj. Franklin. The notes marked with red ink were probably memoranda made by himself. J. Q.'

One of these notes showing Franklin's jealous care for the history of the commonwealth of his adoption appears on the margin of a page opposite one of the underscored passages:

> Such is the account given of the advantages of their situation by New York writers. But when these facts are considered, that New York was a well-advanced colony long before William Penn began to settle his province; that though there have been always in the territory of New York great tracts of land unsettled, strangers have rather chosen to sit down in Pennsylvania; that numbers of families, particularly the Germans,

have actually abandoned the former for the latter; that most of the emigrants from New England crossed the province of New York to settle beyond it, that Pennsylvania now far exceeds it in population; and that wheat, though equally good, is generally cheaper at Philadelphia market than at that of New York; it seems as if those boasted advantages were either much exaggerated, or over-balanced by some disadvantages accompanying them, or by greater advantages in Pennsylvania which these writers do not mention.

A volley which places Franklin high in the ranks of writers of long (and telling) sentences. The book is now in the Boston Public Library.

Among the minor experiences of Park Street days there are a few incidents which illustrate that consideration of others which is a characteristic of certain people. Clarence S. Bement of Philadelphia was interested in engraved colonial currency. Calling at the shop on one of his visits to Boston he selected a few pieces from a box that contained odds and ends of old currency. One item he withheld from the lot. 'And how much for this?' he inquired. At random I replied, 'Would five dollars be satisfactory?' 'If it is to you, it will be to me,' was his answer. 'Suppose, however, we say fifteen dollars, which I shall be glad to pay for it.'

Another pleasant incident of the same nature occurred when Maude Adams was putting on the spectacle of *Joan of Arc* at the stadium in Cambridge. Her secretary came in one day when rehearsals were going on, saying, 'What have you in old French prints? Miss Adams is very anxious to get some which show military evolutions.' By chance I had a lot of military engravings of French subjects which, while not actually of the period, appeared to answer Miss Adams's needs. Her secretary took these on approval and promised to make a report on them, but failed to do so before Miss Adams left town. As the prints had no particular commercial value I thought of dropping the matter, but finally decided to make a nominal charge of three dollars and sent a bill for that amount. That was in the spring. I heard nothing until autumn when a letter came from Miss Adams's business agent in which she said that Miss Adams had received my bill for the prints, but that she did not agree with me in my estimate of their value and enclosed a check for twenty dollars.

If collectors occasionally do benefit by an accidental bargain, the dealer profits by it as well. Few persons under these circumstances resist the temptation to boast, and the seller is thus recompensed by the advertising which he receives.

Andrew Lang, in discussing book-buying ethics, once asked, 'Is a gentleman ever justified in taking advantage of the ignorance of a bookseller?' Replying to his own question he said, 'I don't know, for I never had the chance.' [1] My own feeling is that in the dealings between collector and bookseller, the former is entitled to any bargains he may find. It is the business of the dealer to know the value of his stock, on which he has ample opportunity to inform himself.

When the dealer buys from a private owner the case differs. I am of the opinion that he is bound to pay to an uninformed owner a reasonable proportion of the amount he can get for the goods. This is especially so if the owner of the material has not placed him in competition with others. Naturally

[1] The collector of Leigh Hunt, if he should recall *Men, Women, and Books,* will pause at this statement and meditate on the change brought by time. Ninety years ago, in the comfortable enjoyment of a newly acquired pension, Hunt wrote: 'Your second-hand bookseller is second to none in the worth of the treasure which he dispenses; far superior to most; and infinitely superior in the modest profits he is content with. So much so, that one really feels ashamed sometimes to pay him such nothings for his goods. In some instances (for it is not the case with every one) he condescends even to expect to be "beaten down" in the price he charges, petty as it is; and accordingly, he is good enough to ask more than he will take, as though he did nothing but refine upon the pleasures of the purchaser. Not content with valuing knowledge and delight at a comparative nothing, he takes ingenious steps to make even that nothing less; and under the guise of a petty struggle to the contrary (as if to give you an agreeable sense of your energies) seems dissatisfied unless he can send you away thrice blessed — blessed with the book, blessed with the cheapness of it, and blessed with the advantage you have had over him in making the cheapness cheaper. Truly, we fear that out of a false shame we have too often defrauded our second-hand friend of the generous self-denial he is thus prepared to exercise in our favour; and by giving him the price set down in his catalogue, left him with impressions to our disadvantage.'

there are difficulties here, for it sometimes happens that a piece is either unique or of such unusual scarcity that no market value is immediately ascertainable. Then the buyer has to protect himself and make a safe purchase, but if the sale, when made, results in an unexpected profit, ought he not to share the increase with the original owner, even though under no legal obligation to him?

Quite a number of years ago Miss Georgiana Boutwell, whose father was Secretary of the Treasury in Grant's administration, sold me some books which I selected from her father's library. There was but one book of importance in the lot. That one being of uncertain value I included it with a few others in a consignment to an auction sale. To my amazement it brought sixteen hundred dollars, a sum I thought far in excess of its value. This put me in a dilemma. I had paid what I believed to be a fair price for the book. What should I do now? I finally decided to put the case before Miss Boutwell and ask her view of the situation. Quite to my satisfaction she referred me to her lawyer, pleading her own ignorance in matters of business. As I related the circumstances to him he asked with a quizzical smile, 'What do you propose?' I replied, 'Well, I don't know what you think of it, but supposing that I were to divide with Miss Boutwell the amount realized above cost and expenses. Would you consider that satisfactory?' He thought it would be, and we settled the matter in that way.

It is only in recent years that women generally, through a broader education, have come to a knowledge of business which fits them to handle their affairs without recourse to a male adviser. Instances like the following, showing a knowledge of trade practice combined with a sense of equity, were not common in my early experience.

A woman called to sell a small book which I had never seen, nor indeed heard of before. No place of publication was given on the laconic title-page, 'The Holy Bible in Verse. 1717.' It was a tiny volume, two and a quarter by three and one-half inches in size, illustrated by ten crude cuts, and bound in sheep-

WOODCUT FROM *History of the Holy Jesus*

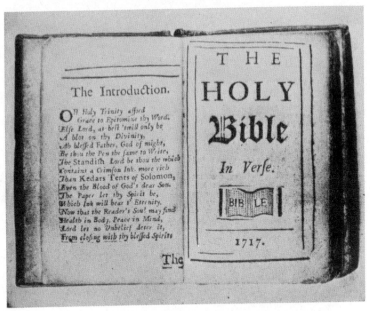

TITLE AND FRONTISPIECE OF *The Holy Bible in Verse*

covered wooden boards. What was it worth? I made an offer which the owner decided to take under consideration. Then I asked if she would leave the book for further investigation which she did. Not discovering much more about it, yet finding more in it of interest than at first appeared, I wrote to her raising my offer to one hundred and fifty dollars. Her reply surprised me by its reasonableness. I do not recall the exact wording of her letter but it was in effect, 'I think your offer for the book is fair and I accept it, but do you think it unreasonable in me to suggest that in view of the fact that you have little information at present concerning it you should, in case you sell it for more than double that amount, divide the surplus profit with me?' What could mere man say to such a fair request but to assent to it with alacrity and resolve that the maker should profit through her proposition? Surely such confidence ought not to meet with disappointment, and I decided that we must do our best to get a good price for the book.

I need not enter into our further research except to say that it identified the author of the book as Benjamin Harris, well known for his connection with another small book, that most widely circulated of all New England juvenile literature, the *New England Primer*. The ten pictures which illustrated *The Holy Bible in Verse* are also found in the earliest copies extant of its famous prototype.

Other facts, not known to us at the time concerning this book, show that it was not published in Boston, but in London, where the first appearance of it antedated our Boston issue by twelve years. It also appeared that a prefatory caution made by the publisher against a spurious edition did not, as we had supposed, refer to William Bradford, the colonial printer of New York, but to a pirate-publisher abroad.

Had these facts been known at the time we sold the book, the woman with whom I was dealing would not have fared as well as she did, for I should certainly not have asked, even in those favorable times, the seven hundred and fifty dollars for which we sold it. In the present year we have disposed of another copy (this but the fourth example recorded as known) for less than half the amount just quoted.

American juveniles of the early eighteenth century are of great rarity. Although thousands of copies of the *New England Primer* must have been printed before 1727, no copy of an earlier date has yet been found. I did not take note of the text of *The Holy Bible in Verse*, but judging from the size of the book it must have been a severe condensation of the original Scriptures. A friend tells me of a perhaps similar abridgment, or rather paraphrase, of Holy Writ which an old character of Thomaston, Maine, used to croon as he sat before the fire. My informant describes his habit of swaying to and fro, rubbing the palm of one hand crosswise against the other as he half-recited, half-sung in a quavering voice some doggerel lines beginning:

> When Ad-a-a-r-m was cre-*a*-ted
> He lived in Eden's shade
> As Moses has rel-*a*-ted
> And soon the bride was made
> Ten thousand times ten thousand
> Of creatures swarmed around
> Before that Eve was for-med
> And Ad-a-a-r-m's bride was found.

Who has seen a copy of the 'Wicked Primer' so-called? No one living, so far as I know. And yet there can be no question that an edition of the *New England Primer* was printed about the year 1750 which contained features that must have been highly obnoxious to the public for which it was designed. Not that anything on the title-page indicated a departure from other editions of the *Primer* nor that the text was in any way different. The offence lay in an incongruous juxtaposition of text and cuts. A few years before the 'Wicked Primer' appeared, the Reverend Thomas Prince, pastor of the Old South Meeting House in Boston, introduced some new couplets in the alphabetical part of the *New England Primer* to replace certain ones of the original issue which he deemed too secular for the edification of children. In the reprobated edition, Mr. Prince's

verses were illustrated, not by the new and appropriate cuts
supplied for them, but by those in the *Primer* as it was first
published. For example in the old copies, opposite the lines

> The cat doth play
> And after, slay —

a cat was shown playing with a mouse.
   Prince's substituted couplet

> Christ crucified
> For sinners died —

was accompanied by a picture of the crucifixion. In the so-
called 'Wicked Primer,' this couplet by Prince appeared with the
old cat-and-mouse cut substituted for that of the crucifixion.
Several other verses were treated in a similar manner. The
existence of this curious example of accidental transposition is
revealed in a letter signed 'A child's instructer' (*sic*), printed in
the *Boston Gazette* of September 24, 1759. A copy of this typo-
bibliographical oddity would be of very great interest to collectors of children's books and would undoubtedly command
a high price.

   Yet another juvenile, also typical of the books designed for
children's use in the eighteenth century, is the *History of the
Holy Jesus*. The earliest copy we have had of this publication
was one of the sixth edition, published in Boston in the year
1749, about the date of the two books of which I have just
written. It can hardly be said to display much facility of
composition, as witness these lines:

> Unto *Jerusalem* again
>   He comes at the Feast Time,
> And heal'd a Man that was diseas'd
>   For thirty eight Years Time.

> And there apologizes with
>   The Jews that would him slay
> Because that God his Father was
>   He openly did say.

The cuts in all the editions of the book are also of unbelievable
rudeness. The specimen given here is from a later edition, 1774.

It is to such works as the foregoing that we must look for the sources of instruction — intellectual and spiritual — of New England children from the latter part of the seventeenth century to the time of the Revolutionary War. To ridicule the theology of these epitomes and to deride the poverty of their thought is the custom of some modern writers. It should be remembered, however, that such publications, designed to inculcate morality and religion in the minds of youth, expressed the limited culture of a new country with no environment of literary activity, and that their theological instruction, although now outmoded, accurately reflected the dominant Calvinistic doctrines of its day. That theology with its uncompromising temper and its insistence on duty was the chief factor in the development of the New England character, an inheritance which none of the sons of New England need feel ashamed to own.

Man is prone to exaggeration, and horticultural catalogues have acquired considerable reputation as works of fiction, and as author of many catalogues, I may be tainted. ELLIOTT: *Adventures of a Horticulturalist.*

IV. CATALOGUES AND COMMENTS

THE old bookseller's catalogue is not a bit of ordinary trade propaganda. Much of its contents is commonplace, and the ill-considered superlatives which the compiler attaches to his descriptive notes may be justly criticised, but with all of its defects it is the tabloid of the book-collector. The homeward-bound commuter snatches his shocker-sheet from the news-stand with no more eagerness than the book-lover seizes an old-book catalogue from the hand of the postman.

London, which contains the largest number of secondhand bookshops of any city in the world, sends out the greatest quantity of old-book catalogues. There are lists covering almost every conceivable subject. Specialized lists, lists of miscellaneous books for the general reader, the rare-book catalogue, catalogues of natural history, of topographical works, of chess, sport, travel, economics — in fine the body of catalogues industriously compiled by the English trade furnishes a summary of the field of book-buying. American booksellers as a rule have not attained the same skill in the preparation of catalogues, for the larger part of their trade usually comes from buyers who frequent their store, although when they are located in a city aside from the greater routes of travel they are forced to depend upon the agency of the mail to increase their business.

Goodspeed's first catalogue appeared in October of 1899 near the close of my first year. I remember with gratitude, Ernest Dressel North's generous comment on it in *The Book Buyer* — 'a very creditable effort for a first catalogue' (quoting from memory). Having in mind that my knowledge of books had been acquired in the casual contacts of secondhand shops and auction rooms, Mr. North's commendation seems perhaps justified; and when I now consider my inexperience and the small capital with which I started, I wonder that the business survived the critical period of its existence with a stock of sufficient variety and interest remaining to justify a printed list. The first catalogue was described on the cover as a 'selection' from my stock. It was hardly that, but rather a listing of most of the saleable books which I had. In compiling these early catalogues my limited education, lack of intellectual training, and general ignorance of the broad field of literature led me into minor errors, and what was worse, to occasional solecisms which greatly to my mortification dogged my path for years. To quote an example of the former: one day Doctor William Everett of Quincy, the learned and eccentric son of the famous orator Edward Everett, was in the shop when mention was made of the fads of collectors. He exclaimed, 'My hobby is collecting *errata*. For example' — here he snatched a copy of this first catalogue of mine, opened at random to the thirty-fourth page, to which he gave a hurried glance, and then shouted — 'look here, "Thackery" should have two *a*'s!'

It was my practice occasionally to print at the beginning or end of the catalogue some quotation which seemed sufficiently interesting to attract the attention of readers. The very first entry printed on the second page of the purple cover in catalogue No. 1 was an extract from *The New English Canaan* of Thomas Morton. Morton's entertaining work, published in Amsterdam in 1637, is familiar to all students of American history, but as this passage may not be known to others I reprint it here. My own residence is in a part of Quincy near to which Morton lived and gave the suggestive name of 'Merrymount.' For that reason and also because Morton's lines contain the most eloquent description of the New England country given by a contemporary writer, I chose them to precede the business part of my first venture in cataloguing. The extract, headed in my catalogue 'New England in 1620,' follows:[1]

> And when I had more seriously considered of the bewty of the place, with all her faire indowments, I did not think that in all the knowne world it could be paralel'd, for so many goodly groves of trees, dainty fine round rising hillocks, delicate faire, large plaines, sweet cristal fountains, and clear running streames that twine in fine meanders through the meades, making so sweet a murmuring noise to heare as would even lull the sences with delight a sleepe, so pleasantly doe they glide upon the pebble stones, jetting most jocundly where they doe meete and hand in hand runne downe to Neptunes Court, to pay the yearly tribute which they owe to him as soveraigne Lord of all the springs. Contained within the volume of the Land, Fowles in abundance, Fish in multitude; and discovered besides Millions of Turtledoves one the greene boughes, which sate pecking of the full ripe pleasant grapes that were supported by the lusty trees, whose fruitful loade did cause the armes to bend; which here and there dispersed, you might see Lillies, and of the Daphnean-tree; which made the Land to me seeme paradice; for in mine eie t'was Nature's Master-piece; Her chiefest Magazine of all where lives her store; if this Land be not rich, then is the whole world poore.

Sometimes in the early days of my catalogue work I had the courage to insert a sententious paragraph of my own composition. The following sample, artificial and trite in sentiment as it is, will nevertheless show what kind of thoughts I harbored at the time it was written and may also illustrate to some readers the influence of Ruskin which I have already mentioned.

1861 — 1911

> The Blue and the Grey! Our eyes are blurred by the pathos of thinned ranks and tottering steps, but not to us is it given to feel the sternness of purpose, the high fidelity to the right as it was revealed to them, which thrilled the nerve of the

[1] I print this as it appeared in the catalogue mentioned, but I cannot imagine the source of the text, for it differs considerably in spelling and punctuation from the original work, to which both the reprint of the *New English Canaan* in Force's *Tracts* and the edition prepared by Charles Francis Adams for the Prince Society conform.

country when our fathers fought and our mothers prayed and the world saw and wondered at that awful strife! If we today are to show ourselves worthy inheritors of the fruits of their sacrifice let us, while holding fast to the priceless blessings of peace, make no truce with injustice or any form of social tyranny or the more subtle forms of treason to the State. Let us not oppress the poor for his poverty nor condemn the rich for his abundance, but ameliorate poverty and harmonize riches with wealth of life. Let us, while realizing in truth that we have been created in the image of God 'a little lower than angels,' cherish at least so much of humility as may make us see our faults before those of our neighbors, and rate our own poor virtues after theirs. So far as it is allowed us to judge, let us judge each man by his effort rather than by his achievement, and let those who aspire to greatness remember that it has been said of great men that they 'see something divine and God-made in every other man they meet,' and are 'endlessly, foolishly, incredibly merciful.'

I find not much in my first catalogue worthy of mention here, although there is a quotation from Varlo's *A New System of Husbandry* appended to a listing of the Philadelphia reprint of 1785 which may interest someone. It describes 'An Infallible Cure for the Galloping Consumption,' that all-devastating malady now happily mastered by modern medical practice. Varlo's specific reads:

> Take half a pound of raisins of the sun, stoned, a quarter of pound of figs, a quarter of a pound of honey, half an ounce of Lucateller's balsam, half an ounce of powder of steel, half an ounce of flower of Elecampane, a grated nutmeg, one pound of double refin'd sugar pounded; shred, and pound all these in a mortar; pour it into a pint of sallet-oil by degrees; eat a bit of it four times a day the bigness of a nutmeg; every morning drink a glass of old Malaga sack, with the yolk of a new-laid egg, and as much flour of brimstone as will lie upon a sixpence; the next morning as much flour of Elecampane, alternately; and if this will not cure you, the Lord have mercy upon you.

This book was first published in York, England, in 1770. There was a singular episode in the life of the author. Soon after the Revolution certain documents (of questioned authenticity) in the nature of grants from Charles the First to Sir Edward Plowden came into Varlo's possession. With these he came to America and entered a preposterous claim to one-third of the lands of New Jersey, his expectations rising to the height of anticipating a reception as Governor of that Province.

How it came about that nostrums like this one recommended by Varlo attained a reputation for medicinal virtue does not appear to the layman; like folklore, to which department they belong, they are the results of an evolutionary process possibly known to the student of therapeutics. In another of our catalogues a 'Collection of Receipts for the Use of the Poor,' a pamphlet published in Newcastle-upon-Tyne in 1745, is described. In this empirical medley there are offered eleven cures for rheumatism, of which these four will suffice for specimens: 'Dry Elder Flowers picked from the stalks, and put them up in Canisters; drink Tea made of these twice a day for a month; Or, live fourteen Days on New Milk Whey and White Bread: Or, infuse Earth Worms in White Wine, and drink a Glass twice a day: Or, take twenty-five grains of toasted Rhubarb every other night.' Excepting the earthworm remedy, which published the usefulness of the humble *Lumbricus* a century before Darwin raised it to a preëminent place in the service of man, these rheumatism prescriptions savor less of extravagance than do most of the old remedies. If we are inclined to ridicule the ignorance which made the acceptance of such mixtures as these possible, we should remember the extraordinary advance which medical science has made in our lifetime. The introduction of ether as an anaesthetic agent was made by Morton less than ninety years ago, and it is only sixty years since Lord Lister made his successful fight for antiseptic surgery.

Before passing on to examine the contents of these old lists, and at the risk of being tedious, I copy a poem found inside the last cover of my second catalogue. It was taken from a volume of poems by A. Mary Frances Robinson. The lines mirrored the sentimental habit of my own mind; the last verse particularly apologizes for an attitude which was then and, I suppose I should say regretfully, is still my own.

THE BOOKWORM

The whole day long I sit and read
  Of days when men were men indeed
And women knightlier far;
  I fight with Joan of Arc: I fall
With Talbot; from my castle-wall
  I watch the guiding star...

But when at last the twilight falls
  And hangs about the book-lined walls
And creeps across the page,
  Then the enchantment goes, and I
Close up my volumes with a sigh
  To greet a narrower age.

Home through the pearly dusk I go
  And watch the London lamplight glow
Far off in wavering lines;
  A pale grey world with primrose gleams
And in the west a cloud that seems
  My distant Apennines.

O Life! So full of truth to teach
  Of secrets I shall never reach,
O world of Here and Now;
  Forgive, forgive me, if a voice,
A ghost, a memory be my choice
  And more to me than Thou!

Descending to prosaic ground I notice that some collector in 1900 bought from my catalogue, for seventy-five dollars, two volumes that would seem bargains today if offered for many times that amount: *A Week on the Concord and Merrimack Rivers* in the first edition inscribed by Thoreau to his sister, and the author's own annotated copy of *Walden,* each in the original binding, the *Walden* in pristine condition. Two other Thoreau rarities picked up by someone at Goodspeed's in those days were original proof-sheets of *A Week on the Concord and Merrimack Rivers,* 1849, and a copy of Emerson's *Nature,*

1836, with a fine presentation inscription from Thoreau to a classmate at the time of their graduation in June, 1837. These, probably once the property of Thoreau's poet-friend Channing, were brought in to me by Frank B. Sanborn, of whom more presently.

The walls of a stately marble structure on Capitol Hill in the city of Washington shelter one of the eight great libraries of the world. The Library of Congress ranks in importance with the libraries of Harvard University, the British Museum, the Vatican, the *Bibliothèque Nationale* of Paris, the sister libraries of Leningrad and Moscow, as also with the great New York Public Library, one of the most useful of American libraries. There are in the Library of Congress more than five million printed books and manuscripts. Its preëminence in the future cultural life of our country seems assured.

In my catalogue for February, 1911, I listed a modest pamphlet of ten pages. This rarity, published in Washington City in 1802, contains the first catalogue of the library described as a 'Catalogue of the books, maps and charts belonging to the Library of the two houses of Congress.' There were only nine hundred and sixty-four books in the library in 1802, and the maps in the Library, now represented by a stout quarto volume of eleven hundred and thirty-seven pages, then numbered nine pieces. Such is the growth made by our national library in one hundred and thirty-five years.

Although the 1802 catalogue is very rare, it appears to have been valued by me at only five dollars; it was an interesting bit of *Bibliotheca-Americana*, but its importance escaped me in 1911.

Now that I know more of the Library of Congress, I am moved to say a few words about it as an institution. Although from its name this vast institution might be thought to serve merely the Congress of the United States, and while it does function primarily in the interest of that body which takes a proper satisfaction in the growth of the child of its begetting, what interests me is the fact that it has become in reality the library of the American people. As such, every American should take pride in its development and seek its welfare as he finds opportunity. In the past, the Library of Congress has not received the support from individuals which its importance deserves. It is true that in recent years public-spirited citizens have contributed many special collections to its shelves, including the Houdini collection of books on magic, the Yudin collection of Russian literature, and Jacob H. Schiff's library of Judaica. Besides these, there should be mentioned the seven thousand volumes received from the Chinese Government, Andrew W. Mellon's collection of Chinese manuscript maps and atlases, and also the John Boyd Thacher, Toner, Holmes, Cushing, and Rockhill special collections, all indicating a growing appreciation of the Library. In the department of fine arts, the Library has received notable accessions of Whistleriana and Pennelliana from Joseph and Elizabeth Robins Pennell, the important Freer collection of prints, gifts of Japanese prints, wood engravings of the late nineteenth-century American School, and the Schreiber collection of over thirty thousand early wood engravings, which includes the marks of ten thousand printers and publishers, presented by Doctor Otto H. Vollbehr. In the manuscript division, supplementing earlier acquisitions, gifts by Edward S. Harkness, the sons of President Garfield, Mrs. Benjamin Harrison, the Honorable George B. Cortelyou, Mrs. Brand Whitlock, and Miss Margaret W. Cushing have brought material of great value to the Library. It should be a matter of satisfaction to owners of historical and literary property of national interest that so enduring a depository is available. This paragraph is written also in the hope that more voters will encourage their representatives in Congress to advocate liberal appropriations for the Library's support. Money now wasted on schemes of benefit to none but a few politically serviceable individuals might be spent wisely in the advancement of letters. In these days of lavish spending, two hundred thousand dollars a year seems inadequate for the proper accessions to so great a library.

Similar claims to these of the Library of Congress may also be advanced for other institutions of specialized or regional usefulness. Ranking in its field with the most important of these is the great Americana collection of the American Antiquarian Society of Worcester, Massachusetts. This organization, although limited in its membership, generously shares its accumulated records of the past with all students and historical workers. The collections of the Society are unexcelled in importance and extent in the particular fields of its activities. Both the Library of Congress, through the instrumentality of the recently created 'Library of Congress Trust Fund Board,' and the American Antiquarian Society, in its own corporate title, are open to the receipt of testamentary bequests.[1] As these funds and their income gradually increase, the usefulness of both institutions is enlarged and it becomes possible for them to buy and preserve material which might otherwise be lost to the future historian.

Closely following this listing of the first Library of Congress catalogue, another 'first' of government publications appears, the first Census. Censuses have never been popular in this country. I dare say that of the army of enumerators who rang doorbells in the service of the Fifteenth Decennial Census in 1930 a goodly proportion reported the same curt and non-responsive reception of their lawful inquiries as that which greeted jaded and travel-worn government agents on a similar errand in 1790. In 1711 an attempt to number the citizens in the State of New York was frustrated by conscientious objectors who, having in mind 2 Samuel, 24, conveniently forgot the Book of Numbers. It is also conceivable that unlettered people in 1790 imagined a relationship between the census-taker and the tax-collector. Gatherers of material for that census also met with an undercurrent of hostility to the new Federal Government

[1] Three great American libraries, the John Carter Brown Library of Providence, Rhode Island, the Henry E. Huntington Library and Art Gallery of San Marino, California, and the W. L. Clements Library of Ann Arbor, Michigan, were founded by men who, when alive, made, either in whole or part, the collections which now bear their names. Each of these collections is, in its field, supreme.

The name of another equally great American collector, James Lenox, contemporary with John Carter Brown, is perpetuated in connection with the New York Public Library — 'Astor, Lenox and Tilden foundations.'

which, with sectional opposition, made their work one of some difficulty. It took them a year and a half to complete the visitation of less than four million people, whereas in 1930 with a hundred thousand field-workers the returns on over thirty times that number were made in a single month.

The title of this rare Congressional publication I quote from my catalogue: 'Return of the whole Number of Persons within the several Districts of the U.S., according to "An Act providing for the Enumeration of the Inhabitants of the U.S., passed March the first, One thousand seven hundred ninety." '

It was a small octavo pamphlet of fifty-six pages, and, like other early publications of Congress, was printed in Philadelphia. Commenting on its contents, my catalogue gave an abstract from which it appears that the population of Brooklyn, New York, was then 1603, 405 being slaves, and that New York City had 32,328 inhabitants, of which number 2180 were slaves. These might be compared with Richmond, 6985 (3984 slaves); Baltimore 13,503 (1255 slaves); Worcester, Massachusetts, 2095, and Boston, 18,038. The only districts reporting no slave population were Maine and Massachusetts. Of the other New England states, Vermont had 16 slaves, New Hampshire, 158, and Connecticut, 2764. The largest slave population was Virginia's 292,627. The total population of Massachusetts was 387,787, New York, 340,125, Pennsylvania, 434,373. Virginia had 747,610 inhabitants, or more than the combined population of Massachusetts and New York.

In examining the complete returns of the Census of 1930, we find the diminutive pamphlet report of 1790 has grown to an enormous publication of thirty-two quarto volumes comprising some thirty thousand pages. If this set of books were offered to a bookseller, he would refuse to buy it at any price as there is no market for it. The only institutions having sufficient shelfroom to house such bulky works are the larger libraries, which already own this one, and there are no private buyers for it. To a large number of people the printing of innumerable statistics, recapitulations, and tabulations seems a waste of public money serving no real need. This is a mis-

conception of the truth. The vast contents of this report are
invaluable to commerce, education, politics, science, finance,
transportation, and every activity of society. They comprise
material indispensable to the leaders of national life. What is
the first element requisite to any business? Is it not the accumulated facts concerning it? Is not all progress built upon the
knowledge and consideration of those facts? The Decennial
Census of the United States is the great reservoir of this information.

Taking a quick jump from subjects of importance to smaller
matters, I find in one of my catalogues about this time an
amusing extract from the advertising leaves of the Glasgow
publishers of Reid's *Bibliotheca Scots-Celtica* (1832). It would
seem that the literary piracies of that day were not all com-
mitted on the western continent. The Scottish publishers have
this to say concerning their reprint of Lydia Maria Child's
popular American *Little Girl's Own Book*: 'The publishers think
it proper to state that the work has undergone a complete re-
visal, and that all of the Americanisms, so dangerous to children,
have been translated into English. Particular care has also
been taken in excluding what in this country is not considered
properly the Amusement of Girls.' To give some idea of how
the English miss was expected to amuse herself and from what
conduct she was supposed to refrain, I added a quotation from
The Cowslip, an English juvenile of 1811:

> Miss Agnes had two or three dolls, and a box
> To hold all their bonnets and tippets and frocks.
> In a red leather thread case that snapp'd when it shut
> She had needles to sew with and scissors to cut;
> But Agnes lik'd better to play with rude boys,
> Than to work with her needle, or play with her toys;
> Young ladies should always appear neat and clean,
> Yet Agnes was seldom dress'd fit to be seen.
> I saw her one morning attempting to throw
> A very large stone, when it fell on her toe.

Poor Agnes! thus made an early example of the pernicious influence of expressionism!

As I come to Goodspeed's catalogue of January, 1904, I see that in the six years which had passed since I first began to buy books to resell I had picked up what was for that time a respectable stock. Catalogue no. 20 described the accumulation which it offered as 'a superb collection of first editions,' although with one exception there were no outstanding rarities in it. Hawthorne's *Gentle Boy*, Keats's *Endymion* in boards, Longfellow's *Evangeline*, the *Class Poem* and *The Vision of Sir Launfal* of Lowell, Thoreau's *Week*, and *At Sundown*, by Whittier, were all desirable books but none of them could be called of great rarity. In another class, however, should be placed *The Great International Walking Match of Feb. 29, 1868*. This piece is, in form, a folio broadside. It was written by Charles Dickens and described in sporting language the walking match between Dickens's manager, George Dolby, and the Boston publisher, James R. Osgood, which took place on an inclement winter's day in the suburbs of Boston. Only a few copies of this broadside were printed for guests at the Parker House dinner given by Dickens to celebrate the event. The text is quite long and a noteworthy piece of Dickensiana. It was reprinted in full in our catalogue.

In scanning the pages of these old lists occasional bits of pleasant humor enliven their contents. A collection of pamphlet publications by the late Charles Francis Adams, Jr., is the subject of one item in catalogue 37. The twenty-two pieces bound in two half-levant volumes would in themselves offer a tempting dish to the reader who relishes history most when pithily pungent. Mr. Adams's monographs were, however, preceded by a satire on the author himself. This squib, the title 'Boston,' and the author 'A. F. W.,' is written partly in parody of a well-known hymn. It appears to have been suggested by a sentence in Mr. Adams's address in 1899 at the opening of the new building of the Massachusetts Historical Society which dignifies a retired corner in the Fenway district in Boston. In the course of his remarks Mr. Adams had made a comparison of the importance of the events which led to the founding of Rome with those connected with the settlement of New England by the fathers of Plymouth, from which he drew a conclusion calculated to dilate in his auditors that complacency which was natural to the occasion.[1]

The skit commences with an

INVITATION

Come hither, Moses Taylor Pyne, and stand beside my knee
And list the tale of Boston town that I will tell to thee,
Not in cold and distant manner, nor with chilling look and shrug,
But straight outward from my inwards, heart to heart and mug to mug,

and continues with a fling at

THE ADAMS FAMILY

Soon after our young planet on its course through space was twirled
There appeared the Adams family as the oldest in the world.
Everything was fixed to suit them, everything put up their sleeve,
And for Adams express company there was furnished lovely Eve.
Everything made way before them and if there was need to weave
Fig leaves for a coat for Adam, then the fig trees had to leave.

The *exordium* goes on through several stanzas in the same vein to the poem itself, of which I quote the

IDYLLIC FINALE

There is a region lovelier far
Than Eden's vales and vistas are,
Serene and sheltered in repose
From every stormy wind that blows,
A place than all beside more sweet
At once you know it! Beacon Street.
.   .   .   .   .

Lo! Sunday comes! and at their call
The breakfast bean and codfish ball,
Assisted by a slice of pie,

[1] 'I have long held that the history of Massachusetts is the history of the gradual and practical development of certain social and political truths of the first and most far-reaching importance; that the passage of the Red Sea was, from this point of view, not a more momentous event than the voyage of the *Mayflower*, and that the founding of Boston was fraught with consequences hardly less important than those which resulted from the founding of Rome.'

Conspire to raise their spirits high
And fit them for the arduous day
Their fathers reverenced once — while they,
No longer needing God to serve,
Adore themselves with steady nerve,
Why should a man Jehovah fear? —
The Unitarian Church is near.
Yes, God made man they used to say,
Now man makes God up Boston way.

Charles Eliot Norton and Mrs. Eddy are also irreverently juxtaposed in this satirical composition.

In another catalogue, a book, author unknown, describes the outfit of an old book-bindery. The entry in the catalogue reads:

The Poetical Vagaries of a Knight of the Folding-Stick, of Paste-Castle. To which is annexed, the History of the Garret, etc., etc. Translated from the Hierogliphics of the Society. By a member of the order of the blue string.

> I neither write for fame or Pelf
> But merely do't to please myself.

Gotham, Printed for the author, 1815, bds., uncut, $3\frac{7}{8} \times 6\frac{1}{8}$, pp. 143, *two copperplate illus. (one folding).* $7.50

DESCRIPTION OF A BINDERY.

Imitative of the description of a country session.

Three or four cutting-presses and three or four pins,
Three or four dozen of calf and sheep skins,
Three or four setts of letters and eight or nine rolls,
One or two squaring shears and a pan for charcoals,
Three or four gilding-pallets and three or four stamps,
Three or four candle sticks, three or four lamps,
Three or four ruling-pens, three or four rules,
Three or four sewing-benches, and three or four stools,
Three or four setts marbling-rods, three or four brushes,
Three or four burnishers, (agates and tushes,)
Three or four folding-sticks, ivory and bone,
One or two beating-hammers, and one beating-stone,
Three or four shaving-tubs, three or four racks,
Gold, brass and silver-leaf, three or four packs,
Three or four bottles, cups, phials and bowls,
A standing press, press bar and box of charcoals;

One or two polishers and a grind stone,
Three or four skins of Morocco and roan,
Three or four sticks of green, red or blue taste,
A glue pot, a brush, and a bowl full of paste;
One or two knives, scissors, needles and hones,
Type cases, gold cushions and paring stones,
Three or four bottles or cups full of glair,
Tringles and compasses, three or four pair,
Three or four tables for folders and sewers,
Pressing and cutting boards, three or four scores,
Three or four patterns for cutting out leather,
Three or four quires to lay out and gather:
Three or four titles to letter and pare,
Three or four volumes to paste-wash and glair,
Three or four backs to be rubb'd off and draw'd,
Three or four benches of books to be saw'd;
Three or four volumes that are incomplete,
Three or four dozen books all to be beat,
Three or four books to be cover'd and patch'd,
Three or four old volumes all to be match'd,
Three or four jobs to be polish'd and mended,
A *bindery* to hold them and thus th' affair's ended.

Pausing now in the effort to extract some readable material from the office copies of these bygone catalogues lying before me, each one meticulously ticked off with the buyers' names and flanked by neat tabulations of costs and sales, it is a relief to turn to the catalogues of others. One which particularly comes to mind was issued soon after the close of the War by a North-of-England bookseller. I cabled for two items in it which attracted my attention and got both of them. Of the first of these the dealer knew nothing, and his catalogue consequently gave merely a transcription of the brief title:

Memorial to R. G. S. Cambridge, 1864 Sm. 4to. 5s.

Only five shillings for the privately printed memorial to Robert Gould Shaw,[1] containing original contributions by

[1] Shaw was a young Boston soldier who commanded a regiment of negroes in the Civil War. He was killed in the assault at Fort Wagner in 1863. A bronze-relief by Saint-Gaudens which faces the State House on Beacon Street, Boston, commemorates his death.

Lowell and Emerson, a book which had brought two hundred and twenty-five dollars in New York the year before!

The second item was more correctly priced. It had considerable interest as an association book, but the note appended to it by the dealer was even more interesting than President Wilson's inscription on the flyleaf to Matthew Arnold's daughter. Here is the English bookseller's description of the book.

> Wilson, Woodrow. Mere Literature. New York, 1896. 8vo, cloth.   £5.
> Presentation copy with inscription from the author to Miss Arnold.

And here is his characterization of the author!

> By the greatest of American Presidents; the man who saved the Allies in the World War, and who, had he not been basely deserted by his countrymen, would have ended war forever and become the second Saviour of the World.

This reference to an association copy brings to mind one library where a large proportion of the books were inscribed to the owner.

In the early spring of 1909, at the home of a friend in Cambridge's pleasant and serenely select Brattle Street, in the region made historical by the homes of Lowell and of Longfellow, a man died whose name is little known except to the few readers of a delightful book on life in the southern Pacific, *South Sea Idylls*.

Portly and bearded Charles Warren Stoddard, actor, special correspondent, traveller, author, and Professor of Literature in two universities, was generously endowed by nature with a very precious gift, the capacity for inspiring friendship even to the bounds of extravagance. Neither before nor since the time when the Stoddard library came into my possession, upon the death of that author's friend and host of his last days, have I seen such evidence of affectionate regard for one man by others of his own profession as was contained in the volumes of that collection. Later, from Stoddard's sister, I purchased the

CHARLES WARREN STODDARD

From a drawing by W. W. Denslow in the collection of Mr. J. C. Whitney

Stoddard correspondence which exhibited the same feature even more remarkably.

The catalogue in which I listed the more important of the Stoddard books covers a little more than four hundred titles; but these were selected from a much larger quantity. Typical of the hundreds of autographic inscriptions on fly-leaves or title-pages of these books are the following:

For Dear C. W. S., with love, GEORGE CABOT LODGE.

To Charles Warren Stoddard. O, you Singer of the South Seas! How can I write aught else just now, to you who know? There is neither time nor space for love — yet, I can only repeat, O, you Singer! JACK LONDON.

For Charles Warren Stoddard with the cordial regards of EUGENE FIELD.

To Chas. Warren Stoddard from his oldest and handsomest friend, THE AUTHOR (Mark Twain).

Charles Warren Stoddard, from his friend ROBERT LOUIS STEVENSON.

To Charles Warren Stoddard, with grateful and abiding love. His old Hoosier friend, JAMES WHITCOMB RILEY.

To Charles Warren Stoddard, in memory of his immemorable generosity, CLARA MORRIS.

Charles Warren Stoddard, from RUDYARD KIPLING.

W. D. HOWELLS, *with best wishes to Charles Warren Stoddard.*

Charles Warren Stoddard with the very best regards of HENRY CABOT LODGE.

To Don Carlos W. Stoddard my friend & fellow with bushels of love. JOAQUIN MILLER.

Besides the foregoing, the Stoddard catalogue offered Kipling's *Life's Handicap* with title-page autographed, 'This paper is too blotty to write anything on. R. K.,' and his *Plain Tales from the Hills* with autograph, followed by 'And he told a tale. Chronicles of Buddha.' Stoddard's copy of *The Jungle Book* had Kipling's autograph and thirty-two lines of verse ('Morning Jungle'); and on the title-page of a New York edition of *Under the Deodars*, etc., Kipling's autograph and the line — 'Men's insides is made so Comical, God help 'em' — was written. From Mark Twain there were no less than ten presentation copies. No book in this library, however, interested me as much as Lafcadio Hearn's *Two Years in the French West Indies* (although it was not of the first edition) for to its own exotic flavor there was added this poignant note written on the fly-leaf — 'With the sympathy of Henry Adams, 16 June, 1894.' How gladly I would pay today, not the dollar and a half which some buyer gave for it then, but many times that amount, to recover this volume for my own bookshelves!

By the record kept in the back of my catalogue of the Stoddard books, I see that sales from it amounted to less than nine hundred dollars. Nearly twenty-five years later one of our best customers entered the shop, saying: 'Congratulate me! I have just got the only known presentation copy of the first edition of *Tom Sawyer*. How much do you think I paid for it?' I hazarded a guess of — well — say over five thousand dollars (actually the amount I suggested was more than that). His reply indicated that if my estimate was high, it was not absurdly so. 'I am very glad you have it,' I said, 'as it is a book which I owned myself years ago. Here' (turning to the file of my old catalogues and showing him the entry facsimiled below) 'is your copy of *Tom Sawyer*, offered by me in 1909 for ten dollars!'

68 **Clemens.** Adventures of Tom Sawyer. Clo., 6½x8⅜. Hartford, 1876. $10.00
•*• FIRST EDITION.
    PRESENTATION COPY, with inscription on fly-leaf: " *To C. W. Stoddard, from his friend*, S. L. CLEMENS, 1877."
69 **Clemens.** The gilded age. Clo., 5½x8⅜. Hartford, 1876. $7.50

I might have added that the number of people who ordered this extraordinary bargain were exactly three, and if my annotated copy of the catalogue was kept correctly, not a single duplicate order came for any of the six autographed Kiplings, although none were priced higher than *The Jungle Book* with its four-stanza poem written on the end-leaves, which went for the modest sum of twenty-five dollars.

Association books, which the Stoddard books in a true sense were, are prized by collectors for their obviously close relation to the writers. Nowadays authors are to be found 'autograph-ing' their books before perspiring crowds in department stores. These are not real association copies. They convey no senti-ment of intimacy. They are advertising products and should be so rated. Only a few years ago the business of manufacturing pseudo-association copies was still further exploited in ways both novel and ingenious.

The late President Coolidge was sometimes asked to write his name in his autobiography. As in the case of applications for his *ex-libris*, which was given on application to those who contributed five dollars to a certain philanthropic institution in which he was interested, so in this, Mr. Coolidge auto-graphed his book for a similar consideration. It is not difficult to see how this situation could be used to the advantage of a clever manipulator.

We will imagine that someone, let us say a travelling sales-man who is also a book-collector, knowing these circumstances, has secured a copy of the Coolidge autobiography and has the perspicacity to have the inscription made to the name of a prospective customer in his own business. You, my reader, we will say, are that customer. The knight of the gripsack enters your office and after touching discreetly on the weather, politics, or the state of depression, casually remarks: 'I was in Northampton a few days ago and talking with Mr. Coolidge he said to me, "Do you ever call on Mr. Smith of Smithville? I wonder if he would like my book?" I answered that I was sure it would please you very much to have it, and he sat down and wrote your name in it and signed it. Here it is.'

After this, would you send that salesman away without giving him an order? Well, something not unlike this may or may not have really happened; but supposing (which is quite within the facts of the case) your bright tradesman, remembering the value which booksellers put upon books of distinguished association, should prepare for Coolidge's signature a whole list of names, names of men themselves eminent in literature. Is it not evident that these books might be sold for a goodly sum and net a substantial profit to the promoter of the scheme?

I have seen, for example, copies of the Coolidge autobiography variously inscribed by the author to T. S. Eliot, George Moore, Ben Hecht, Robinson Jeffers, A. E. Housman, H. M. Tomlinson, and Ernest Hemingway.

To Ernest Hemingway
With Regards
Calvin Coolidge

Should the reader see Coolidge's *Autobiography* with an inscription to a famous author offered for sale, he should hold both donor and (supposed) recipient innocent in the transaction which places before him a surprising conjunction of names.

There are other instances of guile in such matters. Years ago a Western collector conceived the idea of electing to membership in a fictitious 'Historical' or 'Literary' society bearing a high-sounding name the persons most prominent in a contemporary biographical dictionary. Authors, theologians, statesmen, scientists — it did not matter to what profession the subjects belonged as long as they were famous. The 'Secretary' of the Society, in sending to his victims the official notice of the honor bestowed on them, suggested that inscribed copies of their works for the shelves of the library of the Society would be appreciated. It is surprising to see how many persons both in this country and abroad were taken in by this device. The originator of the scheme received in response to his letters a large number of books and autographs which were eventually sold at auction, bringing low prices, as might have been expected.

Many collectors — such men as W. H. Arnold, the Reverend Roderick Terry, and W. F. Gable — were on the lookout for presentation books in their day, but the most earnest collector in this line amongst my customers was the Honorable Francis A. Gaskill of Worcester — gentleman, scholar, and Justice of the Superior Court of Massachusetts. His interest centred about Walpole and Walpole's time, as did many another of our local collectors, but he had a catholic taste and might be counted on to buy any good association book whatever its origin. He was a genuine lover of his books and a buyer who was not ashamed to show his enthusiasm; the shop was always a little brighter after a visit from Judge Gaskill. To him, the entire provenance of a book was of interest. He valued not only its first association but took pleasure in tracing each succeeding ownership as well, a point which is growing in the consideration of buyers.

In the endless stream which passes through the bookseller's hands there are certain books that might be put in a class of their own, although I do not know just how to label them. Books of unconscious humor, the products of abnormal minds and marked by eccentricities of structure, by inconsequence, or by incoherent thought, would be placed under this head; though there are writers ordinarily sane who at some time have written poetry which has one or more of these peculiarities. A few of our own *literati* whose work qualifies them for admission to this circle are William Cook, versifier and craftsman of Salem; Lord Timothy Dexter and his henchman, Jonathan Plummer, of Newburyport; J. Gordon Coogler; Julia A. Moore, Sweet Singer of Michigan; Bloodgood H. Cutter, the Long Island farmer-poet; A. Clifford Hawes, erudite versifier of New Bedford; and hen-loving Nancy Luce of Martha's Vineyard. Perhaps, in courtesy to a Poet-Laureate of England, Alfred Austin should be admitted as an honorary member in this company. I have read only one volume of Austin's poems and it is probably an unfair sample on which to pass critical judgment, but I have never dared to try another book by him, fearing that I might find him descending to the merely commonplace. The work of Austin's which I have in mind is entitled *The Human Tragedy* published, I believe, in 1862. Not all the stanzas are as good as the following but they are all enjoyable:

> You see that there were reasons of the strongest
> Why Mary's parents should approve his suit.
> He was betrothed, and went away to shoot;
> He little knew to what he owed his conquest,
> That Mary, had her sire bid her do't,
> Had married the first man who came, or next one;
> I almost think, she would have wed the sexton.

The eccentricities of Timothy Dexter in composition and punctuation have often been reprinted; the poetical effusions of Plummer, 'independent Preacher and Poet Laureat to his Excellency Sir Timothy Dexter,' may be represented here by the opening stanzas of his Dexter eulogy:

> Lord Dexter is a man of fame,
> Most celebrated is his name;
> More precious far than gold that's pure
> Lord Dexter shines forevermore.
>
> His noble house, it shines more bright
> Than Lebanon's most pleasant height;
> Never was one who stepped therein
> Who wanted to come out again.

In Bloodgood Cutter's volume of verse narrating the voyage of the steamship *Quaker City* his eye falls on a fellow-excursionist:

> One droll person there was on board,
>   The passengers called him Mark Twain,
> He'd talk and write all sorts of stuff
>   In his queer way, would it explain.

These lines are doubtless respondent to the advertising which Mark had given to Cutter in his own famous record of the same voyage (*Innocents Abroad*), wherein he immortalized the poet as the 'Larriat.'

Julia Moore's effusions have run into several editions and are familiar to so many that I will not quote from them, but the artless lines of Nancy Luce, although locally exploited for the author's gain on several occasions, are not so well known. Domestic-fowl pets inspired Nancy's muse:

> Lines Composed by Nancy Luce About Poor Little Tweedle Tedel Bebee Pinky, When She Was A Little Chicken. And You Will Find More Reading In the Book About Her.

> When poor little heart Pinky
> Was about six weeks old,
> She was taken with the chicken distemper,
> Chickens died off all over the island.

> She was catching grasshoppers and crickets,
> In the forenoon smart,
> At twelve o'clock she was taken sick,
> And grew worse.
> . . . .

> I gave her a portion of epsom salts,
> With a little black pepper in it,
> I wept over her that afternoon,
> I prayed to the Lord to save me her life.
> . . . .

> The next day I gave her
> Warm water to drink,
> The third day she was herself,
> Got well and smart.

Nancy's literary remains comprise a large box of manuscripts which, with her family Bible, photographs, and other Luce-ana, were sold after her death to reimburse the town for her burial charges. They are now in my possession, awaiting the advent of an enterprising publisher.

In the brilliant E. P. Mitchell days of the New York *Sun*, geniuses like A. Clifford Hawes were not allowed to pine away in local solitudes. The *Sun* frequently printed Hawes's poems, dubbing him in the columnist's style of the time *Anacreon* Clifford Hawes. The poems of this writer were notable for two points: first, the irregularity of their construction, and second, the frequent use of an irrelevant terminal idea or image. When

Hawes saw the dead-end of his verse ahead of him, his mind was usually about out of gas, but instead of putting on the brakes and stopping to cogitate the situation as most dabblers in literature would do, he pounced jovially upon the first thought which came to him and with its assistance bumped to the close in fine fettle. The result was more incongruous although not so ludicrous as in Austin's productions.

Here, from Hawes:

> I've just been looking inside the Browning
> Home in Venice; strange place that with frowning
> Plain walls and strict simplicity. His ways
> Were different from mine and, too, his lays.

> I should have said I saw his home by picture,
> But never mind, it's just as well I'm sure;
> Mistakes will creep in and of course I'm human
> Though quite different from an old woman.

But whose protesting shade is this demanding the admittance given to another Englishman in our symposium? Enter, Owen! As a bookseller, I blush to have forgotten your book, the best-seller of its day.

Come then, *Lucile* —

> Lord Alfred, when last to the window he turn'd,
> Ere he lock'd up and quitted his chamber, discern'd
> Matilda ride by, with her cheek burning bright
> In what Virgil has call'd, 'Youth's purpureal light.'
> (I like the expression, and can't find a better.)
> He sigh'd as he look'd at her, Did he regret her?
> etc., etc.

Reader, if you have not seen it, buy a copy of this choice morsel of Victorianism. You will find *Lucile* on every old-book stall. It is well worth the dime it may cost you.

For another favorite stanza I can give no one credit, as it comes from an old nursery favorite. Most of such productions are unfortunately of unknown authorship and I suppose they have been subjected to so many changes since they were first written that their original authors might not recognize them now as their own productions.

NANCY LUCE
From a photograph

(The curtain rises — brothers to the rescue!)

> When Bluebeard they saw
> With his scymeter drawn
> And their poor sister kneeling
> In sorrow forlorn
> With her ringlets dishevell'd
> (So beauteous and long)
> They shrewdly suspected
> That something was wrong.

This screed, too long drawn out for a trivial subject, was begun as an introduction to the Reverend William Cook of Salem, Massachusetts, of whose productions I offered a group in a catalogue of twenty-five years ago.

Apart from his labored attempts at versification there were features in Cook's personality of interest. Like Timothy Dexter of near-by Newburyport, he was an eccentric, but, unlike his irascible neighbor, Cook was a gentle, kindly being who, to their credit, was treated with consideration by his Salem townsmen. Cook's verse was on the whole rather dull, and the forty-three pamphlet publications which he peddled along Salem streets between 1839 and 1874 are all written in a didactic or religious vein, not excepting *Fremont* in which the subject is historical. One verse from this poem will give some idea of the style of his writing:

> How envy with co-working peers
>   Goaded Fremont right hard
> Such rapt Poet will illustrate,
>   When moving each sympathetic chord,
> He will ope the fountain of tears —
> Anon raise his hearers to cheers,
> As triumphant virtue appears,
> Laurels obscured at Washington,
> In new lustre will shine each one.

On the page opposite this stanza the 'rapt poet' is portrayed in the appropriate act of reciting his verses.

Lawrence W. Jenkins, in a paper read before the American

Antiquarian Society, quotes from a newspaper a pen-picture
of Cook which pleases me:

> William Cook was a man of quiet habits, temperate and
> courteous to all. He was never morose but always cheerfully
> accepted conditions of life as they came to him, even when
> funds were low and food scarce, as at times was the case;
> and when relief came through unexpected sales of his books,
> he gave hearty and devout thanks to Divine Providence to
> whose guiding hand he always attributed his good fortune.
> He was of stocky build, a little below medium height, of dark
> complexion and with bushy, iron-grey hair. He was a great
> walker and had a short, quick step. As he walked he held his
> head up with his eyes well opened. He usually wore a dark blue
> cape or cloak of the fashion of 1840–1850, with a soft hat, and
> was a familiar sight on Salem streets in the days when most
> Salemites were known to each other and he always received a
> pleasant greeting for, with amusement over his eccentricities,
> there was mingled a certain respect for his industry and ability
> to support himself. A well-informed man and level headed in
> the practical affairs of life, it is most unaccountable that he
> should have been so irrational whenever his imagination came
> into play.

To Mr. Jenkins I am also indebted for additional information. It seems that Cook's courtesy title of 'Reverend' received
its justification from the fact that after his student days (at
Phillips Andover Academy, Yale College and Trinity College,
Hartford, followed by two years of private instruction by the
Rector of Saint Peter's Church, Salem), he was admitted to
holy orders and ordained a deacon. Receiving permission to
read in Saint Peter's Church a sermon by an approved
author,

> misfortune overtook him, for he unhappily began to read an
> ordination sermon and discovered his mistake too late and was
> obliged to read it through to the amusement of the congregation
> and the mortification of the Rector. This incident began and
> ended his clerical career. But he could not wholly resign the
> ambition of his life and afterwards frequently conducted re-

REVEREND WILLIAM COOK
Engraved on wood by himself

ligious services in his own house, preaching to his immediate
family and such neighbors and acquaintances as might attend
from curiosity. At one time he built a small wooden building
on top of one of the highest hills in the Great Pastures, which
he frequented for prayer and exhortation, and when this
building was burned he attempted to replace it with one of
stone which was never finished. His religion seems to have
consisted of emotion and ecstasy and lacked thought and well-
ordered expression.

These 'Cook books,' as the pamphlets are sometimes called,
were, I suppose, unique in American bookmaking at the time
they were published. The author was his own illustrator,
printer, and binder. The pictures which he drew he also
engraved with a jack-knife on birch blocks and heightened some
of the cuts with pencil or colored crayons. It is the ensemble
of the production which makes it of interest to the collector.
His typography — the type a newspaper's discard — was
crudely amateurish in composition and the printing wretched.
It is locally reported that Cook's two-hundred-pound sister
aided the impression by the weight of her body. In conception,
his drawings when describing such ideas as 'Great omen-
character' approached the weird, while others were merely
the brightly colored childish picturings of a rural-minded
imagination. These features, encased in homemade linen or
hand-decorated paper covers, harmonized perfectly with
Cook's text. One might almost think of him as a crack-brained
Yankee who had been inspired by William Blake but who had
not a whit of Blake's inspiration.

Culling the abundant material of this sort, an interesting
collection of books might be formed. Whatever value the
students of pathological literature may attach to them, most
readers are satisfied to find them entertaining by reason of
their absurdity.

Goodspeed's catalogues now number more than two hundred
and eighty. For the most part they are relatively small in
size; the earlier ones ranging from about thirty-two to forty-
eight pages with occasionally one of double size. The few scat-

tered selections given in these pages do not include the more valuable items in them, but have rather been chosen for some oddity or unusual interest, and these chiefly from the catalogues issued before 1914. One catalogue, the outstanding one of our history issued much later, that is in the year 1927, was perhaps as important as any catalogue of Americana issued by an American bookseller, and so may properly receive separate notice.

The material of which it was made came into our hands in an accidental way. Towards the end of the previous chapter of this book I described the purchase of *The Holy Bible in Verse.* Had I not bought that book, Goodspeed's catalogue no. 168 containing 308 pages of rare Americana would never have been issued. It came about in this manner: I was seeking other copies of that 1717 juvenile when it occurred to me that a certain collector, whose purchases from Littlefield were made before I was established in business, might have one. Although the owner of the library was reported to be unresponsive to letters from booksellers, I made the inquiry, and although I did not find the little book for which I was seeking, it resulted in our buying the library — the most important purchase of books we ever made. Our catalogue, of which this collection formed the nucleus, comprised nearly twenty-five hundred titles, many of exceeding rarity. The first item in it was an outstanding piece of Americana.

George Littlefield had once said that one book in this library was worth ten thousand dollars. On our first inspection of the collection no book of this value could be found, but later we discovered a pamphlet bound with a few others in a shabby old volume that might qualify as the piece Littlefield had in mind. This rarity was a small quarto of but seven pages whose undistinguished appearance was emphasized by its unconventional title-page. John Winthrop's 'Declaration of war against the Narragansets,' as Roden describes the piece in his history of the Cambridge Press, was 'printed by Stephen Daye during the summer of 1645....' Continuing in the words of the same authority:

The pamphlet was so rare in Governor Hutchinson's time that he reprinted it, in his 'Collection of papers' from a manuscript copy 'having never met with it in print.' Nevertheless, Winthrop's copy was in existence and is now in the library of the Massachusetts Historical Society. . . . A second copy was unearthed in England by Henry Stevens in the middle 60's but was declined, at the reasonable price of ten guineas, by both James Lenox and John Carter Brown. The less capricious Brinley took it with eagerness in 1868, and at his first sale it went to the New York Collector (Lenox) who had previously refused it, costing him two hundred and fifteen dollars . . . and is now in the New York Public Library (Lenox Collection). . . . After the sale of Brinley's copy, a third example was obtained by the late Charles H. Kalbfleish . . . evidently the one which passed into the Hoe library and which was sold to Mr. Huntington for ten thousand dollars in 1911.

We sold our copy of this pamphlet, the fourth known, to the John Carter Brown Library for more than three hundred times the amount which the founder of the library refused to give for it fifty-seven years before. The title reads: 'A Declaration of Former Passages and Proceedings between the English and the Narrowgansets, with their confederates, Wherein the grounds and iustice of the ensuing warre are opened and cleared. Published, by order of the Commissioners for the united Colonies: At Boston the 11 of the sixth month 1645.' After the *Bay Psalm Book* and the Harvard Commencement broadside for 1643, this is the earliest printing by the Cambridge Press of which any copy is known.

To the statistically minded it may be of interest to know that these two hundred and eighty catalogues of ours list over a quarter of a million titles and, of course, cover a much larger number of individual pieces. The review of them brings to mind many scenes of interest to me and revives the memory of friends whom I have not seen for years. It also calls to mind many pleasant letters and messages which the catalogues have brought me from time to time. Of all these I recall none which gave me as much pleasure as a telegram which came from a lady at the close of a December day years ago:

CLASS OF SERVICE

This is a full-rate Telegram or Cablegram unless its deferred character is indicated by a suitable sign above or preceding the address.

WESTERN UNION

NEWCOMB CARLTON, PRESIDENT   J. C. WILLEVER, FIRST VICE-PRESIDENT

Form 1201 B

SIGNS

DL = Day Letter
NM = Night Message
NL = Night Letter
LCO = Deferred Cable
CLT = Cable Letter
WLT = Week-End Letter

Received at 169 Congress Street, Boston, Mass.

PB438 59 BLUE 5 EXTRA.

CHAS GOODSPEED.

CARE GOODSPEED BOOK SHOP .7 ASHBURTON PLACE BOSTON MASS .GOOD AFTERNOON MR GOODSPEED YOUR VERY NICE CATALOGUE ARRIVED LAST MONDAY MORNING AND MONDAY EVENING A SMALL SON CAME TO LIVE WITH US WASNT THAT A PRETTY BIG DAY WOULD LIKE TO PURCHASE NUMBER THREE FIVE EIGHT CHIPPENDALE DIRECTOR FIRST EDITION WILL FORWARD CHECK AT ONCE IF BOOK IS AVAILABLE BOTH BABIES SEND REGARDS.

Who would not count a message like this as one of the felicities of life?

What is the style of engraving — line, stipple, mezzotint, or etching? What do we know of the artist who painted the original picture? What do we know of the engraver or etcher? If it is a portrait, what do we know of the person represented? If a 'subject' composition, what are its pictorial qualities that should make the engraving of it desirable?

SALAMAN.

V. PRINTS IN THE BOOKSHOP

PAUL REVERE, versatile silversmith of Boston, hero of an exploit commemorated in a poem of national fame, solid in person, worthy in achievements, has been highly celebrated by posterity. Whether he ranked as high with his contemporaries may be questioned. The subject of a famous poem acquires renown which in fairness should be divided with the poet. Also, in the interest of historical accuracy, it must be mentioned that in a letter which found its first publication in recent years, one Henry Pelham reproaches Revere for plagiarism. Pelham says that Revere copied his design of the *Boston Massacre*. Possibly, although Revere is not alive to reply to this attack posthumously delivered. Admitting that Revere was a copyist, what then? There is no dispute of the fact that he was a stout patriot and a talented silversmith.

Historians may criticise its caption as conveying a false interpretation of that event which took place in Boston on the evening of the fifth of March, 1770, but his picture of 'The Bloody Massacre perpetrated in King Street Boston on March 5th 1770 by a party of the 29th Reg^t. Engraved, Printed & Sold by Paul Revere Boston' has fixed the popular conception of that tragic fracas and is now the most famous print of Revolutionary days.

The subject is poorly engraved and crudely colored by hand. Being produced in Boston, where it was chiefly sold, specimens are not infrequently offered locally. How many of them have passed through our hands I cannot say, but they would number at least a dozen — possibly more. The first of these was bought by me in the year 1901, shortly after the sale of the F. W. French library, where a copy brought eight hundred dollars; mine was sold for six hundred and fifty dollars. Although not a rare print relatively, it possesses many attractive features, not the least of them being the engraver's fame for which, to Longfellow — many thanks!

There are six [1] different engravings on metal of the *Boston Massacre* done in America. First, there is Henry Pelham's. Only two copies are known. It bears no engraver's name and differs materially from the others. Next in order we suppose is Revere's. This was reproduced in smaller size on type-metal by an unknown engraver for *The Massachusetts Calendar* for 1772. Then, and possibly preceding the foregoing, comes another engraving of the subject presumably copied from Revere and even more poorly executed than his, by Jonathan Mulliken, craftsman of Newburyport and Revere's contemporary. Mulliken was more skilled as a clockmaker than as an engraver, for he once produced a musical clock which played seven different tunes upon twelve bells. It does not appear that he did any other engraving than the *Boston Massacre* and decorative work on clock faces.

The two remaining *Massacre* prints of American origin are of later date. In 1832 a Boston artisan reëngraved the Revere print on pewter. The engraver's name (William F. Stratton) is not on it and excepting the words 'Copy Right Secured,' engraved below the verses, the only mark of identification is the publication line at the bottom reading 'Boston, (Fac-Simile) Re-Published, at 15 Water St. March 5. 1832.' On most copies this line is so faintly printed that it is difficult to read. Finally, in 1911, Sidney L. Smith made a new engraving of the subject which I published in an edition of seventy-five copies. All of the foregoing, except the one in the *Massachusetts*

---

[1] Sabin (and Evans, apparently quoting him) describes the edition of the *Short Narrative* published in Boston in 1770 as containing a plate, an error which he seems to acknowledge, for in his second, the title entry, of the book he does not mention a plate. See *Bibliotheca-Americana* titles 6739 and 80668. Sabin was probably misled by the Brinley catalogue no. 1665, where a frontispiece is recorded, although even there it is described as having been inserted.

Calendar, were hand-colored. Uncolored prints bearing Revere's name but lacking the descriptive verses are frequently seen. They are restrikes from the original plate which is now in the State Archives of Massachusetts. Three other plates of the *Massacre*, two in octavo size, one, on a larger folded sheet, were engraved in England for books [1] contemporaneous with Pelham's and Revere's prints. They were not colored.

Historical writers are not of one mind in interpreting the event portrayed by the Revere print. Students belonging to the ultra-critical school look upon the affair as a street-brawl between the soldiers and a small crowd of town rowdies. Recent writers generally incline to this view. The martyr theory was held by the older, conservative historians, especially those of the 'filio-pietistic' type to whom patriotism was of more importance than the truth and it also has some racial support as one of the victims of the affray was a negro.

Whichever aspect is the right one, there is no doubt that the populace of 1770 was wrought to a degree of excitement. The *Boston Gazette* of March 10 following the affair spread the news over a black-bordered sheet and headed the text with a show of coffins. There is a facsimile of this paper (there may have been several of them) which is often offered to us as the genuine issue. To convince the owners of their delusion is a thankless undertaking; the knowledge that the sheet has been a family possession for more than one generation satisfies them we are mistaken or are acting from self-interest.

I recall an unusual experience connected with the purchase of one of Revere's *Boston Massacre* prints years ago. It was brought to me one morning by a stranger of middle age, a decorator by trade, from Hartford, Connecticut. The condition of the engraving was not of the best, and my offer did not satisfy the vendor. 'That is just what I shall have to pay

---

[1] These publications were: W. Bingley's edition of the *Short Narrative* (which was advertised by Bingley as published on May 5, 1770, and is, therefore, presumably the first English plate); another edition of the same pamphlet reprinted for Dilly and Almon, also in that year, and the *Freeholder's Magazine* (London) of May, 1770.

for it.' 'Very well,' I replied, 'it is all that I can give for it in that state.' Two days later he returned to accept the proffered amount.

About that time I had received an inquiry from Doctor Rosenbach in New York for Revere's *Boston Massacre* and I sent this one to him. A fortnight had passed when the man from whom I bought it reappeared, much agitated. He gave an account of his relation to the print as follows: An auctioneer of his acquaintance was the owner of a lot of absorbent cotton and he was trying to sell it for him. Not meeting with much success he asked for money for travelling expenses. His appeal being refused with a plea of 'no funds,' the possibility of selling the *Boston Massacre* then hanging in the auctioneer's office was discussed. Finally the auctioneer told him that if he could sell it for a certain amount he might apply the money to his expense account. With this agreement he went out to make inquiries about the engraving, and after his conversation with me, returned to get it. The auctioneer was out so he took it from the wall, brought it to me, and after taking time to consider my offer, sold it as narrated above. After making this statement he said, 'Now, Mr. Goodspeed, this fellow denies the agreement, says that I took the print without authority, and has had me arrested for larceny!' 'When does the case come up?' I asked. He replied that he was summoned to be in court that morning.

Of course there was nothing for me to do but to go up to the Courthouse and see the thing through. It was just a clear-cut case of two parties denying *in toto* the statements made by the other. One was lying. Which one was it? I think the judge was puzzled, and his decision bears out that thought, for although he found my man guilty, he put him on probation.

This left me in the embarrassing position of having purchased, sold, and delivered a print in which I had no title. I therefore wrote to Doctor Rosenbach explaining the matter. Fortunately he was able to help me out of the dilemma by returning it. I then telephoned the legal owner to call for the print, but he failed to do so. After various reminders he called me six months later and said, 'Why don't you buy that print of me? You'll never get anything out of the man from whom you got it; perhaps you can sell it and get your money back that way.' He was wrong in thinking that I would not get my money refunded, as I had already been reimbursed three-quarters of the amount. I got the balance later. However, I said, 'I will give you just what I paid for it before.' He accepted the offer and the engraving then became my property.

Far exceeding in rarity and of greater historical interest than this Revere engraving are the prints which visualize the opening events of the American Revolution. They were drawn by Ralph Earle and engraved by Amos Doolittle of New Haven, both men contemporary with the events which they depict. There are four in the series, entitled: I. The Battle of Lexington, April 19, 1775. II. A View of the Town of Concord. III. The Engagement at the North Bridge in Concord. IV. A View of the South Part of Lexington. The third plate illustrates the scene which Emerson described on the tablet marking the spot:

> By the rude bridge that arched the flood,
> Their flag to April's breeze unfurled,
> Here once the embattled farmers stood,
> And fired the shot heard round the world.

In 1902 I employed Sidney L. Smith to reëngrave this set for publication in a limited edition. For this purpose I borrowed one original from the Pequot Library of Southport, Connecticut, and the others from the Bangor (Maine) Historical Society. By a coincidence each of these libraries had the prints of the set lacking by the other. Those owned in Bangor were unfortunately destroyed by the great fire in that city a few years afterwards.

I have owned a very few of the separate prints of this Concord and Lexington series but only one complete set. This was brought in at closing-time one day by an antiques dealer from Vermont. He did not offer to sell them, but inquired where he might go to have their defects repaired. 'Moore of

Brooklyn, New York,' I replied, 'is the only person to whom
I should advise you to entrust them, and he may or may not
take them, as he has usually more work than he can handle.
Would you sell them?' 'Yes, at a price.' 'How much?' 'One
hundred dollars!' The purchase was quickly made and I
turned the Doolittle engravings over immediately to my best
customer at a very moderate profit. It was a great bargain for
the buyer, as we resold the set on his account years later for
a handsome sum.

How oddly things happen! A long time after this transaction, while looking over some papers found in a large collection of Americana which we had bought, I found an envelope bearing this note: 'Doolittle Prints of Lexington Battle.
See inside address of woman who had a set.' This information
cost me a hundred dollars! I received no reply to the letter
which I wrote to the address given on the envelope, but a
personal visit to the woman disclosed that the prints bought by
me fifteen years before had been hers and that she had sold them
for the pittance of twenty-three dollars! I was under no obligation, and it was out of my power at that late date, to rectify
the injustice of another person's dealings, but the check I sent
to the woman was for a fair portion of my profit on the turn-
over of her prints and after all she had a claim in equity on
somebody.

If I were asked to list the five most important engravings
of early American events, I should, after naming those of
Concord and Lexington (as one title) and that of the *Boston
Massacre*, give three others. They are: I. Blodget's Battle of
Lake George, 1755. II. The Landing of the British Troops,
1768, by Paul Revere. III. Romans's Battle of Bunker Hill,
engraved in 1776.

The second print named above, by Paul Revere, is described
as 'A View of Part of the Town of Boston In New England and
British Ships of War Landing Their Troops! 1768.' The old
plate of this engraving, cut down, still exists; impressions from
it in this state plainly show its present incompleteness. There
is a modern copy of the original with a publication line (some-

TWO ENGRAVINGS BY SMITH AFTER DOOLITTLE
From the Concord and Lexington set

times cut off) which reads: 'This *Fac-simile* of Paul Revere's Picture of *One Hundred Years Ago* is issued by Alfred L. Sewell, Publisher of The "Little Corporal" Chicago Ill.'

The dedication of the original engraving is a bit of a mystery. It is found on a cartouche at the right-hand corner and reads: 'To the Earl of Hillsborough, His Majest^s Secy of State for America. This View of the only well Plan'd Expedition, formed for supporting ye dignity of Britain & chastising ye insolence of America, is hum'y Inscrib'd.' What explanation can be made of this language by Paul Revere — 'supporting the dignity of Britain and chastising the insolence of America'?

I offer a conjecture which, although not satisfactory, does, at least, fit the facts of the case. The print was advertised as 'just published' in the *Boston Gazette* of April 16, 1770, roughly a year and a half after the event it crudely illustrates. The regiments shown disembarking were ordered from Halifax by General Gage under Hillsborough's instructions. Hillsborough, then Secretary of State for the Colonies, was actively hostile to Americans. On May 18, 1770, the Duke of Richmond introduced his conciliatory resolutions which were carried by the Lords. Is it a plausible supposition that this print was made and sent to London in anticipation of the debate on this measure — a pacifist gesture from America? Or was Revere merely satirical?

Such other contemporary prints of Revolutionary scenes as exist are inferior in importance to the four described above.

Blodget's picture of the battle at Lake George enjoys the preëminence of being the earliest engraving produced in this country representing an American historical scene. The title reads (in part):

> A Prospective Plan of the Battle fought near Lake George on the 8th of September 1755, between 2000 English with 250 Mohawks under the command of General Johnson and 2500 French and Indians under the Command of General Dieskau in which the English were Victorious, captivating the French General with a number of his men, killing 700 and putting the rest to flight.

There are process reproductions of Blodget's *Plan* and from one of these (published in the *Proceedings* of the Massachusetts Historical Society) there hangs a tale.

A copy of this reproduction contributed by a patron hangs, with other historical views, in the hall of an inn at Charlemont, a village lying on the Mohawk Trail at the foot of the Berkshire Hills of Massachusetts. One day a New Yorker stopping there for lunch spied it on the wall. 'How much do you want for this?' he demanded. 'It is not for sale,' was the answer. The inquirer, insistent, made an offer for it only to meet a second rebuff. Thinking this the device of a shrewd Yankee to get a large price for the picture, he increased his bid to one hundred and fifty dollars — a bargain, of course, had it been one of the original engravings. A quietus on further attempts was put by the proprietor, who said, 'This print is not for sale. It was given to me by Judge Aiken and you could not buy it for five hundred dollars.' The judge bought it from me for seventy-five cents.

Romans's Bunker Hill is entitled: 'An Exact View of the Late Battle at Charlestown June 17th 1775.' A small print of the battle of Bunker Hill that appears in the *Pennsylvania Magazine* for September, 1775, seems to have been made from the same drawing, but neither engraving gives the artist's name. A copy was published in London in 1776.

Besides these five prints which are the landmarks of American historical engraving, there are three others, earlier, which do not come in quite the same category, as they represent places and not incidents. They are also rarer than those described. I refer to Burgis's *Harvard College*, 1726, and his views of *New York*, ca. 1717, and *Boston*, 1723. Of the first of these only four impressions are known; one in the Harvard College Library, and two of the others in the cabinet of the Massachusetts Historical Society. One of the last two named was discovered in a curious way: the wooden panel upon which the second state had been pasted became cracked and on removing the print, a unique impression of an earlier state, with contemporary coloring, was found beneath. It was this impression which I used for the reproduction made by Sidney L. Smith and published in an edition of fifty copies in 1906. The fourth Harvard College is in the New York Public Library. The second state was issued in 1739 or 1740.

It must not be supposed that any of these prints are often found. Of the eight described above the *Boston Massacre* is the most common. I have already spoken of the frequency — or infrequency — with which that and the Doolittle *Battles* appear — at least in my own experience. I have never owned one of the *Harvard College*. Of Burgis's *Boston* in its 1743 issue[1] I have had two, and of the second state of Burgis's *New York*, one; one also of Blodget's *Lake George*, five of the *Landing of the British Troops* by Revere, and two or three of Romans's *Bunker Hill*. This is a reasonably accurate statement, covering a collecting period of nearly forty years.

These old rarities in line-engraving are entirely antiquarian in their interest and it may be said generally of eighteenth-century American engravings that they are almost wholly deficient in artistic merit. The most notable exception to this statement is found in the work of Edward Savage, an artist of a somewhat later date than that of which I have been speaking.

Savage was a native of Princeton, a small village lying on the slope of Mount Wachusett in central Massachusetts. He is supposed to have been self-taught in the rudiments of engraving, but his real progress in the art doubtless came from the instruction which he received in London during his stay there in 1791. The fine stippled engraving of the Washington family published by him in 1798 is said to be the only one made from life studies. Other beautiful examples of Savage's copperplate engraving in the stipple manner are to be found in his small head of Washington and the portrait of General Knox. Savage's most notable work, however, was done in mezzotint,. and the series of folio engravings executed in this beautiful style are highly treasured by those who own them. The sub-

---

[1] No copy of the first issue (1723) is known to exist. The only copy of the second (1736) extant is in the British Museum.

jects of these engravings are Washington, Franklin, Doctor
Benjamin Rush, and David Rittenhouse, the Philadelphia
astronomer.

A good collection of Savage's work, which also includes
some miniatures, may be seen in the Worcester (Massachusetts)
Art Museum. That museum, by the way, bought from me in
1910 a collection of early American engravings which it had
taken me twenty-odd years to assemble. There were over
four thousand prints in the lot representing the work of about
four hundred engravers, suitably lettered, mounted, arranged,
and boxed, forming the most comprehensive collection of the
kind then existing. It was a fortunate sale for me, coming at
a time when the family need of a new house was pressing
and the six thousand dollars which I got from the sale provided
a substantial amount of the cost of the building. In that house
where I now live is my library.

I am not one of those who think that the term 'library'
should be used only in connection with a vast quantity of
books. If I choose to call my comfortable room which shelters
something less than a thousand books a library, whose concern
is it? If the man who has eight thousand books in his house
thinks that they do not constitute a library that, too, is a
matter for his own consideration. Let him call his collection
what he chooses; but if the owner of even a hundred well-
chosen, cherished volumes which serve him speaks to me of his
library, I do not quarrel with his use of the word, Samuel
Johnson in disagreement notwithstanding. Indeed (the subject warms me), should we booksellers not stand up for the
interests of the small buyer, the man whose *Boswell* is not in
boards, uncut? Why let the big fellows get away with all the
fun in this book-collecting game?

Engravings are not ordinarily a part of the bookseller's
stock. My interest in the subject was generated through
association with early customers who collected American prints
and book-plates and to whom I have referred before. Those
prominent in following the book-plate hobby were Doctor
Clark of Lynn, Frank E. Marshall, Clark's Philadelphia cor-

IN THE AUTHOR'S LIBRARY

respondent and friend, John P. Woodbury of Boston, James Terry of Hartford, Doctor H. C. Eno of Saugatuck, and W. E. Baillie of Bridgeport, Connecticut. Doctor Clark's fine collection, containing examples of every book-plate engraved by Paul Revere, was sold by me to a customer in Cleveland after his death. The collection made by James Terry was purchased by the American Antiquarian Society and that of Doctor Eno was dispersed by auction some years since. The Marshall collection, now augmented by Mr. Woodbury's book-plates recently presented by his son, John Woodbury, as well as by many other gifts and purchases, is now in the American Antiquarian Society's library at Worcester. The combination of book-plate collections last mentioned makes the Antiquarian Society's collection of American plates the best in existence.

Soon after the Antiquarian Society had acquired the Marshall plates, Mr. Baillie called on me on his way to Worcester. 'What about this Worcester society which has been buying up bookplate collections and has got Frank Marshall's?' he asked. 'What kind of a man is this Brigham, the librarian?' 'I can tell you what kind of a man Mr. Brigham is,' I replied. 'If I guess rightly you are going to suggest to him that there are two or three plates in the Marshall collection which you would like to get (and I know how badly you want them!). You will suggest to Brigham an exchange and offer from your duplicates twice the same number of equally valuable plates not in the Marshall lot. That is your plan. You won't get them, but before you leave Worcester you will agree to leave your whole book-plate collection to the Society in your will. That is the kind of man you will find Brigham to be.' Here I was in error. Just how it happened I do not know; possibly my friend Clarence Brigham was away on that day and missed Baillie's call, or it may have been a unique occasion when his persuasive powers were not registering one hundred per cent; possibly it was due to a bit of Scotch resistance on Baillie's part, but whatever the reason may have been, when Baillie died his book-plates went to the Metropolitan Museum of Art.

Mention of the reproductions of Burgis's *Harvard College*, the

Boston Massacre, and the Doolittle *Battles of Concord and Lexington* brings to mind the engraver whose copies bore so faithful a resemblance to the originals. Sidney Lawton Smith was a talented artist. Skillful in design, apt in the use of the burin, his facility with the etching needle was marvellous in its handling of minute detail. In person he was spare in build, six feet in height, blond, with bold, well-proportioned features and a heavy mustache. His manners were genial to those whom he knew and liked, but he was impatient of dullards and pretenders. With a client who offered a reasonable scheme for him to work out, no one was more considerate or coöperating; he would have nothing to do with one whose ignorance offended his sense of artistic fitness. Possessing the temperament of an artist, he had the artist's attitude towards his work and when crossed in that further dealings became impossible. Earlier Smith had worked on stained glass with John LaFarge and was afterwards employed by the Century Company in book illustration; the decorative features in the *Century Dictionary* are Smith's work. When I first knew him he was engaged on book-plates, for which he always had a good number of orders in his portfolio. Doctor Clark, one of my three earliest customers, introduced me to him, Clark being his friend and client. He might have been Smith's patron as he brought him many orders, but Smith was not a man to be patronized. Clark was, as many others have been, a great admirer of Smith's work and was not ashamed to shine in the light of his acquaintance. I myself share the enthusiasm of Smith's friends. In my conception, Smith was by far the greatest etcher of book-plates the country has seen and that is a large claim when we remember the work done by E. D. French, J. W. Spenceley, W. F. Hopson, and A. N. Macdonald, to mention but a few of the admirable workmen in this field. Smith, however, showed a greater variety of design with a more delicate and sure control of the needle and the burin than any of the others, possibly excepting the purely decorative features of E. D. French's work.

Another devoted admirer of Smith, also his neighbor and

WILLIAM H. CHASE
From the painting by Harry Sutton

friend, was William H. Chase, whom I have already mentioned in connection with N. J. Bartlett and Company, the
Cornhill booksellers; a twinkling-eyed, eager-voiced, quietly
jocular, pipe-puffing bachelor familiarly known as 'Chasie' in
the Smith household. Having but a few intimates, Chase
spent many of his evening hours smoking tobacco and gossipping
in the studio with Smith as the latter worked. He was not a
great bookman, but he had cultivated a serviceable knowledge
of English literature and was well-read in eighteenth-century
history and memoirs. To Americana, first editions, and the
rarer books as a class, he paid little heed. His interests as a
bookseller lay more in the lines of general literature, and as
his customers' tastes fell largely within this domain, he was a
useful guide to them in their purchases. He had a love of good
reading which was contagious. Not having much knowledge
of prints, however, I do not think that he was the most intelligent of the Smith enthusiasts, but nevertheless he was a
good companion to his friend. Some entries in Smith's diary,
printed in the memoir of him which his daughter edited a few
years ago, give glimpses of the two men together.

Once Chase gave Smith a small print picked up by him in
his English travels. Smith was delighted with it, but Chase
was like the critic in *Fanny's First Play* who, when asked for an
opinion, answered: 'If it's by a good author, it's a good play,
naturally. Who is the author? Tell me that and I'll place the
play for you to a hair's breadth.' Chase, in similar case, puzzled
perhaps with Smith's eagerness, demanded, 'Who made it?'
'I haven't the slightest idea,' was Smith's answer. 'What does
it matter, anyway?'

One year when Chase returned from his London buying trip
he brought with him a miniature book, an English dictionary
which the Oxford University Press had recently published.
It was a tiny volume only one and one-quarter by seven-
eighths inches in size. Smith, noticing his pleasure in the
book, as a surprise engraved a diminutive book-plate for it.
He copied Chase's plate, of which the main feature was an
open page bearing the Aldine anchor device (engraved by

him years before), in the smallest compass of any plate he had ever done, and inserted it in the book. The engraved surface is half an inch high and eleven thirty-seconds of an inch wide. Only six copies exist. Mine cost me a hundred dollars.

Smith's charges were moderate — in one instance, at least, they seem absurdly small. For the beautiful work which he did in illustration of *The Iconography of Manhattan Island*, he charged Mr. Stokes at the rate of ten dollars per day. His prices for book-plates were around a hundred and fifty dollars. As I remember it, he charged me a little less than that for the Greek plate (the *Demeter of Cnidos* subject) which he made for me. My other plate, the one having for its subject Revere's *Boston Massacre*, was a present from him to me. I consider both these plates, entirely different as they are in design, outstanding examples of Smith's art. Any reader who may have access to the Greek plate will see, if he examines the statue of the goddess under a glass, how accurately the etcher has reproduced even the slight chipping of the nose on the marble.

Another enthusiastic admirer of Smith's work was the late Ruthven Deane of Chicago. Deane's book-plate by Smith, although not one of the best examples of the artist's work, is interesting for its design of wild-life. The central panel shows a lake with ducks, and a moose in the middle distance. Portraits of two extinct birds, the great auk and the passenger pigeon, are in the border, with likenesses of Alexander Wilson and John J. Audubon almost microscopic in detail at the corners of the plate.

One of Deane's regular calls on Smith when visiting Boston was responsible for a good dog story. As Deane was standing on the steps of Smith's house in Cumberland Street waiting for an answer to the bell, a dog quietly took a place beside him. As the door opened both Deane and dog walked in, the man to be ushered upstairs to the studio and the dog to be led to the kitchen for hospitable entertainment by Mrs. Smith. An hour later when Deane descended to the door the dog passed out into the street with him. Six months afterwards Deane was again in town and made his usual call at the Smith house.

JADE BOWL

From the etching by Sidney L. Smith

Same steps, same dog, same man and dog entry. On Mrs. Smith's remark, 'That's a nice dog you have,' Deane replied, 'That is not *my* dog, Mrs. Smith, I don't know anything about him.' 'Oh dear!' Mrs. Smith said and cast a stern look dogward. On which the crestfallen animal, conscious that his ruse had been discovered, dropped his tail and slunk out of the door.

One episode in Smith's career, bearing on the difficult subject of the relations of an artist with his employer, may be briefly told. Heber R. Bishop of New York had a collection of valuable art objects carved in jade which he wished to have engraved for a sumptuous catalogue. Smith received the commission. It was a task that must have appealed to him, for he had studied work of a similar kind by French artists and had attained a proficiency which brought him far on the road to preëminence in reproducing the subtle play of light upon peculiar surfaces like that of jade. Certainly no similar work had even been attempted in this country and there seemed to be every prospect that Mr. Bishop's catalogue would bring credit to the owner and merited distinction to the artist. Alas! the fates were perverse. The etchings were all under way and well along towards completion when, breakers ahead! The proofs!

The working proofs of an engraver have been considered to belong to him. As evidences of his skill they are necessary to his future progress. Bishop thought otherwise. Apparently, to him, the engraver was a workman whom he hired; why then should he not receive all of the product of his time? This may or may not have been the client's reasoning, but at least the demand was made that as the plates were proved, the impressions without exception should go to him. Smith remonstrated in vain. Bishop would not yield the point. The artist, too, was inflexible. I do not know the details of the settlement, but Smith was paid for what he had done and kept his proofs. Bishop, however, although he took the plates would not use them and employed a French engraver to make a new set for the catalogue. Smith, after exhibiting these exquisite etchings at the Chicago Fair in 1892, returned them to his portfolio whence they came into my possession in 1929.

Smith's most important work for me was in the reproduction of antiquarian prints which, as I have said, he did with great skill. Besides the set of Doolittle *Battles* and the Revere and Harvard engravings, he reproduced an unpublished drawing of Boston Common in 1768 by Christian Remick and Johnston's *View of Yale College*. He also engraved or etched for me other views, some portraits (including a Roosevelt, nearly life-size, for which he made studies in the White House at Washington), and a few book illustrations. The latter include some of the most delightful specimens of his work and are as fine examples of naturalistic etching as I have seen.

It is probable that Smith could have doubled his fee for book-plates during the last five years of his life had he chosen to do so. As it was, he gave out physically and had to decline many orders. The last commission which he undertook was the book-plate of Calvin Coolidge. The Coolidge house at Plymouth, Vermont, and the signing of the Pilgrim compact in the cabin of the *Mayflower* were to be the pictorial features of the plate; it never got beyond the drawing. Had it been possible for Sidney Smith to etch the plate, what a finish it would have made to his career! The original sketch is now in the unrivalled collection of Smith proofs, the artist's own set, in the library of the American Antiquarian Society.

As years went by and my book business increased, I was in constant receipt of miscellaneous prints. Occasionally these lots contained a few that were valuable, but much of the material comprised copper and steel plates which had come from old books. For a long time I undertook to preserve these, minutely classified in drawers, and at one time I boasted that any one of the hundred thousand or so small portraits and views in my stock could be located in thirty seconds. Eventually I found that it cost more to care for this stock than it was worth. There was, however, one excuse for bothering with these prints aside from their frequent convenience to customers; they furnished useful material for the 'extra-illustration' of books.

UNFINISHED SKETCH FOR COOLIDGE BOOK-PLATE
Drawn by Sidney L. Smith

Just how the business in this line was first started I do not remember, but in a few years 'extra-illustrated' books came to be an important feature with me. A few subscription booksellers and some private buyers of our own supplied a market for books of this class which have been roundly abused of late, although the business in them has now gone by. The work of putting appropriate pictures in an otherwise unillustrated or inadequately illustrated book has been criticised, but on what good grounds it is not easy to see. The old argument that books are being destroyed to furnish the engravings won't hold. There are enough prints lying about to supply all the books which will be 'extra-illustrated' in a hundred years. Certainly many extra-illustrated works are not for the rare-book collector, but not all buyers of books are in that class. Take one specimen of the books which have been castigated which even a collector would not be ashamed to own. It is a pamphlet publication which I extra-illustrated in 1904, the Reverend Jonas Clark's sermon preached at Lexington in commemoration of the affair at Lexington Green on the nineteenth of April, 1775, which he delivered on the first anniversary of that event in 1776. It was described in an old catalogue of ours as having four prints inserted:

> I. A View of the Green in Lexington Where the British Troops first fired on the Americans in 1775, (From The Massachusetts Magazine, 1794). II. Colored engraving, Battle of Lexington. Drawn by Earle and engraved by A. Doolittle in 1775. Re-Engraved by A. Doolittle and J. W. Barber in 1832. III. Portrait, 'The Hon'ble Samuel Adams, Esq.' engraved by J. Norman (1781). IV. Portrait, 'The Hon'ble John Hancock, Esq'r.' engraved by Paul Revere (1774).

What is wrong with that book?

During the time when we produced these books we employed a man who was highly skilled in the delicate work of inlaying, splitting, and mounting prints. The splitting process was employed when we wished to use but one side of a print or page. The operation itself is not difficult; the print is pasted between two pieces of cloth which are then pulled apart leaving half of the paper on each piece to be soaked off and mounted afterwards. The procedure sounds quite simple, but it requires dexterity and much practice to gain proficiency in the operation. Once, coming upon a pamphlet having a cover of spongy texture which bore the heavily scrawled autograph of Rufus Choate, I showed it to Herbert Jackson, the expert then employed by us on this work and asked him if he could, by splitting it, make two signatures out of one, as it were. Jackson performed this feat successfully, and doubtless could have split the two pieces again as he has often split a magazine leaf into four perfect sheets.

Cotton is useful to man; so is wheat. One clothes, the other feeds him. But when the mouths are all fed, and all the uses of cotton are satisfied, what is a surplus good for? The principle holds with all merchandise whether it is potatoes or prints. No market, no value. The supply and demand law operating in relation to prices was demonstrated to me by an early business experience.

William E. Marshall was a household name seventy-five years ago. This artist, by an excellent line-engraving, brought the Athenæum-Stuart portrait of Washington into thousands of homes. In 1866 he translated the popular conception of Lincoln's face in a painting. This, through an engraving made by him on steel, found its place in a vast number of households otherwise destitute of pictorial adornment. A recent writer has said, 'Many homes cherish among their best examples of art Marshall's interpretations of the "Father" and the "Saver" of our country.'

So skillful was Marshall in the execution of this likeness (based presumably upon other paintings and photographs) that his engraving became generally accepted by the public as the standard portrait of Lincoln. The poet Whittier saw in it 'the pathetic sadness, the wise simplicity and tender humanity of the man.' In both its painting and in the engraving after it, this picture was the most perfect exemplification of American attainment in popular portraiture of its time. Impressions from the steel plate were widely sold at twenty dollars each; those on India-paper brought thirty dollars. Two years later a companion portrait of General Grant was published. After a while as the sale of both prints declined, the unsold copies were stored and forgotten.

Later, through the breaking-up of households, the Marshall prints of Lincoln became articles of secondhand merchandise and as such were in frequent demand, the market price being around five dollars for prints and ten dollars for proofs.

These were the conditions when, in 1904, I was offered what seems to have been the whole lot of the old unsold copies, of both Lincoln and Grant. There were about five thousand of them, about one-fifth being of Lincoln. The price was twenty-one cents each, which, estimating the larger number of Grant as worthless, made the cost of the Lincoln engravings about fifty cents each. At first this seemed a good purchase, but I soon found that it was not easy to dispose of such a large quantity. Grant, of course, no one wanted, but I had to get rid of them somehow, so I offered the two, Lincoln and Grant, at three dollars for the pair. A good proportion of the lot were proofs on India-paper and for these I asked five dollars.

My education in the value of 'remainders' then began. I found, as others have in similar circumstances, that the sale of a new article offered in response to a need is quite a different undertaking from the effort to revive a dying interest or to create a new market for an old product. The quantity to be disposed of was so large that, had I sold them for a dollar, I might not have got rid of that large number in many years. My only recourse, as I discovered, was to wholesale them in hundred lots, which doing, in time they were all sold. A trifling incident resulting from the attempt to sell them individually shows the result of an experiment in advertising which I essayed in the columns of *The Youth's Companion*. The *Companion* was at the time a prosperous paper having an enormous circulation and consequently in favor with advertisers. I invested fifty dollars for one insertion of a half-inch advertisement running something like this: 'Lincoln. Marshall's world-famous steel-engraved folio portraits of Abraham Lincoln and U. S. Grant. Original, brilliant impressions. Suitable for home or school. Published at $40.00. The pair, $3.00, postpaid. Money refunded if unsatisfactory.' Two responses came. One inquired if the price included framing; the other was a post-card order from a boy which, for luck, I filled. My confidence in the credit of his parents was justified by their prompt return of the prints!

With prints, as with books, my first interest at Park Street was in those of an antiquarian nature, yet as the business developed and I acquired the services of an enthusiastic print-lover to take charge of the tiny back room of our Park Street shop which we called the 'gallery,' it was inevitable that our print business should broaden and to some extent include modern work. Although Louis A. Holman had not the same knowledge of Americana which I had gathered, he had, through previous study and by practice as a draftsman, a general acquaintance with art and also a knowledge of etching which I did not possess. It thereby came about that modern etching gradually grew to be of importance in our business, although our main efforts in this line have been directed to the work of three men — George C. Wales, Samuel Chamberlain, and Hans Kleiber — for all of whom we have acted as publishers. Mr. Wales is a Boston architect. He has been a sailor of boats from childhood days and has expressed his love for ships in many beautiful water-color drawings and etchings which combine a sense of artistic values with such accuracy of drawing that, in the most minute details, from topmast to hull, they are beyond criticism. Samuel Chamberlain is another artist whose training has an architectural background. He is as exact in his drawings of French cathedrals as Mr. Wales has been of Yankee ships, and in his etchings of their sun-flooded façades he is equally successful in the difficult task of being definite while avoiding the sin of 'tightness.'

From Old France to Wyoming is a far cry. The richness of Gothic spires contrasts sharply with the wild beauty of far western mountains, yet the wide-spaced, wild-life-tenanted etchings by Hans Kleiber do not suffer in comparison with subjects which represent human grace and skill. Mr. Kleiber was formerly in the United States forestry service and has been self-taught in etching. His work has a freshness and a virility in keeping with the scenery that it represents and adds a welcome variety to our print gallery.

In looking for old prints, it is even now possible to resurrect occasionally something of value from such dusty closets and attics as are yet undisturbed by the passing years, but the day of wholesale finds is past. One is not likely to come upon such a stock of Currier and Ives lithographs as I once found in the portfolios of an old printseller on Sudbury Street. They were as fresh and bright as when the lithographer lifted them from his stone in the seventies, and the lot would have been a rare prize had it remained there twenty-five years longer when the Currier and Ives craze reached its height. When I bought them, however, their value was not more than a tenth of what they would bring now.

At another time I bought a large lot of lithographic portraits from the family of an artist who drew on stone shortly before the Civil War. Nowadays there are few buyers for portraits, but I had then a good customer for them. Charles H. Tyler, a Boston attorney whose suite of offices occupied a floor in the Ames Building, was furnishing his walls with American portraits — orators, statesmen, lawyers, authors. I suppose that he had a hundred framed pictures in his offices and hallways. Once he impatiently said to me when I unrolled for him half a dozen portraits — Sumner, Webster, Cass, and others — 'Don't bother me with a few of these. Bring me a big lot. I want slathers of them.'

Tyler was usually engaged when I called and often, waiting in an anteroom for his leisure, I sat and chatted with one of his partners, a genial, dark-haired young man who was never too busy to make himself agreeable to the young print-peddler. I little thought then that Owen Young would so soon rise to international fame, or that he would one day become the purchaser of my most valuable book.

The Currier and Ives prints which have so aroused public interest that they have almost monopolized old-printsellers' activities in recent years, cover a very wide range of subjects. Many of these have neither interest nor value. Those in greatest demand are the ones which show country scenes, the homesteads, farmyards, sleighing-parties, husking-bees, and rural holiday festivals, redolent of pungent country odors and displaying the restrained gaiety of the New England scene.

Equalling these in value and appealing to a variety of tastes are the top-notchers of the Currier and Ives firm, the élite, as it were, of their productions. How fascinating they are, these brightly colored pictures! They show us, as our fathers or grandfathers saw them, the original scenes of their day; the life of the pioneers and the prairie-adventuring railroad. In them we enjoy the exhilarating sport of ice-fishing or, running before a spanking summer breeze, troll for the savage blue-fish. We repose in the idyllic woodland camp of the trout fisherman or follow upland gamebirds over the crisp October pastures. Enticing views, calling us back to the simple pleasures of earlier days.

If, however, prices are a measure of interest, sea-life is the subject which has outstripped all other Currier lithographs in popularity. The price of a fine clipper-ship, which could have been had for a few dollars before the War, has now risen to a figure which only the wealthy buyer can pay. The picture market has for years been steadily absorbing the paintings which New England shipmasters brought home from China, Marseilles, and Liverpool. The lithographic prints of clipper-ships — *Redjacket, North-Star, Dreadnaught, Charter Oak*, and the like — were designed to supply the wider demand for these pictures from a public stirred to enthusiasm by the rapid ocean passages made by them. With this interest there was doubtless then as now the recognition of that beauty of line and grace of motion which is seen in a ship under full canvas. Such features may explain the popular esteem in which certain types of lithographic prints, of which the New York firm of Currier and Ives were the great producers, are now held.

These notes will indicate some of the subjects which, as a printseller, I have found of interest to my customers. To speak of others, not less important — the glorious aquatints and line-engravings of naval actions, the prints which depict the tragic events of the whale-fishery, and the topographical views which show what American towns and cities looked like before their modern transformation took place — would extend the chapter unduly. Two more episodes may be given to illustrate the business of the print-room' and bring the chapter to a close.

Prints and drawings are so closely associated that a concern which sells the one is likely to handle the other also. Some time ago we bought a pencil sketch of the Mormon Temple at Nauvoo, Illinois. It was well drawn with the technique of an architect. The delineator had affixed his signature in printed letters, 'Edward Everett, Q.R.' Who was 'Edward Everett' and what title or degree was represented by the initials 'Q.R.'?

The name of Edward Everett was, of course, familiar. It was the name of a distinguished son of Massachusetts, a member of Congress, Speaker of the House of Representatives, President of Harvard College, and Minister from the United States to the Court of Saint James's. Yet it seemed out of question that he was the one who made the drawing, and casual investigation failed to identify the draftsman or disclose the meaning of the obscure initials attached to his name. As often happens, the obvious source of information was turned to last. Consulting the Everett family history in our genealogical room, all was clear. The sketch was made by a namesake of the famous orator. In 1843 this young Everett went from Boston to Quincy, Illinois, where he joined a local military organization and participated in its service at Nauvoo during the Mormon troubles there. The initials 'Q.R.' after the artist's name stand for *Quincy Riflemen*.

It took some years of business experience to teach me that time invested in research pays profitable dividends. Here is an incident which happened before I had acquired that useful bit of wisdom.

Edward R. Lemon, the last landlord of the famous Wayside Inn at Sudbury, Massachusetts, before Henry Ford undertook that rôle, was a buyer of antique furniture for the furbishing of the old hostelry. He saw in my shop one day the life-size profile portrait of a man with hair dressed in the manner of a century and a quarter before. It was drawn in crayon on pink paper and I had bought it at auction for a few dollars.

The value of a drawing more often comes from the reputation of the artist than from the subject, but in this case, both to Lemon and myself, the only question of importance appeared to be, of whom is this a portrait? Neither of us knew. My price was six dollars. Lemon held out for a dollar reduction. Some demon of chance must have inspired me that day, for I said, 'No, I won't cut the price, but I'll do this: I'll toss a coin with you to see whether you get it for five dollars or pay me ten.' He accepted and lost.

For years that gamble has troubled me, whether due to an upbringing in the Puritan tradition or to a quite different cause, I leave to the reader to decide. The drawing, as I learned afterwards, was from the pencil of Charles Balthazar Julien Fevret de Saint-Mémin.

*W*hat duller looking volume than a Parish Register? ... What is it, but a barren abstract of the annals of mortality? ... But suppose an aged man to open this same volume, and, seated in the midst of a circle of his fellow-parishioners, run his eye along the time-discoloured pages, and relate his recollections. ... HARTLEY COLERIDGE.

VI. THE GREAT, THE NEAR–GREAT, AND SOME OTHERS

TO MANY of the names which honor the pages of the guest-book of our shop no claim of intimacy or of frequency of visit may be made. Those persons of distinction whose autographs are found there were, in the main, tourist-visitors, birds of passage brought by favorable winds to our doors. A brief hour favored with their presence and they are gone. Nevertheless, no tradesman would regard lightly the compliment implied by such visits. It is something to remember that on such and such a day Fritz Kreisler told you of his collection of incunables, that on another Sarah Orne Jewett favored the shop with her gracious presence; or that you once talked to Mrs. Sothern, the lovely Julia Marlowe, to whom, as *Rosalind*, you indited in your salad-days (tempted by a counterfeit spirit of poesy) such a jingle as this —

> A winsome face, a woman's grace,
> A charm which everyone endears
> As precious quite, as the mingled light
> Of April's dimpled smiles and tears —

(How many readers can plead guiltless of such follies!)

Could we gather in one group all of the persons whose names are written in this book they would make an interesting company, although the roll of celebrities recorded there is far from complete, for from sheer negligence on our part, it omits many persons of equal prominence who were frequent callers.

A large number of the writers in the album are dead. Thomas Wentworth Higginson, Nelson A. Miles, Francis E. Wilson, Charles Follen Adams, Thomas Nelson Page, George E. Woodberry, Robert W. Chambers, Samuel McChord Crothers, John Drinkwater, W. D. Howells, Albert J. Beveridge, Charles M. Loeffler, George Herbert Palmer, Basil King, Gamaliel Bradford, Childe Hassam — these are all gone, but of the illustrious living I find inscribed the names of Christopher Morley, Bruce Rogers, Mark Sullivan, Edwin Markham, H. M. Tomlinson, Gluyas Williams, Owen D. Young, D. B. Updike, Arthur Rackham, Margaret Deland, Fritz Kreisler, Joseph C. Lincoln, Laura E. Richards, with others equally well known.

Amongst these persons there are some with whom an incident is connected, or who bring to mind through association other names worthy of recollection. For example, we find here the signature of John Burroughs. No other autograph appearing under the date of September 2, 1913, we might infer that Burroughs was unaccompanied on this the first and only time that he entered the Park Street basement, but we should be mistaken. The reason why the autograph of Burroughs's companion is not there with his own is found in the fact that this album being intended to record the visits of celebrities, everyday folk like automobile manufacturers were not invited to contribute to its pages. That is why Goodspeed's album, now to the chagrin of its owners, lacks Henry Ford's signature. Yet the two men came in together, Mr. Ford to buy for Mr. Burroughs the book for which they were inquiring — a sumptuous edition of *Walden* published by the Bibliophile Society. John Burroughs was a rare migrant; we never saw or heard from him again, but Ford's orders for old schoolbooks, country-dance music, and Longfellow first editions since then have not been inconsiderable. To bring Mr. Ford seriously into the book-collecting class, however, has exceeded my efforts. What I believe the last personal communication received from him by Goodspeed's was a telegram which I found on my return from lunch fifteen years or more ago. It read something like this: 'Please wire description inside and outside of Longfellow's village-smithy shop. Mr. Ford would appreciate reply today.'

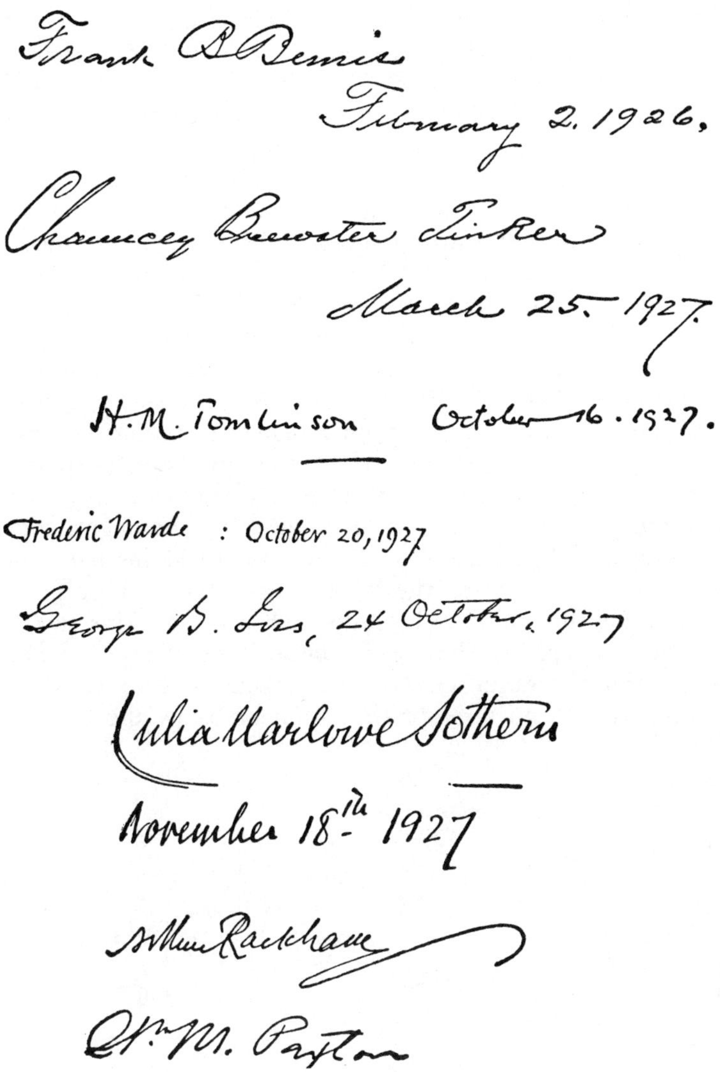

Frank B Bemis

February 2, 1926,

Chauncey Brewster Tinker

March 25, 1927.

H. M. Tomlinson   *October 16. 1927.*

Frederic Warde   : *October 20, 1927*

George B. Ives, *24 October, 1927*

Julia Marlowe Sothern

November 18th 1927

Arthur Rackham

Wm M. Paxton

PAGE FROM GOODSPEED'S VISITORS' BOOK

And how would a bookseller, the old blacksmith's shop being no longer in existence, handle that order? By happy chance there is a rough sketch of the building available, one made by the poet himself. But I challenge the reader to write such a concise description of that simple structure as would not exceed the ordinary limits of telegraphic communication. The only way to make this kind of message intelligible is to forget the price-per-word charge, and let the pen run loose. Ford received a reply before five o'clock and probably he did not mind the toll, although it was a fairly stiff one.

In the Park Street shop, rear, there was a wide shelf topped with a stone slab doubtless of some culinary use in the old-time kitchen. Lester G. Hornby, the etcher, was standing near it as I left the shop on a certain evening. Entering the next morning, I found him, an early visitor, in the same place. I greeted him with the wish that he had not found the stone slab too uncomfortable a resting-place for the night, and recalling just then that he had never inscribed his name in our album, I presented the book to him for that purpose. Responding, he added to his autograph a pen-and-ink sketch intended to represent himself in the attitude of repose. The next visitor of note to the shop was a humorist who wrote his autograph with an appropriate sentiment below the Hornby sketch:

Sandwiched between the autographs of Percy MacKaye and Louise Homer I find the following written in our album by the greatest collector of books on magic when calling on us. 'Secure knots, secures not Houdini. Dec. 24, 1921, 11.31 A.M.' As Houdini already owned most of the odd works on legerdemain and the occult sciences which came into our stock, his purchases were mostly of original material, autographs of dramatic performers and magicians. In whatever part of the world Houdini travelled, his collection on magic (and the theatre) — which at his death ranked with the world's largest — was ever in his mind. The cards which Houdini sent to his acquaintances at Christmas were original and amusing.

Rudolph Valentino's name is on a leaf of our guest-book. His signature is dated 1923, but his first visit was several years before. It was at the earlier time that, busy in the rear of the shop, I was called aside by our stenographer who whispered excitedly, 'Do you know who that man with black hair out front is?' 'No,' I answered, 'who is he?' 'That,' Helen replied in a hushed voice, 'that is Valentino!' 'And who,' I replied, 'is Valentino?' Not being then (when, as I imagine, most of the film-star admirers were shopgirls) nor now, in these days of universal movie-appeal, a reader of film news or a regular addict of the screen itself, the fame, or even the name, of Valentino had not reached me.

Miss Amy Lowell came to the shop often. Her autograph, seen in our guest-book, is precise and elegant. She was kind in heart and liberal in her purchases of books as befitted a great collector. No dealer had cause to find fault with her in either of these respects, yet if he were sensitive the half-hour of her call might be a questionable pleasure, for she had a sharp tongue. The directness of her expression left no doubt as to what her views were on any point under discussion, and her dominating spirit was likely to beat down the opposition to a cause which she might espouse. The tea-table campaign which she carried on successfully against the plan to remove the Boston Athenæum Library from its grey walls at the downtown end of Beacon Street to a more central and socially de-

sirable site in the Back Bay is an instance of this. Once, unknown to Miss Lowell, perhaps, I competed with her for the
purchase of the manuscript of Keats's *Ode to Autumn*, then
owned locally. In the contest the odds seemed to favor me, as
I was backed by Frank Bemis, a client who was liberal in his
purchases, but there were strong personal factors which prevailed in Miss Lowell's favor. That manuscript is now in the
Poetry Room in the Harvard College Library having been received with other Keats material by bequest on Miss Lowell's
death.

What most impressed me about Miss Lowell was her attitude
of mental curiosity to which Professor Lowes has somewhere
referred. She had the most alert mind of any woman I have
known which, with her poetic gift and aggressive personality,
made her an outstanding figure in the development of contemporary literary ideals. I saw her at a dinner given in her
honor on the eve of her intended sailing for London in the
spring of 1925. It was a pleasant party not untempered in the
minds of some by forebodings, for she was not in good health.
There was a large company gathered in the ballroom of the
Somerset. As a dozen speakers offered their tribute of appreciation, eulogy, essay, or impromptu remark from the orchid-
adorned table, Miss Lowell smilingly sipped coffee and smoked
the inevitable cigar. When the speaking was finished she read
two poems, received an offering of flowers in a silver bowl,
bowed, and the affair was over. I wonder how many of those
present sensed the shortness of her hold on life or realized that
this meeting with her was the last.

Another caller at Park Street who may be mentioned here,
although it does not appear that his autograph was solicited
at the time, was Franklin D. Roosevelt. He dropped in to see
us with some regularity on his way to Cambridge during the
World War. Mr. Roosevelt was then on the board of Harvard
Overseers and on his visits he enjoyed rummaging in the sub-
terranean regions of our premises in search of odd or rare naval
books, in which he was then, as since, keenly interested.

I turn now from names found on the guest-book leaves to

Gentle friend, it may
be shocking,
But I'm in your
Christmas stocking

In your service I
am tied –
Couldn't get out
if I tried

HOUDINI
278 W. 113th St. NYC, USA

the pages of memory. By 1898 the group of authors who made New England literary history in the middle of the nineteenth century had finished their work. Emerson, Hawthorne, and Thoreau, Longfellow and Lowell, Holmes and Whittier were no longer familiar figures on Concord, Cambridge, Boston, or Amesbury streets. Only a few of the minor authors of their time were living when our bookshop was opened. Of these, still in health, his tall form but slightly bent with years, Frank B. Sanborn was one who became a frequent visitor. Sanborn was in early manhood the tutor of Emerson's children. When John Brown, the Osawatomie sheep-farmer, appeared bearing the incendiary torch of insurrection, Sanborn became his ardent partisan and narrowly escaped Southern vengeance for his activities in Brown's behalf. Later he became Brown's biographer. He was in his youth an acquaintance of Thoreau's as afterwards he was in close association with Alcott and his School of Philosophy. At the time I knew

Sanborn he was the Boston correspondent of the *Springfield Republican* and as a lecturer was much in demand for parlor talks on literature and literary history. As I got to know him I saw that he was likely to be of use in many ways. Having no ready source of general information, he became my first recourse when I needed help with unfamiliar books, although his assistance had to be received with caution. Colonel T. W. Higginson once said to me, 'Sanborn has the most encyclopædic mind of any man I know — and the most inaccurate.' If I showed him a book about which I knew nothing — the subject, the author, and the language all being strange to me — Sanborn's response might be on this order: 'What have we here? Why, this book must be very rare! It is by that famous German philosopher, So-and-So. If you like, I will take it home and look it over.' The next day the book would be returned with a helpful typewritten note concerning it.

In his newspaper writings Sanborn was critical of 'economic royalists,' a fact which gives some point to the following incident. It happened during one of the few calls which the Quincy-kitchen shop received from J. P. Morgan. I was turning for Mr. Morgan the folio sheets of a collection of Audubon's bird plates when Sanborn entered. Walking to where I was standing with Morgan, and opening a folio volume of Piranesi which was on the table beside us, he disregarded the other visitor's presence as he exclaimed, 'Why, here is that famous book of Roman views by Piranesi!' Mr. Morgan quietly remarked that he had a complete set of Piranesi's works, upon which Sanborn looked at the stranger with lifted eyebrows and an air which I cannot describe as he responded, 'Indeed! Perhaps you know that they are very rare!'

From time to time Sanborn sold me books and manuscripts of interest. Thoreau's college themes in manuscript came to me from him. I also bought from him the galley-proofs of *A Week on the Concord and Merrimack Rivers*. About the time of which I write there was an increased interest in Thoreau and he was becoming popular with first-edition collectors. Previous to this time I had published a collection of Whittier's letters in a small edition; the book was one of Bruce Rogers's designing and was printed for me by Houghton, Mifflin and Company. Having now established a working acquaintance with Sanborn, I thought it worth while to inquire if some ore might not be extracted from the tailings of his reminiscences. He proved receptive to the idea and the first result of his exploration of the old mine was a brief but interesting paper, *The Personality of Thoreau*. This, illustrated by an exquisite etching of the red-winged blackbird and nest made by Smith after Herbert W. Gleason's charming nature photograph, was printed for me at the Merrymount Press. A companion volume by Sanborn on Emerson followed. When the first of these was published, the printer had designed the book so beautifully that, knowing his interest in Mr. Updike's work, I sent a copy to Professor Charles Eliot Norton, who acknowledged the gift in a graceful note of appreciation. Following this self-introduction I ventured to inquire if Professor Norton would write another 'Personality' book for the series which I hoped to make (a 'series' which never went beyond the *Emerson* volume), say, *The Personality of Ruskin*. This was as unfortunate a suggestion as could have been made, for Norton had expressed his opinion that too much had already been written on Ruskin. Politely declining the invitation he asked me to call on him to discuss another work which he thought we might undertake together.

Thomas Gray, whose fame rests on the great *Elegy*, besides being a poet and letter-writer, was an amateur entomologist. Norton owned Gray's copy of the *Systema-Naturæ* of Linnæus, in which the poet's elegant Latin notes were beautifully written and illustrated by his own figures of insects and birds on interleaved pages. The volume, once Ruskin's, had been presented to Norton by Mrs. Arthur Severn after Ruskin's death. Professor Norton now proposed as a joint enterprise that we should have some of the more interesting pages of Gray's manuscript reproduced and, with a prefatory essay which he would write, ask Mr. Updike to make a small book for me to publish. The idea seemed a happy one and the book, when printed, proved highly satisfactory in all respects. Professor Norton wrote me saying that it seemed to him as nearly perfect as a mortal thing could be. Nevertheless the venture was unprofitable, and afterwards, when we found a substantial portion of the edition unsold, Norton wrote me enclosing his check for one-half of the loss. I do not think that he ever called at the shop, but I saw him several times at his home. When leaving Shady Hill no servant was summoned to show a visitor to the door. Norton performed this courtesy himself, conveying by an irresistible smile the impression that you were a very dear friend whom he delighted to honor.

Daniel B. Fearing of Newport, Rhode Island, was a mighty collector in his day. This statement might be taken in two ways, but it has no reference to the size of his body. His great hobby was fishing and he gathered omnivorously books, pamphlets, broadsides, book-plates, pictures — even picture postcards — in fact printed matter of every sort — on both fish and fishing.

More discriminating collectors along such lines prescribe for themselves narrower limits. The subject of angling alone covers in its variety of detail subjects diverse though related in interest. There are the technical features — tackle, equipment, mechanics, and the skill of fly-casting, with the debated question of sunken or floating lures — as well as the more general aspects of the fisherman's art — poetical, romantic, and historical — subjects on which there is enough literature to form many collections. The Fearing collection, however, is all-inclusive, embracing as it does *The Compleat Angler* of 1653 and Statutes governing the North Sea herring industry; bulky reports of the United States Fish Commission and dainty brochures of the North Country anglers' songs. Pollock or salmon were both for the Fearing net. The old-time angling collections of Bethune and Bartlett and later accumulations such as those of Heckscher and Dean Sage were left far behind when Fearing entered the race. No collector exceeded him in enthusiasm. 'Well, what have you got for me today?' was his morning greeting as ruddy and rotund he rolled in from the door of the shop radiating good-fellowship and expectancy.

The kernel of Fearing's library, like that of most collections of fishing books, was *The Compleat Angler*. He sought for every edition of this book and when one which he lacked appeared for sale he was not likely to come off second-best in the bidding. One morning a letter came from him asking about an edition of this book which he had seen in Libbie's auction catalogue. It was described as printed by Septimus Prowett, London, in 1826. 'Of course,' Fearing wrote, 'there is no such book. The cataloguer has got this book mixed up with Walton's *Lives* which Prowett published; its companion volume, the *Angler*, has the Pickering imprint. Check up on this for me, please.' I went to Libbie's as requested, examined the small volume and reported that the book was catalogued correctly — Prowett *was* its publisher. Mr. Fearing became greatly excited — a Walton unknown to *Bibliotheca Piscatoria!* — and he instructed Libbie to buy it for him without limit. Unlimited bids are dangerous, especially when there is a serious competitor in the field. Nathaniel C. Nash of Cambridge was as keen for a unique Walton as Fearing was. His buying agent, Frank C. Brown, received the same instructions as Mr. Fearing sent to Libbie. The bidding was spirited, but Brown finally let the book go to Libbie and Fearing got it for three hundred and thirty dollars. This issue being unique, is well worth the amount which Fearing paid for it, although its cost astonished him at the time.

There are two books on my own shelves which came from Fearing. One is the printed check-list of his collection as it was in 1901, which he 'loaned' me subject to a recall never made. The other is his copy, checked and annotated, of Westwood and Satchell's *Bibliotheca Piscatoria*. At the top of the cabinet which contains the choicer volumes of my collection of Complete Anglers, on a narrow ledge, there is a miniature bust in bronze of Izaak Walton. This effigy of Fearing's patron saint, made for him by Tiffany and Company, was given to me by Mrs. Fearing after the death of her husband. I prize these mementoes of one who was both a generous customer and a friend.

Although mail orders from him were not infrequent, I do not remember meeting Sir William Osler, a great collector of medical books, the greatest, I believe, of his time. As one of our transactions with him has reference to his last days, it may be worth recording here, although Doctor Harvey Cushing has made incidental reference to it in his *Life*. I should preface the account by saying for the information of any who have not read Doctor Cushing's great biography that Osler had been a lifelong collector of the writings of Sir Thomas Browne. A few days before he died (of pneumonia contracted during a motor ride from Newcastle to London in the days of the railway strike of the autumn of 1919) Osler called for the Ticknor and Fields (Boston) edition of *Religio Medici*. This was his favorite edition,[1] of which I had sold him many copies. Doctor Cushing writes:

> What he looked for is apparent; for in this, the Ticknor and Fields edition, his 'constant companion' for fifty-two years, remarkably free from annotations of any kind, considering that it had been so long in the possession of a man who read pencil in hand, he has written this marginal note on page 345 of the 'Urn Burial'; 'Wonderful page... always impressed me as one of the great ones in B. 6. xii. 19. W. O.':

> But the iniquity of oblivion blindly scattereth her poppy, and deals with the memory of men without distinction to merit of perpetuity. Who can but pity the founder of the pyramids? Erostratus lives that burnt the Temple of Diana; he is almost lost that built it. Time hath spared the epitaph of Adrian's horse, confounded that of himself. In vain we compute our felicities by the advantage of our good names, since bad have equal durations; and Thersites is like to live as long as Agamemnon. Who knows whether the best of men be known, or whether there be not more remarkable persons forgot than any that stand remembered in the known account of time? Without the favour of the everlasting register, the first man had been as unknown as the last, and Methuselah's long life had been his only chronicle.

[1] Dr. Osler's fondness for this edition must have come from its typographical excellence. The editorial work of James T. Fields was severely castigated in a contemporary criticism of several pages wherein the writer declares that Fields 'has put in all the intelligence furnished him by previous editors, and all the ignorance peculiar to himself.' (*The Philobiblion*, vol. 1, pp. 30–34.)

Oblivion is not to be hired. The greater part must be content to be as though they had not been, to be found in the register of God, not in the record of man. Twenty-seven names make up the first story, and the recorded names ever since contain not one living century. The number of the dead long exceedeth all that shall live. The night of time far surpasseth the day; and who knows when was the equinox? Every hour adds unto that current arithmetic, which scarce stands one moment.

This, however, is aside from my anecdote. There had been on our books for a long time an order from Sir William for *The Boston Medical and Surgical Journal* for 1846, the year in which the use of sulphuric ether as an agent of surgical anæsthesia was demonstrated by Doctor William T. Morton in the Massachusetts General Hospital. The year before his death Osler had written to Doctor F. C. Shattuck in Boston, '... Drop in at Goodspeed's & jog his memory about the Bost. Med. & Surg Jr. *Vol* 35 which has the ether papers & I want BADLY Morton's original papers'; and not many months later Doctor Shattuck's son, returning from London, brought me a similar message. It was about two months before Osler's death that an auction house catalogued for sale a long run containing the desired year of this periodical. To show the extent of Osler's acquaintance and the number of physician friends who had his interests in mind, I mention the fact that even before the catalogue containing this title had reached my desk, a letter came to us from a physician in Portland calling attention to the *Boston Medical and Surgical Journal* in the sale and reminding us of Sir William Osler's need of it. We bought the set, took from it the volume which he wanted, and unaware of Osler's illness forwarded the book to him in London. Doctor Cushing writes:

> On recovering from the anæsthetic on the day of his first operation, he said to Malloch: 'Well, it's good to have gone so long with so little wrong with me. But I feel with Franklin that "I have been too far across the river to go back and have it all over again." Did you ever read Franklin's Life? — a

wonderful book.' When about this time there arrived a package
forwarded from Boston by C. E. Goodspeed, containing the
numbers of the Boston journal giving the early accounts of
ether administrations which he had been wanting so long for
the Bibliotheca Prima, he asked Malloch to write in the 1846
volume: 'All things come to him who waits, but it was a pretty
close shave this time.'

Twenty-four days later, on the afternoon of December 29,
1919, Osler died. Early in January following, Laay Osler
wrote to me of the pleasure which the long-desired volume
had given her husband and enclosed a check in payment for it.
That same month I sent to her for addition to the Browne collection a book which it would have gladdened Osler to see,
his favorite 1862 Ticknor and Fields issue of *Religio Medici*, one
of three copies only on large paper made in that size for the
private use of the printer. That was a volume which, alas!
came too late.

It may seem absurd to couple the names of Osler and Fearing
as book-collectors. A comparison between their libraries would,
of course, be impossible. They offer, however, points which
are noteworthy in contrast. Fearing's fishing library of more
than eleven thousand volumes given by him to Harvard College
was all-inclusive, rejecting nothing. It was made by an enthusiast on a recreational subject which being of slight utilitarian
value, the importance of the collection from that standpoint
is relatively small. Its value lies in its extent and the degree
of its completeness. Osler writing to an old McGill student
once said:

> I am collecting on two lines — books that are of historical
> importance in the evolution of medicine, and books that have
> interest through the character or work of their authors. In
> that way I limit the field, which is large enough!

As a contribution to the world-history of medicine, Osler's
Bibliotheca Prima, now at McGill University, is of enormous
value.

Frank Brewer Bemis was a Boston banker, sportsman, collector, and philanthropist. He was the most modest of men

concerning his possessions and, though few men have had as good reason for pride in their collections as Bemis, no one whom I have known has shown such reluctance to allow the nature and extent of his library to be known. Not that it was especially large as collections go, but, considering the average quality of its volumes, the size was, nevertheless, impressive. Bemis had an antipathy for publicity and the remotest thought that his books might become the means of self-advertising was repellent to him. This trait was indeed carried to a point where, for an American, it might be thought extreme. His gatherings were not like those of some others of his day, the result of prodigal disbursements of wealth acquired in the flush of speculative dealings; they represented the patient watching and intelligent purchasing of many years. A large part of his books came from London, both from dealers and from the salesrooms through his agents. I doubt if he ever purchased in the auction room in person. He was also a liberal buyer in this country — in New York from the most recent importations of the larger dealers, and in Boston chiefly from Mr. Foley and myself from our local acquisitions. One book which he purchased of me was a copy of *Evangeline* in the first edition, presented and inscribed by Longfellow to Hawthorne. For this book, of very special interest from the fact that Longfellow was indebted to Hawthorne for Evangeline's story, he paid two hundred and fifty dollars.

Due to the reasons mentioned above few persons outside of the group of book-dealers with whom he had business relations, a few students, and the circle of his personal friends, have known that Mr. Bemis left, when he died, what might perhaps be described as the best private collection of first editions of English literature in America.

Had Frank Bemis been less diffident he could have entertained his friends with many interesting tales of his collecting experiences, but he could not be prevailed upon to break his reserve even in the privacy of the Club of Odd Volumes, although often urged to do so.

One anecdote I tell not only for its own interest but also

because in a way it answers a popular curiosity concerning sources of supply to the rare-book market. To explain my own connection with the story I should say that, some months before (it was in 1922), I had spent the night at Beverly and had been shown by Mr. Bemis his library as it was at that time. The next morning while at breakfast, I was asked concerning any deficiencies in the library which I might have noted. The outstanding omission, to me, was William Blake and I so told my host. The immediate result of this criticism was his purchase of the *Songs of Innocence*, 1789. The next year he bought the book now to be described.

There came to me from London in December, 1923, an auction sale catalogue which included Blake's poem, *Milton*. This work is very rare; no copy had ever appeared at public sale, and but four examples were known. The copy was described as containing an extra page of text not found in the other known copies and was in other respects the largest and finest of the four. To increase its value still further the three others are all owned by public libraries (including the Huntington Library in that description).

This catalogue I sent to Mr. Bemis who cabled to Pickering and Chatto, his agents in London, asking for their estimate of what the book might bring. The estimate was far more than Bemis wished to pay, but he decided to bid on the item, though for a less amount. Through some mischance his instructions were delayed and only got on the cable at the last minute. However, the message was delivered in time and Pickering and Chatto secured the book, although they went beyond the limit given them. Notwithstanding this increase, Bemis accepted the book. It was received by him on a Saturday afternoon. We were about to close shop for the day when he came in, book in hand. 'Here is the *Milton*,' he said, 'and as you are responsible for my getting it, I want you to take it home over Sunday and have the first pleasure of looking it over.' The poem, with the title-page and two other plates reproduced in color, was reprinted by the Club of Odd Volumes of Boston.

This is only part of the story. The next summer in London

FRANK B. BEMIS

the elder Massey of Pickering and Chatto, one of London's leading bookmen, now gone, told me that Bemis's cabled bid was brought to his desk about noon of the sale-day. As Massey was occupied with other matters at the time, the envelope remained unopened for half an hour. When he finally got to it he found to his alarm that the hour lacked but a few minutes of the time of sale, and the *Milton* was well up to the front in the afternoon session. Snatching his hat he dashed for a cab which soon got into a street jam. Hastily thrusting his fare into the cabby's hand he leaped to the sidewalk and ran all the way up the street to Sotheby's door, arriving in the room just as the book was placed on the auctioneer's desk. The competition for this book was keen, but Massey was successful and Blake's *Milton* was knocked down to him and forwarded to America.

Still the story is incomplete. The conclusion (in sequence of narrative, though not in chronology of event) follows. One day prior to the events described above, an elderly lady from one of the Channel Islands brought in to the Sotheby rooms in New Bond Street a parcel of books to be sold. After looking them over the auctioneer's assistant told her that they might fetch a matter of, say, forty or forty-five pounds. That sum being insufficient to meet some special need of the seller, she took from her reticule a thin volume and inquired if that would have any value, adding that she had been reluctant to sell it because it was a favorite book of her childhood days on account of the bright coloring of its pages. That was the Windus copy of *Milton* which was bought by Bemis for thirty-four hundred pounds!

During Mr. Bemis's lifetime there had been speculation concerning the future of his library, and not until after his death in 1935 was it known that it had passed from his ownership ten years before. While retaining possession of the books for life, they had been conveyed by him through a deed of trust to two friends to be disposed of after his death at such time and in such manner as they should determine. The Children's Hospital of Boston is the beneficiary of that trust.

One of the two trustees of the Bemis library, Harold Murdock of Chestnut Hill, died two years before Bemis. The relations between them were close. Mr. Murdock was a banker who, after retiring from business, became the Director of the Harvard University Press bringing to that department of the University his business ability plus an intimate knowledge of books and typography gained through the studies of a lifetime. The sound judgment of book values which Bemis acquired, and that intimate acquaintance with their contents which confutes the thoughtless, oft-repeated libel on book-collectors were, I believe, in no small measure due to the influence of Murdock's long experience and studious mind. With this influence and the inspiring contact of great literature in the earliest form of its issue, Bemis became a student as well as a lover of his books.

Harold Murdock was a no less earnest collector than his friend. His interests varied with the years but centred about the Georgian period. The famous group of Johnson and his friends, their books and their relationships — personal, literary, and political — were the subject of his study, but contemporaneous with, and related to, that galaxy, Murdock gave especial attention to the local conflicts between the British and the Americans during the early years of the Revolution. His brilliant monographs, written with sympathetic regard for the Tory interest, not fairly treated by American historians in the past, dramatize the affairs of Concord, Lexington, and Bunker Hill in 1775. These monographs, with the exhaustive and scholarly work of Allen French, are our most trustworthy account of those events. A part of Murdock's collection which, though not one of the largest, was most distinguished, especially by many autograph letters of prime importance from the chief participants in the scenes of the time and others of great literary value, has been presented to Harvard College Library by his friends in his memory.

In casual acquaintance Mr. Murdock was at times austere; in fact his manner seemed rather forbidding in his early visits to my shop. Whether a closer relationship brought by the passing years or the mellowing influence of time was responsible

HAROLD MURDOCK

for a change in his aspect I cannot say; it may have been both. Anyway his visits came to be a regular feature, and on the days when those visits were, for any cause, omitted, there came that uneasy feeling of unfulfilled expectancy which follows any break of routine. When in later years Murdock had retired from business life, his mornings were spent in Quincy Street overseeing the affairs of the Harvard University Press. From Harvard Square, by subway over Charles River Basin and under Beacon Hill, ten minutes brought him to the Union Club for lunch; after which a few steps uphill for the half-hour at Goodspeed's while waiting for his car to carry him home to an afternoon with Jane Austen or the evening gathering with Johnson and The Club. Murdock's retentive memory and penetrating mind made the daily discussion, bibliographical or personal, of great value to me and also to my son to whose desk-side he gravitated during the last years. On one point only was there serious difference between us: Murdock's views on the relative values of books rebound and those in original covers did not agree with ours as, curiously for a collector, he thought that the value of a book should not be seriously diminished by rebinding. On this point our own opinions were supported by auction-sale prices.

Our dealings one with another, which on my part were more intimate and extensive than those with any other customer, covered a period of thirty or more years. In all of that time he was a wise counsellor and a constant friend. In rectitude of thought no less than in probity of deed, Harold Murdock was both my inspiration and my ideal.

Percival Merritt was another one of the group of Bostonians actively prominent amongst book-collectors. He was a man of culture and personal charm, admitted through his scholarship to the first rank of bibliographers on both sides of the Atlantic. A student of our New England colonial history, he wrote extensively on particular phases of the life of that period, but it is to his contributions to the bibliography and life of Horace Walpole that we are most indebted. Merritt became widely recognized as an American authority on Walpole and made a superb collection — at the time perhaps the most nearly complete of any in America — of Walpole's works and the books printed for him at the Strawberry Hill Press. These and his other Walpole material Mrs. Merritt generously gave to the Harvard College Library after her husband's death.

It was in the year 1907 that Theodore N. Vail came to Boston as president of the great Bell Telephone System. His first purchase of books from me depleted my stock of American humorists — Mrs. Partington, Orpheus C. Kerr, Philander Q. Doesticks, Artemus Ward, Josh Billings and their kin. Mr. Vail's massive, shaggy head, genial face, and impressive figure marked him as an exceptional man, but he was so little known in Boston at the time that a customer, a highly placed banking-house officer whom I asked concerning the credit of this new-comer, confessed that he had never heard of him.

Although Vail became a good buyer he was never an important collector and I fancy that the high position to which he was called absorbed his attention so completely that he had no time for serious book-collecting. My shop, then a one-man establishment, could not spare me the time to wait in an anteroom of Vail's office, so it was not long before I had to employ an outsider when I had a book which I thought he might like. One expensive set of books which he purchased in the days when he called at the Park Street shop was a ponderous edition of Granger's *Biographical History of England*, converted into a veritable portrait-gallery of English worthies by some old-time extra-illustrator. It contained thousands of engravings, from octavo to folio in size, bound in huge volumes, how many I do not recall. The set was bought by me from Maggs Brothers of London, and when Vail died I bought it again at the auction sale of his library. It now has a permanent home in the library of the Boston Athenæum.

Another customer, also a telephone official, of lesser renown than Vail although by no means unknown to fame, and of high technical achievements, was General John J. Carty, a vice-president of the American Telephone and Telegraph Company and at the time of his death in charge of its mechani-

cal department. General Carty was an old friend and customer of George Emery Littlefield. We had a standing order
from him for all copies of Perry's *Expedition to Japan*, a stout
three-volume publication of the United States Government,
copiously illustrated by tinted lithographs wherein the results
of Commodore Perry's momentous voyage to the Island
Empire are set forth in full detail of narrative and scientific
report. I think that these purchases were in some way related
to a visit which General Carty had made to Japan years before
and Perry's *Expedition* may have been bought for presentation
to Japanese friends, although why he needed so many copies is
not clear.

The names of many other customers might be cited for
some incident or mentioned for some unusual personal trait
which gave zest to their relationship to the bookshop. Thomas
W. Lawson, once a celebrity of local fame, though now forgotten, was one of them.

Tom Lawson, as he was commonly called, had a meteoric
career of a militant sort. He tilted against the magnates of
Boston and New York with an audacity that, while it supplied
spectators with an entertainment of the bullfight order, must
have exasperated his victims beyond measure. The epithet
'that gentile-plated jew' applied to one adversary is a specimen
of the picturesque language he employed in *Frenzied Finance*, a
book published in the early nineteen hundreds which greatly
scandalized the vicinage of State and Wall Streets. In person,
Lawson exemplified his character. He dressed in a shepherd-
plaid suit, wore a bright red tie and wore a carnation in the
buttonhole of his coat. This attire, with his black mustache,
the outcropping of a head of wavy hair, gave him a rakish
appearance suggesting a modern freebooter with a touch of
the dandy added.

I met Lawson but once when he came into the shop to look
at Savage's engraving of *The Washington Family* which he saw
through the window as he passed. Later, when I wrote him
soliciting his order to 'extra-illustrate' a book of his choice,
he inquired in reply what it might cost to produce in this

manner the finest possible set of Poe's works. The price quoted and agreed upon was, according to my recollection, two thousand dollars — a mere trifle to the man whose fortune for a brief season has been rated at fifty millions.

This commission was not altogether easy to follow out, for where, except in the various engravings of Poe's portraits and in illustrations from other editions of his works, could we find suitable pictures? Luckily the *Chapter on Autographs* which Poe once wrote furnished an opportunity to use original letters by the writers whose handwriting Poe discussed. It also occurred to me that it might be interesting to secure short original estimates of Poe's genius from contemporary authors which would make a unique addition to the biographical volume of the set selected for the extending. Most of the writers whose assistance in this direction was solicited responded favorably; some gratuitously, others for a compensation. Frank Sanborn was one who accepted the invitation; Thomas Wentworth Higginson was another, and there were more whose names I do not now remember. Henry van Dyke's name I recall very clearly, for he was one who curtly, though I cannot say unreasonably, refused compliance with my request. When the Poe work was completed and the set was ready to bind, Lawson ordered for it full green *limp* levant morocco, a binding unsuitable by reason of its impermanent color (green leather always fading when exposed to the light) and also on account of the impossibility of making a leather cover unsupported by mill-board stand properly on its shelf. Another peculiarity of the binding concerned the decoration. Lawson specified that all ornamentation should be carried out with due regard for his *penchant* for the numeral three (the reason for which I never knew). Panel lines, rosettes, fleurons, or whatever form the binder's decorative fancy might take, were to be applied in threes or the multiples of the same.

I believe that this was my only sale of books to Lawson. When, after he died, I appraised his books in the village of Egypt, Massachusetts, his library showed that he had been more of a general reader than a collector of books. Yet Lawson was a collector of other things. The Egypt house, located in extensive grounds enclosed by long stretches of rose-covered fencing, was, figuratively speaking, filled with figures of elephants: elephants for umbrella stands, elephant-supported bookracks, elephant-bearing candlesticks, and about the rooms single elephants, made of various materials in all sorts of attitudes and of many sizes.

Lawson's farm was of moderate extent, located not far from the shores of Massachusetts Bay. It was well stocked with fine cattle and a good stable and he took great pleasure in the latter, being especially interested in his horses.

The Lawson belongings are now scattered, dispersed by auction after his death, but ironically, the Egypt estate retains the significant name selected by the owner — *Dreamwold*.

With baked, and broiled, and stewed, and
toasted,
And fried, and boiled, and smoked, and
roasted,
We treat the town.

VII. SALMAGUNDI

UNDER this name I have thrown together some miscellaneous notes not altogether related to each other; but as I have just told of my early adventures in publishing I may as well finish that account first.

In all of the undertakings in this business which were done at my own risk, my desire was to produce books of literary merit in a manner which would appeal to collectors of limited editions. A fair proportion of them, I believe, met the requirements. It is, therefore, to be regretted that I should have allowed myself in a few instances to be the sponsor for indifferent publications. I had no intention of going into a general publishing business, though not unwilling to be led in that direction should my primary efforts meet with success.

Fred Holland Day had become associated with Herbert Copeland some years before I entered the book business. The list of Copeland and Day publications is not long but it includes some important works. Notable are *The Black Riders* of Stephen Crane, Carman and Hovey's *Songs from Vagabondia*, the poems of Father Tabb, and several of the books of Alice Brown and Louise Guiney. They also published the American edition of *The Yellow Book*. Mr. Day had what is popularly described as an 'artistic temperament' and the books produced by his firm were fairly successful in their attempt to improve on current publications both in typography and binding, Bertram Goodhue being a valuable asset in the matter of decoration. In a general way the name of Copeland and Day became associated with the idea of superiority in bookmaking. Their enterprise achieved but a moderate success and not long after my appearance in Park Street the firm dissolved. Both partners retired from business; Day to carry on his photography in which he had done notable amateur, and, in some particulars, pioneer, work.

Edward Carpenter, the English writer, was a correspondent of Day's, and one day the latter brought to me a new book which Carpenter was bringing out in London. It was an anthology of friendship, entitled *Iolaüs*. Day asked me if I would take the sheets of the American issue with my imprint on them, bind them at my expense, and market them for the author. I accepted the offer and, although Carpenter's vogue at the time was enough to dispose of the small edition furnished me, I imagine that I did not express much enthusiasm for the book. At all events I was not asked to become the American publisher of the works by Carpenter which followed. Day may have been offended by the binding of *Iolaüs* for which I was responsible. It was indeed an atrocious mauve affair of ribbed cloth; not much worse in its way as it afterwards seemed to me, however, than the English typography of the book. Not long after this affair a break came in my relations with Day which, in spite of efforts for reconciliation, to my regret was never healed. It was caused by a trifling matter, but one which touched Day on a sensitive point — his photography. He had undertaken to photograph my young daughters. The proofs submitted were, as I now think, quite charming, but an incidental comment made on their 'fogginess,' as I suppose the absence of focus shown in his style of treatment was considered by us, was enough. The commission was thrown up and I was cast into Philistine darkness never to be restored to his favor. When, after his death two years ago, we bought Day's library of more than five thousand volumes, a photograph of Bruce Rogers taken by him was found amongst his papers. It is reproduced here as an example of Day's work in portraiture. To me it is a good representation of Rogers as I first knew him when the photograph was taken twenty-five years ago.

Two other books undertaken unfortunately, when considered in relation to the really worthy books which comprise

Photograph by F. H. Day

BRUCE ROGERS

most of the meagre list of Goodspeed publications, were the *Bacon-Shakespeare Parallelisms* and *Francis Bacon Our Shakespeare* of Edwin Reed. Reed, an amiable, scholarly man, inoculated by the Baconian virus, had secured financial backing from a Boston lawyer of social standing whose interest in these books was probably more potent with me than the subjects of which they treated. While there was nothing discreditable in the appearance of the volumes, they were in no respect superior to the ordinary output of commercial printers. I was, therefore, much surprised recently to read in an autograph letter that George Moore wrote to the New York publishers who had his collected works in preparation, a strong recommendation of our *Bacon-Shakespeare Parallelisms* as the model to be followed in planning the typography of his own works. I should, myself, be far from suggesting these editions of Reed's books as examples of superior bookmaking.

More happy than either the works of Carpenter or Reed were three early books also published by me on other accounts than my own. Two of these, brought to me by the printer, Daniel Berkeley Updike, were Trumbull Stickney's *Dramatic Verses*, and Burne-Jones's *In the Dawn of the World*, books differing widely both in format and typography, but marked by that appropriateness of treatment which, to me, is the distinguishing feature underlying the other qualities of Updike's work.

While I am on this subject, it is fitting that I should say something about my relations with Mr. Updike and the Merrymount Press. Having no organization or prestige to aid me, it was evident that if my publications were to find buyers they must (merit of contents being assumed) be printed in a superior manner. Of this, the work of the Merrymount Press was more than sufficient guaranty, and my own knowledge of typographic principles being nil (although I do not think that I was wholly lacking in taste in judging appearance of the work) I have placed all but a few of our publications unreservedly in its hands.

One abortive attempt at a more ambitious undertaking, and a mention of three of our latest books from the Merrymount

Press, and I am done with the subject of publishing, space compelling me to omit the other books on our list of publications excepting the bare mention of two especially interesting works not done by Updike. These are the catalogue of George C. Wales's etchings and lithographs of shipping and Louis Holman's important and ingenious folio work entitled *The Graphic Processes*.

I do not remember whether the idea was Updike's or my own — I think it was his — but, in talking over publication possibilities thirty-odd years ago, Jane Austen was mentioned. As far as either of us knew, there was at the time no edition of her works on the market worthy of a place beside the better editions of other English novelists. It seemed as though our own enthusiasm for 'the fair and witty Jane' must be shared by enough people interested in fine books to carry such a project to success, so with specimen page and prospectus I set to work. I got as far as the broadcasting of these announcements through the medium of our catalogue list and made a trip to New York to canvass the book trade for advance orders. The results were not encouraging. I remember that in Putnam's I gained access to the head of the house who grudgingly agreed to take twenty-five sets, but lessened the value of the subscription by reading me a lecture on my presumption in entering the publishing field, a homily which I then thought gratuitous although it may have been salutary.

My feelings may have been those of the panhandler who, when a prospect whom he accosted said to him, 'If you had the sense to ask for a nickel instead of a quarter, you might have got it,' replied, 'Sir, you may do as you please; give me a quarter or give me nothing, but please don't tell me how to run my business.'

Of the three late recent publications to which I have referred, one, *The Complete Angler*, was in keeping with a personal hobby. As a devotee of Izaak's art and a collector of his most-read book, I aspired to make this newest edition of the old classic worthy of the author and a credit to the craftsmanship of our day. I had in mind a size which would allow the book to be slipped

Photograph by Albert Petersen

D. B. UPDIKE

into a pocket of reasonable capacity. It was to be printed, of course, at the Merrymount Press. Also, it should have an introduction of merit and, if feasible, a few illustrations. All these conditions were successfully met. The choice of a scholar-angler, Professor Bliss Perry, for the few pages of prefatory matter and W. A. Dwiggins to supply the decorations, amply satisfied my ideals in these respects. When I saw the final result, I felt like repeating Professor Norton's word regarding *The Poet Gray as a Naturalist*, for I felt that this book indeed approached perfection.

Some years ago, single leaves from an incomplete copy of the Gutenberg Bible with a foreword by A. Edward Newton and a title-page printed by Bruce Rogers were distributed by a New York bookseller at one hundred and twenty-five dollars each. Stimulated no doubt by the success of that publication, in 1929 we exploited in a similar manner some pages from the first American Bible, the one translated by John Eliot into the Indian language and published in Cambridge (Massachusetts) in 1663. The Merrymount Press printed the title-page and the introductory text by Doctor George Parker Winship. The issue was immediately sold at twelve dollars and fifty cents a copy. Three years later, when we catalogued a second-hand copy at thirty dollars, four customers sought it at the advanced price.

In Goodspeed's, coincidences connecting our different departments are not uncommon as, for example, a happening some time after *The First American Bible — A Leaf* was issued. An Indian document, so-called, was brought to our autograph department for purchase. Indian documents, usually deeds to white settlers in the seventeenth century, are moderately scarce. As might be expected the signatures are usually by 'mark.' This particular specimen was not a deed, although of a similar nature, being an agreement between some Indians and their neighbors for the exchange of lands lying south of Worcester, Massachusetts. There were several signatories of both races. There are not many auction records on documents of this kind and our offer for this one was not accepted until after the vendor had tried, unsuccessfully, to get more from other parties. When it finally became our property, the document went into our cabinet without further examination and remained there for some weeks until it was brought out for the inspection of a caller. Then, for the first time, I saw that one of the group of natives concerned in the affair had signed not like the others by 'mark,' but in autograph. He had an odd name — James Printer. Who was James Printer? The answer to the query was quickly found. It appears in the fifteenth page of Doctor Winship's text to *The First American Bible* in which he recounts the history of Eliot's Indian Bible and speaks of the printers of that work as being 'assisted by an Indian boy known in the records as James the Printer.' If there were any question of identity here, a consultation of the local records confirmed the connection. We had, therefore, on this document the autograph of the first native-born American printer to place with a specimen of the autograph of the first American printer of English birth, Stephen Daye, already owned by us.

It will be remembered that it was from Daye's press that the first American book,[1] the *Bay Psalm Book*, came in 1641.

Of our independent publications, the latest and most important of all appeared in 1932. Like Walton's *Angler*, the *Memoir of the Life and Work of Sidney L. Smith* was a labor of love. After Smith's death in 1929, I purchased the contents of his studio, comprising his own large collection of proofs of the

---

[1] Speaking correctly, one should say 'The first book printed in British North America of which any copy is known to exist,' for, in the first place, the fact that no earlier book is known is not evidence that none was printed, and secondly, the statement would be false if applied to America generally, for books were printed in South America in the sixteenth century and there are two and a half shelves of Mexican imprints before 1640 in the John Carter Brown Library, at Providence, Rhode Island. The James Printer document is now owned by The Fruitlands and The Wayside Museum, Inc., of Harvard, Massachusetts.

plates on which he had worked during the mature years of an active life. With these were original coppers of many Smith etchings. Through their possession, aided by the generous coöperation of individuals who owned others, we were able to present an adequate representation of his work printed from the original plates in a single volume which included a biographical sketch by his daughter and some significant selections from his diary. It was an expensive book to produce, but I believe that the result justified the large expenditure.

Having mentioned more than once in these pages what seem to me remarkable coincidences, I shall add a few further examples, although I acknowledge that the subject is not interesting to everyone. The reason for this may be thought the same as in the case of relics. Relics have small value as merchandise because too often their acceptance is a test of credulity. They are unconvincing; by their nature they do not ordinarily carry evidence of reality. A lock of hair said to be Napoleon's must be received as an article of faith; actually, it might be from the sweepings of a barber's floor. As for tales of wonderful happenings, we believe the story told by a friend, but how do we regard a tale by our friend's friend's friend? The following instances of coincidence are, nevertheless, authentic.

The first was told me by Arthur Lord, president of the Pilgrim Society of Plymouth and a well-known Boston lawyer. During the earlier years of his practice in Plymouth, he was called on by a blacksmith to write his will. The paper duly executed and left with him for safe-keeping was placed in a tin docket-box and in time forgotten. Years passed, and one day the dusty box was taken from aloft for inspection. Running over the dockets of the documents left in it Lord came to this will. 'By Jove!' he exclaimed, 'I wonder if that man is alive!' Fearing that the testator might have died and the estate have been settled without his knowledge, Lord took his hat and descended to the street. It was a hot day and but one man passed him as he crossed to the Probate Office to look over the records. Moved by a seemingly irrational impulse Lord accosted him with 'Do you happen to know if a man named —— a black-smith, is alive?' With an astonished look the stranger replied, 'That's an odd question for you to ask me. The man you inquire about was my father; he has just died and I am on my way to his funeral.'

The stories which follow I tell from my own experience. My son, who had then recently come into the bookshop after graduation at Harvard, told me a few weeks before Christmas that, if he could have a gift of his own choosing, it would be the first edition of *The Story of a Bad Boy* — in immaculate condition! Like all juveniles, copies of Aldrich's book, when found, were likely to be anything but immaculate, and as I had never seen more than two or three copies of the first edition in any condition, the chances that my son would get that book for Christmas were small. In less than ten days, however, one of our salesmen, knowing nothing of my son's wish for the book, brought me a superb copy picked by him from a miscellaneous lot of old books recently purchased.

The happening I next describe, one apparently untoward, but nevertheless fortunate in result, was more an accident than a coincidence. Shortly before, I had bought a remarkably fine copy of *An Impartial History of the War in America*, the Boston edition. The work, published in parts but usually found bound, is very scarce; particularly the third volume of but three numbers. The set I acquired lacked the last of these three. On my way to Philadelphia where either a Carson or a Mitchell print sale was scheduled, having seated myself in the train at New York I opened the catalogue, only to discover that I had misread the date. I was right on the day of the week but was seven days ahead of time. Had I not made this careless mistake I should not have gone to Brooklyn, and had I not gone to Brooklyn I should not have visited Neil Morrow Ladd's shop in Fulton Street. On that call at Ladd's I found good material — a volume of early Boston newspapers and a fine copy of the first edition of *The Federalist*, besides minor rarities — acceptable, although not particularly noteworthy, finds. However, on a shelf behind the owner's desk, one of those private hoards where old-book men are wont to keep unidentified or unpriced nuggets, a thin, shabby calf volume lettered 'American War' caught my eye. It was the third volume of the *Impartial History* and, although it lacked the title and many preliminary leaves, it contained the concluding pages necessary for the completion of my set, which I sold shortly afterwards to Bonaventure of New York for four hundred dollars.

One more coincidence. Ezra H. Baker was one of my friends in the Club of Odd Volumes who dropped into the Park Street shop on their way to lunch at the Union Club next door. One day in the summer as we occupied a seat together during the hour's train-ride from the country, he said to me, 'If you should ever happen upon a copy of Christopher Cranch's *The Last of the Huggermuggers,* I wish you would save it for me. I owned it when a boy and I would like to see it again.' My search for it that day took me no farther than P. K. Foley's room in the Phillips Building, for I found a copy there which I sent to Mr. Baker. When I next saw him I commented on the singular fact that the volume contained a stamp bearing the name Baker on the title. 'That is a more curious fact than you realize,' he said, 'for the copy you sent me was the identical one which belonged to my brother and me. The stamp you noticed was the ownership mark placed by us in our books more than fifty years before.'

The bookseller, often looked upon as an encyclopædia and consulted on every conceivable subject connected with books, is frequently called upon for odd services. The Concord Antiquarian Society, generously assisted by the descendants of Ralph Waldo Emerson, a few years ago acquired a fine new brick building to house their possessions. The structure is situated on the main road a few rods from the house in which Emerson lived. The Alcott orchard house and Hawthorne's Wayside residence are not far away. As the Antiquarian Society's brick building was thought to offer a safer depository for valuables than the Emerson homestead, the Emerson Memorial Association, which now owns all of Emerson's property, agreed to house the more important part of Emerson's library in a wing of the new building, and a replica of the room was made for that purpose. This room now holds all the books which were in Emerson's study, as well as its pictures and furniture. As this left the original room bare, we were consulted on the possibility of duplicating the pictures which had been taken from it. They were a miscellaneous lot — old mezzotint portraits, lithographic views, classical photographs, etc. After six months we had succeeded in replacing two-thirds of the pictures with identical copies. Having done this, we were instructed to reproduce the frames at which we were equally successful.

Orders for books in quantity are not unusual. We once received one for fifteen hundred volumes to fill the shelves in a country house. Two conditions were attached: the books selected might be on any subject but they must look like an old lot and the price was limited to twenty cents per volume. There was no difficulty in filling this order; one like it every year would be a stock-reducing blessing.

Someone wishes to know more of the 'finds' which we have made at various times, meaning, I suppose, the discovery of important items amongst material otherwise valueless or of inferior worth. Such discoveries are frequently made in regular daily purchases, and the bookseller has to depend on a certain number of them to compensate him for the losses that result from his mistaken judgment of other volumes. The selling of rare books is a speculative trade and an occasional bargain is due to the dealer's sagacity and technical information, the latter acquired at the expense of time and money. At the same time it is only in the case of the unappreciated treasures of other dealers, his equals in opportunity, that one is justified in taking full profit from the owner's ignorance. When I once found in the poetry section of a London dealer a copy of Joaquin Miller's *Pacific Tales*, a book of poems which the author stung by advance criticism limited to a very few copies, priced at two and sixpence, I thought myself justified in accepting the bargain.

A similar instance was the purchase of Locker-Lampson's

London Lyrics also for a halfcrown. In this case neither the seller nor myself had seen the lightly pencilled annotations in the book, but as I walked with it in hand from Charing Cross Road to New Oxford Street, I came upon them and saw from their nature that they could only have been made by the author himself. The next dealer I called on gave me five pounds for the book. I hope his ratio of profit to cost when he sold it was equal to mine!

These were bargains promptly taken from London dealers, but on the other hand, when I saw the first edition of *Marmion* bearing Scott's presentation inscription on the fly-leaf in an inconspicuous corner of a West End shop marked at thirty shillings, I called a clerk's attention to the mistake (?) in pricing and returned it to the shelf. If the inscription were genuine, the price would have been far too low, and in that shop would have meant an oversight. On the other hand, if I had bought the book and found afterwards that the only feature which apparently gave it special value was a forgery, I would hardly have had the courage to return it.

On my first visit to London I had selected a quantity of books from the stock of the same dealer. In the lot was the ten-volume set of Moore's works published in 1840 which bore a presentation inscription from the author, in this instance on the half-title. As I was reëxamining my purchases this inscription caught my attention. 'Is this not lithographed?' I asked. 'Surely not,' was the answer. Yet a touch of oxalic acid justified my suspicion for the printer's ink did not change. If the inscription had been written in ordinary ink, the acid would have removed it.

No one knows in what odd places treasures will be found. A rarity may come from the next-door building or from a remote place hundreds of miles away. When one is called to examine books at a distance he has to take chances on finding anything of value. Sometimes he is lucky, but often his trip is fruitless. Two women once brought us a couple of books bound in old calf. They contained six New England imprints earlier than 1678 and a good lot of Mathers for which we paid over a thousand dollars. Naturally, when they described the room from which these volumes were taken with the hundreds of books in it, we did not hesitate to make an appointment to visit the town in Tennessee where they were. I do not know what expectant feelings were experienced by Michael Walsh, our Americana expert, as he journeyed to inspect the treasures awaiting his examination. Whatever his hopes may have been, they were doomed. The two volumes that had been brought to us were the only books of real value in the lot. All that remained were worth not more than two hundred dollars.

As typical of circumstances attending the purchase of books, I shall tell of three copies of Hawthorne's *The Celestial Railroad*, a tiny pamphlet in cream-colored paper wrappers published in Boston in 1843.

The first of the three copies was found in New Bedford. I had been called there to examine a library. As I passed through the gate and followed the curving gravelled driveway, a putty-colored, mansard-roofed house of the 1870 period came into view. Approaching this architectural horror I felt sure that there was nothing in it which I should care to buy. When I entered, the marble-top black walnut furniture and the engravings after Landseer which decorated the sombre walls confirmed my impressions. The house contained a lot of books, but they were of inferior value. However, I examined them with as much care as the lot seemed to justify and picked out perhaps fifteen per cent of the whole, offering seventy-five dollars for them. The owner said, 'Well, a local dealer offers ninety dollars for all the books in the house and as we want to get rid of them, perhaps we had better let them go to him.' 'All right,' I replied, 'let him have them. He will bring anything of value to Boston and the ones I want I can buy from him then.'

In one of the chambers of the house a small shelf of books was placed near the head of the bedstead. They were old black-cloth religious works of a kind published in Boston around 1850, and when I glanced at the familiar titles I saw no reason for examining them. The party who bought the library, however, thought these also worth taking away and dumped them in a basket for transporting to the first floor. As he took them down, a few small paper-covered religious tracts fell out from between the volumes. One of them was *The Celestial Railroad*. He brought this pamphlet to Boston the next day and sold it for a hundred dollars.

I found the next copy of *The Celestial Railroad* in the house of a friend who had met with financial losses. He was preparing to move and asked me to look over his books. They proved to be worthless, but in a clothes-basket of newspapers, periodicals, reports, etc., which he brought from the attic, I found *The Celestial Railroad*! As the family gathered around to examine it, my friend inquired its value. I answered cautiously that he might be *sure* of a hundred dollars at least. Amazement! 'A hundred dollars for that thing!' The next day I sent it to my best first-edition customer of the time — S. H. Wakeman of New York. I explained the circumstances to him, that I was selling it for a friend for whom I wished to get the extreme value, and suggested that he send me two hundred and twenty-five dollars for it. Mr. Wakeman, always liberal in his dealings, promptly responded with a check which I endorsed and gave to my friend who was astonished that an insignificant-looking tract of thirty-two pages could bring such a ridiculously large amount.

The third copy of *The Celestial Railroad* was brought into the shop with a handful of paper-covered books for children, and in this case also the owner was as much surprised as my friend had been to find that a trifle, as she considered it, had so substantial a value.

Of course dealers cannot claim all the credit of finding rarities in places where their value is unsuspected. The copy of Cooper's *The Water Witch* which is now before me on my desk was picked up by a customer of ours at Filene's in this city for a dollar and twenty-five cents three years ago. It is the edition in three volumes printed in Dresden 'for Walther,' 1830. Although the book also appeared in London in 1830, two months before its American publication in Philadelphia by Carey and Lea, the Dresden issue, nevertheless, is the first edition of the book, for according to Spiller and Blackburn it antedates Colburn and Bentley's publication by a month. The author was living abroad at the time and this unusual first printing of an American book in Germany came from his efforts to acquire publication rights in three countries. We have it on the authority of the bibliographers that *The Water Witch* is the only one of Cooper's novels which was first published on the Continent. It might be assumed that a book printed in the English language in Germany would have had but a small circulation, and such was undoubtedly the case, for this one is so rare that, although the owner knew that he had acquired an unusual edition worth more than its department-store valuation, he did not know the real value of his find until the auction sale of another copy for seven hundred and twenty-five dollars was reported in the early part of 1936.

In the book I am writing, which it will be observed has offered no promise to be a guide for collectors, matters of bibliography or questions concerning the many details of collecting which interest bookmen have, heretofore, been avoided. One whose personal activities in the trade cannot be extended for many more years is reluctant to enter the lists and participate in the dusty field where bibliographical points are hotly contested by eager warriors of a younger generation. I may, however, comment upon the altered conditions and changed attitude in regard to certain of these matters during the last forty years. Doubtless, there will be amongst my readers those to whom book-collecting is only a 'game,' ranking with other childish sports. Such persons are likely to ask, 'What about this book-collecting anyway? What are "first editions" and what are they good for?' — questions I have no intention of answering directly. At the same time these inquiries induce certain reflections which I shall try to translate into words and offer for the edification of non-bookish readers.

At first thought, there is something unduly selfish in the collector's habit of mind —

But of all of my treasures this one is the king,
For there's very few children possess such a thing,

is too often the motivation of the collector which it would be
embarrassing to try to square with an ideal —

Of joy in widest commonalty spread.

Yet charity to the guild of collectors will credit them with a
more generous thought than the first of these quotations pro-
claims, for they might also say with Stevenson —

The world is so full of a number of things,
I am sure we should all be as happy as kings.

The rationale of first-edition collecting lies, of course, in our
interest in the beginnings of things and in the sentiment which
attaches itself to the particular form in which any great work
of literature first appeared. When this sentiment is appreciated, matters affecting priority of issue, of uncorrected errata,
or even of original binding become of understandable importance, although, through a failure to grasp their real meaning,
the relation of these minor details to the book itself may appear,
to philistine eyes, exaggerated. Simple matters like an inserted
leaf of errata — that word of fear, appalling to an author's
ear — suggesting to a novice inconsistencies really non-existent,
illustrate points of vital importance in collecting.

As a common example take the first edition of Keats's
Endymion. There are two issues of this book, both in the year
1818. The main text of the two is identical; each contains the
same uncorrected mistakes, but the first 'issue' of the book
contains a printed erratum leaf of one line. In copies sold
later, other mistakes in the text having been found, this page
was replaced by a five-line errata. It therefore follows:

1. As all known copies of this book contain one of the pages
   of errata, a copy having neither would naturally be considered
   imperfect.
2. Copies with the five-line corrections, being issued after
   those with one line, are of less value.

Where the errata are printed in the book itself, the case
may be different. In 1926 Sir Leicester Harmsworth of London,
a collector of early English theology, bought at Sotheby's the

first edition of *The Pilgrim's Progress*, 1678. This is one of the rarest of seventeenth-century books. There are only twelve or thirteen copies known and not all of these are perfect. This copy sold for £6800. When he got it, Sir Leicester found an errata of five lines printed on the last page of the book. This feature was hitherto unknown to exist and none of the other extant copies of the 1678 edition have it. Obviously, errors of the text being alike in both, the copy with the errata was a second issue,[1] so the buyer threw the book back on the auction-eers on the ground that they had wrongly described it as of the first edition. Eventually Sir Leicester took the book, but at a reduction of many hundreds of pounds from the sale price.

In one instance, at least, the errata leaf of a book has come to be of more value than the book itself. Cotton Mather's *Magnalia Christi Americana* was published, not in New England, but in London, in 1702. In size it is a small folio of moderate thickness. The author's account of his first sight of the book is interesting:

> Yesterday, I first saw my Church-History since ye publication of it. A Gentleman arrived here, from *New-Castle*, in *England*, that had bought it there. Wherefore, I sett apart this Day, for solemn Thanksgiving unto God, for His Watchful & gracious providence over that Work, & for ye Harvest of so many prayers, & cares, & Tears, & Resignations, as I had Employ'd upon it. My Religious Friend, mr. *Broomfield*, who had been singularly helpful to me in the publication of that great Book (of Twenty shillings price, at *London*), came to me, at the Close of the Day, to join with me, in some of my Praise to God.

Mather's satisfaction in his book was short-lived. As he read it, he might have anticipated the words of Justice Oliver Wendell Holmes, 'As soon as our mistakes are irretrievable, they stand out to our sight flamboyant,' for so large a number of unnoted

---

[1] At least it would so appear, although it has been contended that the *errata* might have been added as the sheets were going through the press and that both these and those uncorrected might have been used, the resulting volume being then issued indifferently. This recondite point is of importance to the collector, but I shall not trouble my readers with a discussion of its merits.

mistakes appeared (*Magnalia* as published containing an errata of only three lines), that he compiled a further list of them which covers three pages. To this second errata he added an apology:

> The *Holy Bible* itself, in some of its Editions hath been affronted, with Scandalous *Errors* of the *Press-work;* and in one of them, they so Printed those Words, Psal. 119.161 *Printers have persecuted me.* The author of this *Church History* ha's all the Reason in the World then to be Patient, tho' his work, be depraved with many *Errors* of the *Press-work.* The common Excuse in such cases is, The Distance of the *Author* from the Press; Here there was the Distance of a thousand Leagues.

Whether this ingenuous two-leaf production is rare because the book was distributed prior to the printing of it or by reason of the neglect of buyers to preserve it we do not know, but I have not seen more than three or four copies. The first edition of Cotton Mather's *Magnalia Christi Americana* can be bought at almost any time for a hundred dollars or thereabouts; a copy of the two-leaf errata might not be obtainable in many years, if ever, and would bring three times the price of the book itself.

Examples of textual variations in books raise debatable questions. Differences found in copies of what appear to be the same edition of a book might be due to the obvious slip of a compositor, or to some error of the author discovered in the printing, or to other changes deliberately made as the book passed the press. It is the bibliographers' job to decide in which state the earliest copies of the work appeared.

Not all collectors are fussy about the points of their books, although they are far more particular than they were a generation ago when, in fact, most of the important variants were unknown, or if known were lightly regarded. Would dealers or buyers forty years ago have known that of two bindings of *Leaves of Grass* the one with edges gilded and gilt used on both covers was the first issue, or, had they known it, would they have thought the point of much importance? In most cases the correct dating and the knowledge that there was no other edition printed in the same year would have satisfied them. Of course, when buying a *Pickwick* the collector might have given consideration to such of the extraordinary bibliographical features of that book as were known, and were he a Mark Twain collector he would search his copy of *Life on the Mississippi* for the cut of the author in flames which Clemens cancelled out of consideration of his wife's feelings, but on the subject of dropped letters, broken type, and the like he was, in the main indifferent, if not happily ignorant.

To continue this discussion of technical matters would probably bore most readers. Those really interested in the *minutiae* which affect priority of editions or issue will find the latest word regarding them in Muir's *Points* [1] wherein is also discussed the involved question of what constitutes an 'edition.' Slater's *Early Editions* (1894) is the pioneer of modern works for the book-collector, as Carter and Pollard's exposé of certain fictitious pamphlet issues of the writings of Victorian authors is the latest contribution to investigations of that kind.

Between the dates of these two works, many bibliographical studies and bibliographies of individual authors have been written for the guidance of collectors. The eleven volumes of the Ashley Library Catalogue supply the widest range of useful information concerning English books, though Wise's conclusions are sometimes open to question; other publications of value include the Catalogue of the Church Library compiled by Doctor George Watson Cole, and the various works issued by the Grolier Club. Ives's *Holmes*, Livingston's *Kipling*, Penzer's *Sir Richard Burton*, Williams's *Lewis Carroll*, Spiller and Blackburn's *Cooper*, Sadleir's *Trollope*, Griffith's *Pope*, and Currier's bibliography of Whittier are mentioned not for their importance to any who do not collect those particular authors but as good examples of modern bibliographical practice. A book of a different sort and of much greater interest than the title might suggest, as it is a careful study and indicates a new drift in collecting, is *First appearance in print of some four*

[1] *Points*, 1874–1930; and the same, Second Series, 1866–1934. 2 vols. London, 1931–34.

hundred quotations. This work was compiled by Carroll A. Wilson, well known to both collectors and booksellers for his interest in bibliographical questions.

These books, though they include some of the more important scholarly works written for the help of collectors in recent years, are far from exhausting the list of those useful to the collector in first editions of *belles-lettres.* Even a tentative list on the great subject of Americana would fill more space than I could give it.

The relations between dealers and the sellers of books are responsible for innumerable stories which show the different situations arising from the transactions between them. In many of those to which I was a party, my neighbor Andrew McCance also figures. He tells this story:

He was called to a house in the suburbs to make an offer for a library. It comprised a large number of books in which the absence of any of especial value was particularly noticeable. Moved by the owner's representation of her destitute condition, he offered one hundred dollars — an amount considerably more than the books were worth. The offer was promptly accepted. Coming back to his store, as he considered the matter, he repented too late of his liberality. The lot came in the next day after closing-time. The boys had gone home and McCance was alone; the men on the truck were half-drunk and left the books scattered all over the shop floor. When, tired out, he had finished looking them over, he was thoroughly sick of his bargain. Nevertheless he sent a friendly letter with his check for the agreed amount expressing a sympathetic regret that he could not give her more. In due time an acknowledgment came. The woman wrote: 'I received your check and, as you say, the amount is very small. However, I am not blaming you; you have to look after your own interests and my necessity is your opportunity!' It did not increase McCance's happiness when I told him the next day that our buyer had gone over the books two weeks before and had bought for a substantial amount everything of value.

Another time McCance had made a bid on a library gathered

by the late master of a famous school for boys in Cambridge. A few days after, I saw McCance and told him that I had just been out to see these books which we had talked about previously. 'It is a nice lot,' he remarked, 'but the books are not worth a thousand dollars.' I agreed to this, but added that my figure was less than that; I intended to offer seven hundred and sixty dollars. Upon this he went to his office and showed me the memorandum of his estimate which was for exactly the same amount! The situation was embarrassing and it was apparent that something would have to be done about it, for the owner would hardly receive two identical bids without suspicion. One of us suggested that one of the offers be increased by twenty-five dollars and that we toss a coin to see which of us should do it. I do not remember who won the toss, but the two bids went in at seven hundred and eighty-five dollars and seven hundred and sixty dollars respectively. The outcome of the matter was that, although we were acting in good faith, the owner of the books was so certain that we were in collusion that he sent the books to a local auction room where they brought only five hundred dollars.

I can plead not guilty of having acted at any time in collusion with another dealer at the expense of a book-owner, although the story that follows might seem to indicate an approach to such reprehensible conduct.

I had been called to examine a lot of some hundred or so volumes in the drawing-room of a suburban residence. The books were of the parlor-table, copiously illustrated, Christmas-gift type. I offered thirty-five dollars. 'That doesn't seem a great deal for so many books,' was the owner's comment. 'True,' I replied, 'but I am not dealing to any extent in modern books; there is only one book here which interests me. If you want to sell Newell's *Songs and Games of American Children* separately, I will give you two dollars for it.' Ignoring the last offer the woman inquired, 'Can you suggest anyone who you think would care more for them than you do yourself?' I gave her Mr. McCance's name, for which she thanked me. The next day I said to McCance: 'You will probably get a letter

from a woman to whom I made an offer for some books. They
are not really in my line, but I think that, as you handle new
books, you may find them useful. I offered her thirty-five
dollars; probably if you offer her five or ten dollars more she
will be glad to sell them, and I think that they would be
worth that much to you.'

McCance continues: 'I went out to look at the books which
Mr. Goodspeed had put me in touch with. It was a very cold
day and when I was shown into the room where the books
were piled on the floor, having my overcoat on, I didn't bother
to go over them individually, but gave them a glance and
offered forty-five dollars which was promptly accepted. Then,
opening the door of an adjoining room the owner said, "Will
you please tell me what you would give for the lot in here?"
Imagine how I felt when I found that after Mr. Goodspeed's
call the books had been separated and that I was now obliged
to make a supplementary offer. However, I bought them all,
although it made the lot rather expensive. When I reported
to Mr. Goodspeed the next day he said, "When the lot comes in,
charge the Newell book to me at two dollars and send it down." '

This is the end of Mr. McCance's story, but there is a bit
more to the transaction. The next morning, the owner of the
books came into my shop with a book in her hand. She said,
'*I have decided to sell you that book on children's games for which
you offered me two dollars, and here it is!*'

There is one class of books for which every bookseller has
call at some time — the old school-readers which someone,
recalling his childhood, wishes to see again. In my business
this demand has been usually for Pierpont's *Young Reader*.
The piece which the inquirer usually quotes when asking for
the book begins with these lines:

> A white old hen with yellow legs,
> Who'd laid her master many eggs,
> Which, from her nest, the boys had taken
> To put in cake, or fry in bacon,
> Was roosting in an outer hovel,
> Where barrel, bird-cage, riddle, shovel,

> Tub, piggin, corn-bag, all together,
> Were put, to keep them from the weather,
> When an old fox stole in, one night,
> As the full moon was shining bright —

The *Young Reader* is moderately scarce. The compiler, the Reverend John Pierpont, great-grandfather of J. P. Morgan, was a fiery preacher and a strong advocate of anti-slavery, prohibition, and other reform movements. In his ministry of the Hollis Street Church, he exhibited the militant traits of his character, vigorously fighting the hostile, influential, rum-selling members of his congregation. The parish having rented a cellar of the church building to a liquor-dealer, a Pierpont partisan penned these lines:

> There's a spirit above and a spirit below;
> A spirit of love, and a spirit of woe.
> The spirit above is the spirit divine;
> The spirit below is the spirit of wine.

Besides the *Young Reader*, Pierpont edited *The American First Class Book* and *The National Reader*, and we used to have occasional requests for both of them. Few schoolboys a century ago failed to memorize the stirring stanzas of *Warren's Address to the American Soldiers before the battle of Bunker's Hill* written by Pierpont for the semi-centennial of that event:

> Stand! the ground's your own, my braves!
> Will ye give it up to slaves?
> Will ye hope for greener graves?
>   Hope ye mercy still?
> What's the mercy despots feel!
> Hear it in that battle peal!
> Read it on yon bristling steel!
>   Ask it — ye who will. —

The series of school-readers compiled by George S. Hillard which had a wide sale in their day were also frequently called for. Hillard wrote a book of travels under the title of *Six Months in Italy* which must have been a best seller,[1] for it is one of three books (the others being *The Diary and Correspondence*

---

[1] It had gone through twenty-one editions in 1881.

of Amos Lawrence and Kane's *Arctic Explorations*) which Boston booksellers never lack. The book last named sold in enormous numbers all over the country. There are, singularly, some publications whose circulation, although very large, has been confined to certain sections of the country. It may seem incredible that a series whose sales are said to have been more than a hundred million copies should be rare in any part of the United States, but so it is that, although we have frequent mail offers to buy or sell McGuffey's *Readers*, yet as far as I remember not a single copy of the McGuffey schoolbooks, of which the first was published in 1836, six years after Pierpont's *Young Reader* appeared, has ever been seen in our stock.

Our Constitution is in actual operation; everything appears to promise that it will last; but in this world nothing is certain but death and taxes. B. FRANKLIN, 1789.

VIII. THE WILLING BUYER TO THE WILLING SELLER

ONE item of the administrative expenses imposed upon the estates of decedents in this country by the Federal Estate Tax law is the fee of the expert appraiser. The amount which 'would have been paid by a willing buyer to a willing seller' in an open market is the Government's interpretation of the statutory requirement that calls for a 'full and fair market value' of personal property. Readers are invited to ponder this bit of phraseology and decide what (for appraisal purposes) a willing buyer would pay to a willing seller for, let us say, a 'large printed Bible' sent by Jonathan Swift to Esther Johnson (if Swift fulfilled his promise to Stella and were the book now in existence); or, in another supposititious case, how much would be given for the original manuscript of *Uncle Tom's Cabin*.

Since the Estate Tax law was passed in 1916, I have been frequently employed to inventory and appraise prints, books, manuscripts, and other literary property. When a bookseller undertakes the rôle of appraiser, he must walk warily. He is then acting in a capacity which may conflict with his own interests, which he must disregard for the time. The following case, wherein I have thought best to omit names, will make this clearer. A Society herein described as the 'Society' and two individuals designated as '*A*' and '*Z*' figure in the story. *A* was a long-time customer; with the 'Society' my relations, both as a member of it, and as a bookseller, were intimate; *Z* was a stranger.

One day *A* said to me, 'I am giving my books to the "Society"';

I have sent many of them to its library already, the balance will go there after my death. I have told the librarian that I know that he will find a lot of them are duplicates, but he can use those for trading with you.'

Some months after this, *A* died. In his will his promise made concerning the books was fulfilled and by it the 'Society' also received a large sum of money. The conditions being known to the director of the 'Society' and myself, it was tacitly understood between us that the 'Society' would select from the shelves of *A*'s library the books needed for its collection and that I should then take the rest directly from the testator's house for credit to the 'Society's' account. Before the estate had been administered, however, I was called on the telephone by a general appraiser who often sent for me to value books for him. 'Can you go out to Marlborough Street tomorrow to appraise a library for inheritance tax?' I answered, yes, and inquired whose estate it was. To my surprise I was informed that the books had belonged to Mr. *A*. The situation was unusual, but there appeared to be no impropriety in my accepting the commission, so the next day I started on the job. I have said that *A* bequeathed his books to the 'Society'; this statement requires a qualification. His will read, 'I give to said "Society" all my books and pamphlets, except such as *Z* may wish to retain,' *Z* being a friend of the testator.

As I was examining the books a friend of *Z*'s was present. I inquired of him, 'When *Z* makes his selection will he do it from the shelves here or from the books listed by me as of especial value?' The friend replied that he supposed the latter.

I had nearly finished my examination when I came to an old-fashioned revolving bookcase in the middle of the room. It was filled with a miscellaneous lot of unimportant books — dictionaries, directories, corporation manuals, and the like — the few books of general literature which it held appearing to be of slight value. One of these was the report of the Lincoln and Douglas debates published in Columbus in 1860. The book is common and worth but a few dollars — not enough to call for separate valuation. What then impelled me to take it from the shelf I don't know, but something made me do it. I opened it casually, glanced at the fly-leaf, and saw what I am firmly convinced had never been seen by the owner — a lightly pencilled autograph inscription from Lincoln to A's uncle!

That was an unlucky discovery so far as it concerned the 'Society,' for, of course, when Z saw the book valued on my inventory at several hundred dollars he grabbed it, whereas, had I not examined the book, Z would not have known of the inscription and would have undoubtedly left it for the 'Society' to take with the rest of the library.

Not all of my appraisal work has been for taxation purposes. Court actions frequently call for expert valuations of books, in criminal as well as in civil cases. I confess that years ago I gave testimony in court once or twice with more confidence than the circumstances warranted. In one case my testimony might have had an unfortunate result. It was given in the trial of certain sharks of the trade who had sold a lot of 'de-luxe' books to a woman for a large sum, over eighty thousand dollars. The amount was so much in excess of actual value that a charge of larceny was made against the sellers.

The District Attorney asked me to value the books. In going over them I came to a collection of memoirs of the First Empire written by various authors. They were translations, in Bentley's good old library editions, assembled as a 'set' and rebound in showy leather lettered 'Napoleonic Memoirs.' The last volume was described as 'Napoleonic Documents,' or some similar title. Upon examination, the documents which made up the contents of this volume appeared to be of small value. I say 'appeared,' for my knowledge of the French language was next to nothing, and my acquaintance with the small fry of Napoleon's time was limited. In appraising them I was, therefore, guided more by the absence of certain names which should have been included in a Napoleonic collection than by the documents contained in the volume which were signed by persons who were apparently obscure.

In due time, the case being on, I was called to the witness

stand. I was young, inexperienced, and probably thought myself a person of some importance as I gave my testimony, but any satisfaction which I enjoyed in posing as an expert on this occasion was dissipated when an attorney for the defendants walked up to me with that unlucky volume of 'Napoleonic documents' in hand, one finger marking a place in the book. At that moment I would have paid liberally for permission to step down from the stand. What could I say? This man was about to show me document after document and compel me to admit, not only that I could not read them, but did not even know who wrote them! I was supremely miserable as I braced myself to receive the blow. It came after my assumed qualifications as an 'expert' had been mercilessly dragged from me. 'You have examined this volume?' My dry lips faltered a feeble 'Yes.' 'And how much is it worth?' 'Twenty dollars' (or some other small amount), I responded. Opening to the place indicated by his finger my examiner demanded, 'Whose signature is this?' I looked and saw 'Louis Xavier'!

No one but myself will ever appreciate my thankfulness as I replied, 'Louis the Eighteenth of France.' Unsatisfied, the lawyer persisted in his laudable but unintended effort to relieve my embarrassment. 'What valuation do you place on this document?' 'Five dollars.' 'Five dollars!' he exclaimed. 'Do you mean to tell me that a genuine autograph of Louis XVIII is worth but five dollars? Where can I buy one for that?' The sun shone once more as I replied, 'At Goodspeed's Bookshop, 5A Park Street.' With this answer the attorney allowed me to retire, which I did with alacrity — grateful but chastened.

An appraisal made some years since at the summer home of the Reverend William E. Barton of Oak Park, Illinois, is mentioned here as it illustrates what kind of collection on a given subject may be gathered by one who works with industry, intelligence, and enthusiasm. Doctor Barton, who died in 1930, spent his summers in the town of Foxboro, Massachusetts. All but a small part of his collection of books, pamphlets, and autographs was housed somewhat precariously in the

Wigwam, a picturesque wooden building of moderate size near the banks of a small pond. It was a beautiful location. The sloping shores of the pond curved gracefully through the woods; robins perched on the tips of pines which had dropped their brown needles into the water, and the grove sheltered early flowers beneath its branches. For retirement and study the spot was ideal and, barring the chill of an unoccupied building in the capricious month of May, the work of examination was a pleasing interlude to the members of Goodspeed's staff who assisted in the work, a task which occupied several days.

Doctor Barton, who made this collection, was a national figure in the Congregational Church; elsewhere he was widely known as a student of Lincoln's life and the writer of a large number of Lincoln biographical works which have had wide popular sale. As the study of Lincoln was Barton's avocation, it naturally followed that his collection was, with the one exception noted below, almost wholly of Lincoln or material related to him. It was probably on account of Whitman's hero-worship of Lincoln that Barton assembled an extensive collection of the works of that poet in their first editions. In addition to the Lincoln collection, however, he had a large and valuable collection of autographs of more general interest; principally of American heroes and statesmen.

In this collection there were about fifty autographs of Lincoln, mostly on documents. These were of no great value for their contents, but a lot of twenty or more legal documents in Lincoln's hand illustrated the variety of cases in which Lincoln appeared, and his signatures to them were interesting as showing his use of the firm names of his law partnerships. Most of Doctor Barton's collecting, however, was of books and pamphlets — Lincoln's speeches, biographies of him, and eulogies delivered after his death. He had the most extensive collection of this material which I have met, and to supplement it he gathered a large miscellany of newspaper clippings, photostats, and similar printed records which were of considerable historical value. A group of this material of curious interest was concerned with the discredited Lincoln-Rutledge love-letters.

The small collection of Lincoln relics of various sorts picked up by Barton could hardly be rated higher than relics generally are. In a different class, however, are the forty-seven sheep-bound volumes of law reports from Lincoln's library, one bearing Lincoln's inscription to W. H. Herndon.

The contents of the Barton library numbered over six thousand bound books and pamphlets and something like sixty per cent of them had reference to Lincoln. The collection is now in the library of the University of Chicago.

If all of the privately owned historical material which I have seen were gathered together, however, it would not approach in interest and value the collections of manuscripts which are described below. There was a large library in the same house with them, but, with the exception of a special collection of rare bindings, the books were such a lot of general literature as any man of leisure and culture might make, expanded along certain lines of Americana in which the owner was especially interested.

I appraised the Clements manuscripts and books at Bay City, Michigan, in 1935. The total value was $265,265.

William Lawrence Clements was an industrialist who had prospered in the manufacture of heavy iron machinery — cranes, wrecking-train outfits, and the like. He was a tall man with a powerful physique, studious of his books and far-sighted in plans for their future use. The collections which he made, and his account of the William L. Clements Library presented by him to the University of Michigan, are evidence of the quality of his mind; the credit which he gives in his book to the librarians and booksellers who guided and assisted him in making his purchases reflects a generous spirit.

To the princely gift of his great collections of rare Americana made during his lifetime to the University, he not only added a library building which was both adequate and beautiful, but also, with rare foresight, provided wisely for its future growth. The building was dedicated with appropriate exercises and in the presence of a distinguished company in 1923.

During the years following this dedication, Mr. Clements

made several purchases of large value, bringing to his residence in Bay City the most important group of historical manuscripts having reference to the French and Indian War and Revolutionary periods in existence. He died in 1934 with these collections in his possession. Such account of them as I find space for must be confined to a brief history, a summary of their contents, and a mention of some of the documents of extraordinary interest which are preserved in them.

These collections, excepting the last two of those named below, were bought by Mr. Clements in groups as follows:

1. The Clinton papers.
2. The Germain papers.
3. The Gage papers.
4. The Stevens collection.
5. The Greene correspondence.
6. The Clements collection of individual purchases.

British military affairs in North America for the period between 1761 and 1781 were successively under the direction of four officers acting under instructions from the ministry in London. These officers were Sir Jeffrey Amherst, Thomas Gage, Sir William Howe, and Sir Henry Clinton. Howe's command was brief, lasting only from 1775 to 1778, and his papers are not found in the Clements Library, as they were destroyed by fire years ago. Most of Amherst's own papers, enormous in number, are in England, but those which he turned over to Gage when the latter succeeded him in 1763, although relatively few, are in the Clements collection. With these reservations, the Clements manuscripts may be described as covering the entire headquarters' correspondence of the British command from the time of Amherst's appointment to Clinton's resignation at the end of the Revolution.

Mr. Clements, having heard of the Gage papers through Allen French and Clarence E. Carter, bought them of Lord Gage in 1929. The purchase was made after examination and report of Doctor Randolph G. Adams, the present director of the W. L. Clements Library of the University of Michigan.

This collection was contained in twelve large wooden chests, dated and initialled 'T. G.' in studded nails on the lids. The contents, tidily folded, docketed, and red-taped, were filed in divided trays resting one on the other.

Gage's chests contained, roughly, twenty thousand pieces — letters, copies, manuscripts, miscellaneous documents, and maps; the copies of his own letters were mainly by a secretary, but there were others in his own cramped hand. Amongst the letters received by him were those from the British ministry — fifteen hundred of them, the largest number from Lords Hillsborough and Barrington. The American letters, complemented by Gage's replies, were from civilians and correspondents, of various rank — colonial governors, military and naval officers, and Indian agents, addressed to him from all parts of the Atlantic seaboard, from Nova Scotia to Florida. There were also in the chests letter-books, accounts, and vouchers, which show the routine of military life. None of Gage's records seem to have been omitted.

Some idea of the fullness of this collection may be had by the selection of a few names. Of Thomas Hutchinson, there are forty-one letters, and one hundred and fifty of Sir Guy Carleton, of particular value as most of the papers of this officer were, I believe, destroyed by his wife. There are nearly two hundred letters from Sir William Johnson, and from Brigadier-General John Bradstreet one hundred and fifty-one. The colorful Robert Rogers of the Rangers contributes fifty letters to the collection, Colonel Bouquet fifty-one, and Major Gladwin forty-seven. There are two letters from Washington to Gage, one of especial interest written from Cambridge concerning reciprocal treatment of English and American officers as prisoners; and as might have been anticipated, the events which took place around Boston at the time of the Boston Massacre in 1770 are well documented here.

Omitting anything more than a mention of the papers of Lord George Germain, which comprise fourteen bound volumes and sundry loose packets numbering sixteen hundred and seventy-nine pieces bought by Mr. Clements in 1927, there come next, in chronological order, the official papers of Sir Henry Clinton, Commander-in-Chief of the British forces in North America from 1778 to the close of the Revolution.

The Clinton manuscripts were bought from a descendant, Miss Frances Clinton, in 1925. They were first brought to Clements's attention by Henry N. Stevens of London, who acted as his agent in the purchase. They are similar in nature to Gage's but the number is smaller; they include between twelve and thirteen thousand pieces. In general there is this difference between the two collections: Gage's papers are of large importance to the story of the French and Indian War and the opening days of the Revolutionary contest; Clinton's cover the thick of the fight for independence. Clinton's include, first, the papers of his father, Admiral George Clinton, Governor of New York from 1743 to 1753. These are mostly concerned with the French and the Indians and are, themselves, of no small importance. As for Sir Henry Clinton's own correspondence, which comprises the bulk of his manuscript collection, a short list will give some idea of its general nature and its extensiveness:

Official dispatches from Lord George Germain to Clinton, 1778–1781. 84 pieces.

'Intercepted' and other letters from American officers — Chastellux, Silas Deane, General Gates, General Charles Lee, Comte de Rochambeau, General Sullivan, Jonathan Trumbull, *et al.* A quantity in 26 'lots.'

Notes of conversations between Sir William Howe and Clinton regarding campaign plans.

Letters from General John Burgoyne to Clinton in explanation of the causes of his surrendering to Gates and on other topics. 18 pieces.

Secret instructions to Clinton to evacuate Philadelphia and attack St. Lucia in retaliation for the French alliance with the Colonies. Signed by George III.

Autograph letter from Ethan Allen to S. Huntington, President of Congress — 'I am determined to defend the independence of

Vermont ... or retire with hardy Green Mountain Boys into the desolate caverns of the Mountains and wage war with human nature at large. ...'

Humble petition of divers loyal inhabitants of Charleston [S.C.] to Clinton and Arbuthnot, 1781, with 141 signatures.

Street Register of Owners and Inhabitants of New York. 12 pp. folio, 1778.

Long letter detailing the Battle of Lexington. Written from Boston by William Sutherland, April 26, 1775.

'Intercepted' letters and documents, American, including Alexander Hamilton (docketed in the handwriting of Major André), Rochambeau (copy in cipher, endorsed by Clinton), *et al.* 50 pieces.

Letters from Generals Gage and Sir William Howe to Clinton relative to the latter's part in the Battle of Bunker Hill.

Letters and dispatches, Sir William Howe to Clinton. 53 pieces.

Group of letters to Clinton from various military and civilian correspondents. About 1300 pieces.

Original articles of capitulation of Charleston, S.C., signed by Gen. Lincoln; autograph letters from Lincoln to Clinton; list of Continental officers on parole (endorsed by André); and other documents relating to the siege of Charleston.

Letters from George Washington. 18.

The original dispatch of some thirty pages from Lord Cornwallis to Clinton dated October 20, 1781, announcing his surrender to Washington at York Town the day before and explaining the circumstances which necessitated his action, with the Articles of Capitulation and correspondence with General Washington.

The foregoing are mostly taken at random from many thousand documents. Even these few samples will indicate how rich a mine is open to historians in the Clinton, no less than in the Gage, manuscripts. I have, however, left for last mention a group of documents of superlative interest. They include the source material of the history of Arnold's treason.

Arnold-André Papers

Letters and documents by Lord Germain and others relative to André's appointment as Clinton's aide.

Poem — 'The Frantic Lover' in André's autograph.

Ticket for the *Mischianza*.[1]

Autograph letter in French, with curious and prophetic sketch for a seal (a man hanging) by André.

Miscellaneous papers mostly in André's hand — drafts of letters for Clinton to write and historical notes including 'Expenditure of public accounts' in André's hand which lists £210 for 'Moore' (Arnold), copies of secret letters, etc.; also cipher letters, deciphers, masks, and keys, 'intelligence papers' addressed to André and docketed by him, as well as letters to him from Tarleton, Rivington, Rawdon, and others; a very large lot.

Note in André's hand of an interview with Arnold; autograph letter, Arnold to Clinton, regarding £10,000 for his services; memorandum in Clinton's hand as to promising £6,000; five letters from Arnold to Clinton; and many other papers, in fifteen lots.

Thirty-five lots of papers which contain various documents. These include (in part) cipher letters in André's hand; a letter of four pages by Arnold, signed 'Edward Fox'; letter from Arnold (signed 'Moore') to 'Anderson' (André) in cipher; drafts of various letters in André's hand signed 'John Anderson'; letter from Beverley Robinson describing André's actions and on his failure to return to ask for instructions; letter from Alexander Hamilton to Sir Henry Clinton suggesting that André might be exchanged for the return of Arnold (Clinton has endorsed this 'Hamilton W's aid-de-camp received after A's death'); Clinton's notes on the André affair and drafts of long letters concerning André and his death; copies of Clinton's dispatches to Lord Germain announcing the capture and execution of André and Arnold's desertion of the American army.

The farewell letter from André to Clinton of September 29, 1780.

[1] An extravagant entertainment produced at Mr. Wharton's country-seat near Philadelphia in 1778 in honor of Lord Howe. Masques, theatricals, and dancing were indulged in. André composed the addresses spoken on the occasion, designed the costumes, and made drawings from which this ticket was engraved.

One more group in the Clinton collection should be mentioned:

Three hundred and ten manuscript maps made under Clinton's command, for headquarters' use in the Revolution, besides a small number which are unfinished; also an important group of engraved maps. Many of these maps are drawn with great care and are excellent examples of the skilled cartographer's art. A detailed account of them is given in the list made by Doctor Randolph G. Adams and published by the William L. Clements Library at Ann Arbor in 1928.

Having given some account of the two principal groups of the Clements manuscripts, it remains to describe the Stevens, Greene, and Clements collections. The first of these lots is of a miscellaneous nature and is the result of various purchases made from time to time by Henry Stevens, Son and Stiles of London. The larger part of the items came from the sale of the Sir Thomas Phillips collection. There were about four hundred and fifty pieces in the Stevens lot when Clements purchased it, but an important portion was transferred by him to the W. L. Clements Library at Ann Arbor.

The Greene papers comprise the Revolutionary correspondence of Major-General Nathanael Greene which had been preserved by a descendant until purchased by James A. Garland. After Garland's death they were placed with Joseph F. Sabin for sale. Sabin eventually purchased them himself and they remained in his hands for twenty years. During that time some of the pieces were sold, but in 1925 the bulk of the collection was, after examination by William Warner Bishop in Mr. Clements's interest, sold to the latter who subsequently made substantial additions to it by purchasing other Greene material at auction. Of the four thousand pieces which make up this collection, the larger part, about twenty-five hundred in number, are letters to General Greene. They include seventeen letters of Washington, fourteen from Lafayette, one hundred and one from Francis Marion, eighty-one from Henry Lee, and twenty-five from Baron von Steuben, to mention a few of the most important ones.

The Clements miscellaneous collection of individual purchases is the result of Mr. Clements's purchases from various sources, chiefly at auction sales between the years 1924 and 1929. To some extent they supplement the other collections and nearly all of them are related to the Revolution.

An attempt has been made to describe, as well as the limited space of these pages will allow, the enormous bulk of manuscript material on the American Revolution which has been brought together by one man in less than a decade. The grand total of pieces is over forty thousand. It includes almost every conceivable kind of military and administrative document, from routine memoranda to letters of the greatest importance.

These letters and manuscripts which now form one collection were written by participants on both sides of the struggle; they were from all sorts and conditions of men — English soldiers loyal to King and Parliament, patriots seeking to establish freedom on a new soil, sailors, rangers, spies, and civilians. They were carried by coastwise sail from distant ports, brought by stage over dubious roads, delivered by hand of horse-riding messenger or brought to their destination by moccasin-shod Indians. They form a store of vast importance to the historian. When they are made available, the military history of their period will have to be rewritten.

As this great Clements collection was, in 1935, the latest important appraisal I had then made, another which I undertook nearly twenty-five years ago was one of the earliest. It was of the books and manuscripts in Craigie House, Cambridge, valued for insurance under instructions from the trustees.

If American poets were put to a popular vote, even in this day there can be little doubt of the result — Longfellow would lead the poll. This popularity does not come wholly from his poetry; there is something in Longfellow's personality, in his placid serenity and breadth of sympathy which attracts men and women. As for his verse, it is perfectly suited to the capacity of the average reader, who understands the message which it brings and enjoys its soothing music. Longfellow is the people's poet.

Thus regarded, it follows that the house in which Longfellow
lodged as a young professor and where he lived from the day
when, on his marriage, it was presented to the young couple
in 1843, until he died there in 1882, is now a national shrine.
In the old Craigie House in Cambridge, there are still preserved the household appurtenances which served the family
through more than one generation. The spacious rooms re-
flect the poet's personality; everything is ample, solid, cheer-
ful. Here is the furniture which Longfellow used, the pictures
which he bought, the books which he read, those which he
wrote himself, and the manuscripts of his poems.

The Craigie House library is very extensive. The books,
covering a wide range of subjects, include a large quantity of
European literature, chiefly French and German. The single
group comprising the so-called Bohn Libraries — standard,
classical, philosophical, historical, antiquarian, scientific, illustrated, ecclesiastical, philological — is the largest collection of
these books I have seen — about five hundred volumes. Although I remember but one incunable — a 1496 Venice
Plutarch — there was a long row of folio Bodonis and other
early nineteenth-century Italian imprints of some typographical value, books of the kind described by the poet himself in
Tales of a Wayside Inn:

> ... many a rare and sumptuous tome,
> In vellum bound, with gold bedight,
> Great volumes garmented in white,
> Recalling Florence, Pisa, Rome.

American books were in the minority; the paper-covered
first edition of *The Raven* by Poe in immaculate condition with
Longfellow's autograph on its wrapper, a set of *The Dial*, and a
few volumes given by Hawthorne to Longfellow (one of
Hawthorne's early juveniles [1] inscribed by him, I found on a
shelf of children's books) were the most noteworthy. These,
and a presentation copy of Dickens's *American Notes*, are the
books I remember as of the greatest interest.

[1] The book was *Grandfather's Chair*, 1841; the inscription — *Longfellow from
Grandfather himself.*

The real importance of the library, however, lies in its great collection of Longfellow's works in their various editions, which include many foreign translations, and in the manuscripts of most of his books, his journals from 1826 to 1882, a large number of his letters of the same period,[1] and his various notebooks. As might be expected, a large group of letters to Longfellow from men and women of many lands is also found here.

I believe that if one excepts the comprehensive Goethe Museum at Weimar, this collection of Longfellow books and manuscripts is as complete a record as is known of the work of one author.

[1] One item in the correspondence is a collection of 508 autograph letters from Longfellow to George Washington Greene, 1830–1882. These I bought for the collection at the auction sale of the Chamberlain first editions in New York in 1909 for $5100.

I am desirous of obtaining information concerning the first volume of verse published by the late Edgar A. Poe, its date, size, contents, etc. It appears to be a scarce book. THE PHILOBIBLION, MARCH, 1862.

IX. THE STORY OF TAMERLANE

POE'S *Tamerlane* was first printed in Boston in 1827. It is a book of no literary value, but it is rated highly in the book market. Even if *Tamerlane* is without poetic merit, its rarity and the fact that it was the first production of a great American writer combine to make it first on the want list of those who collect American authors. If we compare the market value of *Tamerlane* with all other books printed in the United States, we find that it does not stand at the top of the list, for there are many other books which sell for more. However, if we limit such a comparison to the field of American *belles-lettres*, the number of American first editions which bring more than a thousand dollars is surprisingly small. When we mention *The Embargo* of Bryant, Hawthorne's *Fanshawe*, Cooper's *The Last of the Mohicans*, Poe's *Al Aaraaf* and *The Raven*, Emerson's *Letter to the Second Church*, Whitman's *Leaves of Grass*, Longfellow's Dante in the rare issue of 1865–1867, and possibly a few private editions similar to this last, we have mentioned most of them. As for books in the five-figure class — those that would bring ten thousand dollars or more, I know of but two, both by Poe, *Tamerlane* and *The Murders in the Rue Morgue*.

To own one or both of these books has been the dream, usually unrealized, of every bookseller. The finding of not one but two copies of *Tamerlane* was, therefore, to me an exciting and perhaps my most noteworthy experience in book-buying.

It is not necessary to give here an account of the circumstances under which Poe's *Tamerlane* was published, nor to discuss the various causes which have been assigned for its rarity. As to the former, it is enough to say that the book was printed in 1827 during Poe's brief stay in Boston; and as for the rarity of the book, other reasons besides the brief statement given by Poe himself, and quoted below, are conjectural. Stories that the book was never published and that the circulation was limited to a few copies sent for review have, so far as I know, no other support than that which may be adduced from this statement. That only forty copies were printed is another report for which there seems to be no evidence. Our only key to the mystery is a brief note by Poe in his Baltimore republication of *Tamerlane*, with other verses added, in 1829. This note reads, 'This Poem was printed for publication in Boston, in the year 1827, but suppressed through circumstances of a private nature.' For our purpose we shall accept this statement for such significance as it offers and consider the book not bibliographically but as a collector's rarity and the chief treasure of American first editions.

In the year 1925 only four copies of *Tamerlane* were known. Something of the history of these may be of interest.

Seventy-eight years ago, that is in 1859, Samuel G. Drake, then Boston's leading 'Antiquarian bookseller,' as he described himself, sent a consignment of old books to Henry Stevens in London. Stevens had for some time acted as agent for the British Museum in its American purchases even as he numbered the Library of Congress and eminent American collectors amongst his customers on this side of the Atlantic. In a lot of American poetry which, with other works by Edgar Allan Poe, Drake consigned to Stevens, there was a copy of *Tamerlane*. 'It was sent into the Museum in 1860 with many other Boston tracts,' writes Stevens, 'and was paid for in 1867 for one shilling!'

For twenty-three years this was the only known copy of *Tamerlane*. It was rebound and had suffered the loss of its original covers, but it was thought to be unique. Then, some fifteen years or so later, it lost this status, for another copy was found. Richard Lichtenstein, at that time a clerk at

Burnham's Antique Book Shop in Cornhill, while one day looking over a lot of books in the sidewalk box of a neighboring shop, discovered the second copy of *Tamerlane*, and bought it for the marked price of fifteen cents. He realized that the book was valuable, but how valuable neither he nor anyone else knew. He made no effort to sell it and some time after he declined an offer of a few hundred dollars made by Charles B. Foote, then a noted collector of first editions. Afterwards, however, Libbie induced Mr. Lichtenstein to entrust it to him for sale, and in 1892 it was sold at auction, the buyers being Dodd, Mead and Company of New York. It brought what was considered then a large amount — eighteen hundred and fifty dollars.

The next copy of *Tamerlane* which appeared in the market is said to have come from Richmond, Virginia. The history of this copy is involved, but it is worth the telling. It was discovered by E. L. Didier of Baltimore, who sold it through William Evarts Benjamin to Frederic R. Halsey of New York. The book was in fine condition and in the original covers. Mr. Halsey was then the owner of the Lichtenstein copy which had passed from Dodd, Mead and Company to Thomas J. McKee. When the McKee library was sold in November, 1900, George H. Richmond, then a prominent New York dealer in rare books, bought it for two thousand and fifty dollars and immediately sold it to Halsey who had been the underbidder.

In 1915 Halsey sold his library to Henry E. Huntington, retaining the Didier *Tamerlane* and a few other books. He began collecting again, but in 1919 he sold his second collection at Anderson's, on February 17, the Didier *Tamerlane* thus making its appearance at auction.

This copy of *Tamerlane* involved the fortunes of another lot of books — the famous Wallace collection. It is reported that some years before the transaction through which Halsey sold a part of his books to Henry E. Huntington, Walter T. Wallace, meeting him in The Grolier Club, said to him, 'Mr. Halsey, you have two copies of Poe's *Tamerlane*. One of them is of no use to you; why won't you sell it to me?' Mr. Halsey replied, 'I don't know who you are, but I thought this was a gentleman's club and not a bookseller's shop,' and, turning on his heel, left him.

When the Halsey catalogue appeared, Wallace, who already owned copies of *Al Aaraaf*, 1829, *Poems*, second edition, 1831, and other Poe material, saw that he now had a chance of obtaining a copy of *Tamerlane* which would almost complete his Poe collection. He therefore instructed Gabriel Wells, a well-known dealer, to buy this copy at the sale, his limit being ten thousand dollars. Frank B. Bemis of Boston, of whom I have already written, sent a bid through George D. Smith. When Smith found that the bidding was going much beyond his client's figure, he was too much of a gambler to drop out and moreover there was ill-feeling between him and Wallace, whom he probably knew to be Wells's principal. The result was that Smith bought the book for eleven thousand six hundred dollars which Bemis finally paid him, although without any commission.

The sale took place in the evening. Through an error in the newspaper report the next morning, Wallace understood that his agent was the buyer, so he hastened down to Wells's office and expressed his willingness to take the book even though it would cost him nearly two thousand dollars more than he expected. When the mistake was explained to him, he declared, 'Well, if I can't have a *Tamerlane*, I will give up collecting!' The notable sale of the Wallace books at the American Art Association in March, 1920, resulted.

The next copy of *Tamerlane*, one without covers, came from the vicinity of Boston in 1914. Its purchaser was P. K. Foley, from whom it went, through another dealer, to W. A. Clark of California. The other books of the lot Foley bought had no value and the seller, delighted with the amount paid her, hastened to bring in more, also worthless, receiving, in consideration of the previous transaction, a substantial amount which Foley added to the cost of the *Tamerlane*. Failing in her attempts to discover why these shabby old books should realize so much, the woman who brought them to him exclaimed,

'Oh, Mr. Foley, it is such a pity we did not meet before I had a bonfire of old books on my lawn two years ago; I see we might have done a great deal of business together!'

By this recapitulation, it will be seen that the most intensive search of collectors and dealers unearthed but three more copies of *Tamerlane* from the year when antiquarian Drake sent a copy from Boston to London, down to 1914. One of these copies, as we have seen, came from Richmond; the others were found in Boston or its neighborhood. The next one was to come from Worcester, Massachusetts.

The Worcester copy was owned by a woman living with her aged sister on the second floor of a small house in the heart of the city. The rent of the first floor eked out by needle-work comprised the support of the pair. In the mid-summer of 1925 Mrs. Dodd, the owner, was seated in her room reading the *Saturday Evening Post*. An article attracted her notice — 'Have you a *Tamerlane* in your attic?' by Vincent Starrett.

Mrs. Dodd was living in an attic and she had a *Tamerlane*.

The magazine story absorbed the interest of the sisters as they discussed it that evening in the lamp-lighted room, for it told them that a copy of the same thin, tea-colored volume, hardly more than a pamphlet, which they now passed from one to the other, had sold for ten thousand dollars.

But was Mrs. Dodd's the real book — might it not be a reprint? Mr. Starrett, of course, could say and perhaps he would tell them where they could sell it. He was the man to write to, and a letter was sent forthwith.

As days passed to weeks with no reply, the hopes of the old women faded, but on the advice of a friend they consulted the librarian of the Worcester Public Library. Mr. Shaw suggested that they write to Goodspeed's.

When Mrs. Dodd's letter announcing that she had a book entitled *Tamerlane*, and printed in Boston in 1827, appeared in my morning mail, I was as sceptical as the writer in the *Saturday Evening Post* professed himself when others told him that they had the book. In fact I did not even trouble to go to Worcester the next day, but waited for the more convenient weekend. When, however, I found myself in Mrs. Dodd's room and, with trembling hand, she produced her book, I got the first of the thrills which we both experienced that day, for a glance showed that she had what I never expected to see — a genuine and fine copy of the most valuable book in American literature.

It was an interesting moment. Mrs. Dodd was eager, questioning — was hers the book of which Mr. Starrett wrote? Was it worth the ten thousand dollars which he said it had brought? Where could she sell it?

I assured her at once that her book was genuine. As to its value, I had to speak with caution, for I felt there was danger of raising anticipations which might not be realized. The speculative value of the volume before us had to be considered. I explained the situation. 'You might,' I said, 'sell it yourself to a private buyer could you find one; but in that case would you know how much to ask for the book? Again, you could sell it at auction. Without question it would bring a handsome sum, but what that might be, you could not know in advance. As for selling it to a dealer, the last two sales at auction brought roughly one, two thousand and the other twelve thousand dollars. With such a wide variation before him any dealer would have to make a safe offer, which might be far less than the amount you really ought to get.'

These were the conditions. The circumstances were unpropitious for a bookseller's impartial advising, but I felt that they called for an attempt in this direction; yet the nearest approach to altruism of which I then found myself capable was to make the suggestion that she sell her *Tamerlane* through an agent on commission. To this proposition Mrs. Dodd readily assented, and agreed to put the book in my hands to sell for her; indeed, I think she would have accepted any advice which I might have given. Then, to anticipate the cavil of some doubting friend, I wrote a simple contract in which I agreed not to sell the book for less than ten thousand dollars without first obtaining her consent in writing and allowed myself a commission of twenty per cent. After we had each signed this document,

Mrs. Dodd passed the book to me, but I declined to take it just then. Someone would be sure to say to her after I had gone, 'What, did you let a man you never saw before go off with your book without making inquiries about him?' I insisted that, as a matter of business, she must anticipate such a criticism by satisfying herself that I was a responsible person. After several fruitless attempts to connect by telephone with Worcester people whom we both knew, our mutual acquaintance, Mr. Shaw of the Public Library, assured her that she might safely entrust the book to me and I returned to Boston with it in my possession. Half an hour after I left, Mrs. Dodd received an answer to her letter to Mr. Starrett. Unfortunately for him he had been away from home and missed his chance at the book by thirty minutes.

How does one price a book of this sort? I was anxious to get its full value, both for Mrs. Dodd's sake and my own. Furthermore, one does not like to have it said that under any given circumstances another dealer might have done better. I first took counsel of my friend Foley whose general advice concerning the book's value was encouraging. Next, I spoke to Frank Bemis, who at the time owned the fine Didier copy mentioned above. Mr. Bemis was greatly interested in the find and brought his copy of the book for comparison, although it is said that he had never shown it before. With the modesty which was one of his traits, he had been unwilling to have it known that he had paid so large an amount as eleven thousand dollars for a single book.

The copies before us differed very slightly in condition; it really was hard to say which was the better. 'How much are you going to ask for it?' my friend inquired. After talking with Foley, I had decided on twelve thousand five hundred dollars as a minimum price and I was not sure that even that amount was enough. To get Bemis's opinion, I answered him with a query, 'Do you think it worth fifteen thousand?' His answer was, 'I think you can get it.' Very well, I thought, if a Boston collector thinks it is a fifteen-thousand-dollar book, what would it be priced at in New York? My guess was it would stand twenty-five hundred more, so I fixed the price at seventeen thousand five hundred dollars.

It is one thing to price a book, but to sell it and get its maximum value is a different matter. My first offer of the book to Miss Greene, librarian of the Morgan library, was declined on the grounds that Mr. Morgan was not adding to his library books of purely collector's interest. I wrote next to Herschel V. Jones of Minneapolis. He was abroad. Owen D. Young then came to mind. Since his removal from Boston, where he was a frequent visitor at my shop, to New York, Young had become a liberal buyer of rare books. Thinking that he might be induced to buy the *Tamerlane* I wrote to him. His secretary replied:

> Because Mr. Young was obliged to leave town today he asked me to reply to your letter of September 3d. He wants you to know that he is most appreciative of your giving him the opportunity to purchase your copy of 'Tamerlane.' He asked me to say that he has spent so much money recently on books that he does not feel that he can pay $17,500 more now. He realizes how perfect and rare is the copy you have and thinks that the price is cheap and suggests that if you do not sell it readily to someone else, and care to take up the question with him again later, that he might feel less poor and be able to take it.

This ended my attempts at the time to sell the book by correspondence. Although I should have been very happy had Mr. Young bought it at once, I was glad to keep it for my forthcoming catalogue. The sale of any unusual item makes one regret the loss of the advertising which would come from listing it in a catalogue and this was a unique opportunity, as no bookseller had ever before catalogued a *Tamerlane*. Accordingly I made a compilation of the facts concerning the four other copies of the book and assigned it to a place, not at the beginning of the catalogue, but in its alphabetical order — number six hundred and thirty-seven. In this catalogue, issued some months after my correspondence with Mr. Young, *Tamerlane* followed the Eragny Press edition of Pissarro's

The Queen of the Fishes and preceded Poe's *Tales of the Grotesque and Arabesque*, 1840. The other contents of the catalogue comprised books of a 'choice and rare' nature. Lowell's *Commemoration Ode* and the folio edition of Audubon's *Birds* were the only items of large value.

While I was reading the catalogue proofs, I recalled that in my last letter to Mr. Young I had promised to call the *Tamerlane* to his attention again before offering it in a catalogue. I therefore wrote to him, saying:

> Our rare book catalogue is now in the printer's hands, and I have today passed the proof of the page on which the 'Tamerlane' appears. The catalogue will probably appear in about ten days or two weeks, and I am so hopeful that you may decide to take the book before the catalogue comes out that I venture to write to you once more concerning it. Wholly apart from the rarity and the interest of the piece itself, it has a peculiar collector's value, because it gives an added prestige to any collection of Nineteenth Century literature no matter how large such a collection already is in rare material. To be known as the possessor of one of the five copies of 'Tamerlane' is a distinction which no collector would despise, and while it may seem a good deal to invest in one book, it is just the kind of a purchase which the owner is always sure to congratulate himself on having made....
>
> I am not quite sure whether I explained in my former letter that I have taken this book on sale from the owner. I did this rather than purchase it outright because I felt that in the end I could make a better return to her in this way and, as she is an elderly woman in apparently very moderate circumstances, I am hoping that the amount which the book will realize will be sufficient to produce such an income as to provide for her moderate wants. There is a lot of satisfaction to find a book of this kind in the hands of someone to whom the money will really mean a great deal. If you want to see the book, say the word.

I received a brief reply to this letter: Mr. Young was then out of town, but would reconsider the matter on his return. This note came as I was leaving with my wife for a vacation trip to the Adirondacks. On the night of our arrival, while seated in the Lake Placid Club I received a message from home. Mr. Young telegraphed from Atlantic City to me in Boston: 'Could you bring the book over for me to see at my office in New York tomorrow, Wednesday afternoon, which is the only time I shall be there for the next week. Please answer Ambassador Hotel, Atlantic City.'

My son, who had the only other key to our safe deposit box, was also away from the bookshop. I tried to reach Mr. Young by telephone at Atlantic City. The hour was too late, however, but in the morning I talked with him over the wire at his office in New York and explained the circumstances. 'Well,' he said, 'I don't know that it is necessary for me to see the book. I will take it on your description of its condition, but I do not wish it sent to me now, as I am going west for a fortnight; when I return, I will let you know and we can arrange for its delivery.'

In the days which followed, my brother-in-law enjoyed an advantage over me at golf, for my thoughts were very much on the old lady at Worcester and I wondered how she would take the good news which I had to bring her. It happened that I was due to go to Worcester for the annual meeting of the American Antiquarian Society on my return home. Before going to that meeting I made an early morning call.

Mrs. Dodd received me with trembling expectancy. Had I found anyone who was interested in her book? Did I think I could sell it? I answered her cautiously for fear of the effect of a too sudden announcement. I told her that I *had* found a party who was interested in it — very much interested in it, but the customer whom I had in mind had left home for a two-weeks' journey and I reminded her that a great deal might happen in that time. He might become ill or accident might happen to him, but assuming his safe return she might reasonably count her *Tamerlane* as sold. 'And the price?' she asked, breathless with excitement. 'You will remember,' I replied, 'the terms of our agreement provided that I should not sell the book for less than ten thousand dollars — which, less the commission, would net you eight thousand.' 'And am I to get eight thousand dollars?' she exclaimed, incredulous. 'Yes,' I said, 'it is even better than that — you are going to get fourteen thousand!' For a moment I thought she might faint, but in two or three minutes she controlled her emotions, exclaiming with tears on her cheeks: 'It is really so? I can go to Boston to the sales and I can take a taxi when I want to? Why, I'm a rich woman!'

Mrs. Dodd's next reaction to the good news was to insist that I take a larger share of the proceeds of the sale, but I told her that my commission was ample and that we must stand by our contract. 'However,' I said, 'you may do me a favor if you will.' 'Of course I will,' she answered. 'What is it? I will do anything that you wish.' 'Very well, then; promise me that when you get the money, you will put it in savings banks. Use it for yourself as you may choose, but never listen to anyone who wants to invest it for you.'

The promise which she readily made was perhaps too well kept, for when Mrs. Dodd died not long ago the whole of the principal of her little nest-egg was intact. She had used only the interest on the deposit.

A fortnight later I called at Mr. Young's Park Avenue apartment in New York. It was immediately after the breakfast hour. Mr. Young greeted me with his friendly smile and, calling his wife and daughter into the room, remarked that he would make it a family party. All three were curious to see this unusual treasure. It was the quickest business transaction to which I was ever a party, for as I handed Mr. Young the book, he took it with one hand and passed me his check with the other. The *Tamerlane* was his, and although the price may have been more than any American first edition had ever brought, I think that the owner has never considered it a bad purchase.

So far as the sale of this book is concerned, I have come to the end of the story. To the publicity which it received there is, however, an aftermath, illustrating the frailty of mankind.

After the newspapers had published in considerable detail the account of the finding of the fifth copy of *Tamerlane*, six individuals tried to show, directly or by implication, that the book was theirs. One of these persons presented an unqualified claim for the book; others demanded evidence that the book was not one which they had lost or which had been stolen from them.

First there came a letter dated from the Salvation Army office of a western city. The writer stated that he had owned a book of which the title was *Tamerlane. By a Bostonian*, but that it had been stolen from him. He had reason, he said, to think that it might turn up in Boston and asked me to write him if it were offered to me. This clumsy attempt did not require serious consideration.

The second claimant was from Philadelphia. He offered, through the Pinkerton detective agency whose Boston representative called on me, a wild story about a *Tamerlane* inherited from his father and borrowed from him by a workman who moved to New York without returning it. His claim was soon disposed of.

Next there came the most definite and circumstantially maintained claim of them all. A Worcester woman called on me and declared that Mrs. Dodd, whom she had known as a schoolgirl, had seen the book at her home while sewing for her; that she had borrowed the book to read but had failed to return it. Of course the claimant had no idea of its value until she read about the sale in the *Worcester Telegram*. When evidence of ownership in Mrs. Dodd's family for two generations was produced, she made a not too graceful withdrawal.

Nearly a year after I had sold the *Tamerlane*, a man who was once chief of detectives and deputy commissioner of police of New York called on Owen Young in New York in behalf of a client. A New Jersey woman claimed that a *Tamerlane* had been stolen from her in June, 1925. This preposterous claim was quickly disposed of.

Another case was that of one Charles Bruedern of Willseyville, New York, who in 1929 stated that on the twenty-fifth of August, 1928, he had an auction at his place. Amongst some old books which he owned but did not include in the sale was a copy of Poe's *Tamerlane*. After the auction he discovered that the book had been stolen. As a result Captain Daniel E. Fox of Troop C, New York State Police, wrote me asking if I had purchased a copy of this book and if so, demanding from whom I got it. As the alleged loss occurred three years after my transaction with Mrs. Dodd, this claim was soon answered.

The sixth and last of these annoyances was the only one that brought serious embarrassment and that was due to an unusual coincidence. In this case there was no question of the good faith of the persons involved.

In the early part of the year after I sold Mrs. Dodd's book, two women called on me. One of them was the secretary of the Cambridge Neighborhood House, a social welfare organization supported by charitably minded Cambridge women; the other was her volunteer assistant. In August of the previous year, the secretary being on vacation, her assistant then in charge while looking over a pile of books sent in by some contributor noticed a volume with the title *Tamerlane*. Some months later, reading in the newspapers that I had sold a copy of this book, she suddenly remembered that she had seen that very book in the lot on the floor of Neighborhood House some time before. Post-haste she went to the secretary, only to find that the whole pile of books had been sent to Goodspeed's and that Goodspeed's had sent a check for five dollars, saying that they were of no value! My callers were polite, but the inference from their story was obvious; they had sent in a book worth some thousands of dollars to Goodspeed's and had received for it five dollars!

I do not know that I ever had a more unpleasant half-hour than that which followed. I had the evidence to convince these people that my *Tamerlane* came from Worcester and I satisfied them on this point. Nevertheless, one of them definitely recalled the book and the lot in which she saw it was sold to Goodspeed's. Where, then, was *their* 'Tamerlane'? I could only answer that no book of the kind had come from them to our shop and they dropped the matter.

I should have felt less easy had I known that, although it was not among the books sent me from the Neighborhood House, they really did have a *Tamerlane* which the secretary found in her office months afterwards and gave to me. It was a cheap paper-covered modern edition of Poe's poems with the word *Tamerlane* printed conspicuously on the wrapper of the volume. Ten cents would be a fair price for it.

It was hardly a year after this that another *Tamerlane* was offered to me. The owners had read about my sale and came to tell me of the copy which they had bought at an auction sale of antiques some years before. Would they sell it? That depended. What was it worth?

It so happened that at the moment I had a good customer who wanted a *Tamerlane* and was willing to pay more for it than Mr. Young gave me for Mrs. Dodd's copy. I put my cards on the table. I told my callers what was not then generally known — the amount which the other copy had brought and offered them that sum. They decided they would wait. 'It isn't growing any less valuable,' one remarked. 'That is true,' I replied, 'assuming that no more copies turn up soon, but if they do the value of yours might suffer.' 'We will chance that,' he replied, as they took leave.

Here the matter rested for the time, but later I made another attempt to do business with these people. I made an appointment with them, and my son, who was by that time handling the rare-book section of our business, went with me. After examining the book and finding it in fine condition, I said: 'Mr. —— we have been dickering over this book for a year now and have got nowhere. Either you want to sell it or you don't. If you do, we will try to do business; if you don't, we will drop the matter.' 'What is your offer?' he asked. In reply, I took from my pocket a check for eighteen thousand dollars, handed it to him, saying as I did so, 'Here is my offer.' He took the check, looked it over, and handed it back with a cool 'That's a good *offer!*'

It looked like a stalemate. I tore up the check and started to leave the room, saying that if he did not wish to sell the book it was useless to waste time in talking further about it. 'Oh! I will sell,' was his reply. 'How can you sell it if you don't put a price on it?' I asked. 'But I have a price.' 'What is it?' 'I'll sell it for twenty thousand dollars.' At last we had a definite figure. It was a stiff one, but my customer, an Indiana collector, wanted the book, and I paid the amount. This buyer has two other Poe first editions which came from us, the *Tales* and *The Raven* in Wiley and Putnam's Popular Library, 1845 — not great rarities ordinarily, but these copies are in unused condition, the paper covers bright and fresh as when they left the binders. It is doubtful if such another pair exists.

The relation of these transactions may seem unnecessarily detailed, but the celebrity of the book which they concern and the unusual fact of two copies coming to the hands of one dealer within as many years is its justification. Considering the amount which the second copy brought, it might seem unfortunate that Mrs. Dodd's copy was sold so quickly. Hers, however, was a case where a prompt sale was desirable and I was not justified in holding the book for future speculative possibilities. If sold today, it would bring something less than the amount it brought eleven years ago, for the discovery of several copies in the past few years has lowered its value.

How the owner felt about the sale is shown in her note which, disavowing its attribution of magic, I reproduce below:

Worcester, Nov. 4, 1925.

Dear Mr. Goodspeed: The cheques received and everything is all right. It is all so wonderful. Thank you wizard.

Sincerely
Ada S. Dodd

> (*Malvolio.*) *By my life, this is my lady's hand! These be her very C's, her U's, and her T's; and thus makes she her great P's. It is, in contempt of question, her hand.*

X. HANDWRITING AS MERCHANDISE

BUYERS of old books are relatively few. It would not surprise me to learn that there are five hundred persons who collect postage stamps to one collector of books. The bookseller who stocks but one class of books narrows for himself the limits of what is, therefore, at best a small trade when compared with the traffic in any kind of staple merchandise. Some suspicion of these facts was in my mind when I selected 'Anything that's a book' as a motto in 1898. I saw that secondhand bookselling, which was established in this country as a community-serviceable business over a century ago, offered limited possibilities and, at least at the start, such trade as a newcomer might pick up would only be secured at the expense of the existing shops. It was thus necessary to gain through advertising a new clientèle and to find other lines of merchandise not too remote from books which the older houses had not thought worthy of attention — not only for the increased volume of business which these lines might bring, but also for the increased interest in old books which the newer attractions would develop. It was in search of such avenues of trade that my small business in prints took on more importance and that an autograph department came into being.

Before either prints or autographs came to be important as adjuncts to my business, however, I tried other kinds of merchandise and at one time it looked as though I might enter the field of miscellaneous antiques — china, furniture, pewter, silver, and the like. In my early days I did dabble in a small way in all of these. A pair of capacious Liverpool pitchers, a handful of spoons and a silver beaker made by a craftsman contemporary with Paul Revere, a copper kettle said to have been the one which Dickens described in *Barnaby Rudge*, half a dozen old English oak chests collected by a famous London bookbinder, Sangorski (whose untimely death while endeavoring to rescue a woman from drowning happened soon after I bought them) — these, a few of my various purchases of their kind, indicate how near I came to engaging seriously in the business of 'antiques.' The two big Liverpool-ware pitchers, decorated with American ships, which I found in a New Hampshire summer resort hotel remind me that I once bought a dozen plates of the same ware decorated by a topsail schooner and bearing the master's name — 'Ambros B. Martin.' They were brought to me by a Connecticut dealer in antiques who, in his travels, came upon them in the medley of English lower-class household relics — discarded prams, boot-jacks, old crockery, and junk of that sort — offered in the Caledonian Market, a spacious out-of-doors rummage sale conducted in a suburb of London and much visited by antique-hunting tourists. That these marine souvenirs should have turned up in London and by some occult power of attraction find their way back to America, and then from Connecticut to Boston eventually come into the possession of a great-grandson of the old Marblehead shipmaster for whom they were originally made — who already owned other pieces of the same set — is an odd coincidence, but one of a sort not at all uncommon in trade.

Autographs, however, are obviously appropriate additions to the ordinary stock of a bookshop. They are the personal productions of famous persons; they are closely related to books; each specimen is unique, and they take up a minimum of space. These are some of the attractions that autographs offer to the bookseller.

I might enlarge upon the charms of autograph-collecting or give select examples of correspondence, but the subject has been amply treated by both dealers and collectors. An excellent manual, from the professional standpoint, was written some years ago by the late Thomas F. Madigan who was a prominent figure in the American autograph trade. Of books written by

private buyers which were largely suggested by the contents of
their own autograph collections, those of an old-time English
collector, George Birkbeck Hill, Adrian H. Joline, a New
York lawyer (gratefully remembered by the trade as a liberal
buyer), Simon Gratz, and Lady Charnwood come to mind —
books of delightful comment with generous quotations from
unpublished letters and of service to those forming collections.
As I would avoid duplicating the work of these and other writers
on the same subject, I shall select for particular mention only
three of the many thousands of autographs which have passed
through my hands. The first of these, one which we owned
several years ago, was a relic of the dark days in Boston and
Salem at the close of the seventeenth century when, like air
surcharged with electricity, the current universal belief in
demoniacal possession burst in a storm over those communities.

'The Examination of Abigail Hobbs at Salem Village, 19
Apr. 1692 by John Hathorne and Jonathan Corwin, Esq.,'
as its self-description read, vividly recalled that spiritual drama
of death. This document bore, besides the signatures of Hathorne and Corwin, that of the Reverend John Higginson and
Abigail Hobbs, the alleged witch. Hathorne and Jonathan
Corwin were the examining magistrates in the case against the
accused. Hathorne was reared in the strictest tenets of the
Puritan theocracy; Higginson, pastor of the Salem church, was
not actively concerned in the witch prosecution. Probably
the presence of his name on the document is accounted for by
the fact that he was skilled in shorthand writing and may have
taken down the Hobbs deposition. The case was unusual even
in the extraordinary situation then existing. The young Hobbs
woman admitted that she was a witch. She also accused her
parents of the same offence, a charge at first denied but afterwards admitted by the mother, who in turn declared that her
husband and a younger child were likewise guilty. The daughter, Abigail, was condemned to death, but the cases coming as
the witchcraft excitement subsided she was not executed.

Mary, mother of George Washington, comes next in my
autographic memorabilia. The letter of Mary Washington
which I bought in 1912 was from the Hathaway sale at Libbie's.

When it came to the auctioneer's stand, Walter R. Benjamin of New York was seated beside me. I asked him what he thought of it. 'I don't know what to think,' he replied nervously. 'I never have seen a letter of Mary Washington's before, and I have a bid on it. I don't know what to do about it.' The bidding was started by him. When it reached two hundred and fifty dollars, he dropped out and the piece fell to me. The letter had been damaged at the folds by fire and was pasted down on cardboard to preserve the crumbling edges. After I sold it to the Morgan library, it was removed from the mount and found to be docketed on the back by Washington. The text, with blanks representing the portions of the sheet which the fire had destroyed, is printed below. It shows a greater irregularity of spelling than usual even for the writer's day, when vagaries of orthography were common, although such deviations from the standard did not signify the degree of illiteracy then which they would today.

                                        Martch the 17 1782

My Dear Georg
    I was truly unsy My Not being at ho(me?) when
you went throu fredirecksburg it was a un(   ) thing
for me now I am afraid I never shall have that (   )
pleasure agin I am soe very unwell & this trip over the
Mountins has almost killd me I gott the 20 five ginnes
you was soe kind to send me & am greatly obliged to
you for it I was greatly shockt (   )
(   )
ever be driven up this way agin by me (   )
will goe in some little hous of my one if it is (   )
twelve foott squar Benjamin Hardisley has (   ) four
hindred akers of Land of yours ges by George Len(   )
if you will Lett me goe thear if I should be obliged
to Come over the Mounttins agin I shall be very Much
oblig(   ) you pray give my kind Love to Mrs. Washington
& am My Dear George your
                            Loveing & affectinat Mother
                                        Mary Washington
Mr. Nurs desiord me to Mention
his son to you he writs in the
Treasure office of Congres.
                    M.W.

Autographs of Martha Washington are all rare and the following letter is of unusual interest. It was written to Abigail Adams in acknowledgment of Mrs. Adams's condolence on the death of her husband and links in a beautiful way two of the most famous women of the Revolution. My catalogue entry, which lists it, gives only the conclusion of the letter:

> To that almighty power who alone can heal the
> wounds he inflicts I look for consolation and
> fortitude
> May you long very long enjoy the happiness you
> now possess and never know affliction like mine
> With prayers for your happiness
> I remain your cincear
> Friend
> Martha Washington

This specimen was brought to me by a Civil War veteran who had some clerical position at the State House and was, in a small way, a collector. After buying the letter, I began to wonder where he got it. On raising this question, Mr. Pavey satisfied me by producing a letter written to him by the late Charles Francis Adams. Pavey, knowing of Adams's participation in the war as Colonel of a Massachusetts regiment of cavalry, had written an autograph collector's begging letter to him. Introducing himself as a war veteran, he inquired, 'Did Mr. Adams chance to have a Washington autograph which he would give him?' Mr. Adams did and would. Pavey's request was granted and, in superabundant generosity, Mr. Adams enclosed with a Washington signature the Martha Washington letter described above which he said, correctly, was more unusual than the autograph of Washington himself!

A Washington autograph story of unusual nature was told me by R. H. Powel of Newport. The Powels, originally from Philadelphia, have inherited the papers of their ancestors from which about forty autograph letters written by George Washington to Mayor and Mrs. Samuel Powel were stolen from the Powel house in Philadelphia about the year 1840.

In 1931 Mr. Powel was attracted by the announcement of

a sale to be held by the American Art Association Anderson Galleries in New York. Looking over the catalogue of the autographs offered in the sale, he found two letters from Washington to the Mrs. Elizabeth Powel to whom Washington had addressed other letters in the possession of the Powel family. When Mr. Powel expressed the thought that these two letters might be from the lot stolen so many years ago, the head of the Galleries said that they could not have been stolen from the Powel collection, for they had never been sent to Mrs. Powel! An examination disclosed the singular fact that the letters in question, although signed 'M.W.,' were yet, initials and all, in the handwriting of George Washington.

Whether it was a custom in the Washington household for the husband to write letters for his wife to sign, Martha being a bad speller, and George perhaps being fearful that orthographical irregularities might creep into epistles of her composition, or whether in answering a particular inquiry (concerning a steward and cook recommended by Mrs. Powel), it was thought that Washington could reply more suitably than his wife does not appear; but as there was another letter in the same sale written by George for Martha, either conjecture is reasonable. However this may be, Mr. Powel, with a feeling that the wording of these drafts was familiar, bought both pieces. After his return to Newport, he examined the now safely kept Washington-Powel correspondence and found in it the letters which, copied from Washington's drafts but both written and signed by Martha Washington, had been sent to Mrs. Powel.

The legal aspects of autograph-selling, a feature unfamiliar to most people, had not been raised when I commenced business and the few existing court decisions involving rights in this kind of property did not, as far as was generally known, concern the autograph-dealer's business. A brief consideration of these rights will be of interest, for they concern other persons than booksellers.

As property, what is the status of a letter?[1]   To whom does it

[1] Since the above was written a study of property rights in letters written by Roger Randolph has been published in the *Yale Law Journal* for January, 1937. This paper clearly states the problems and court decisions on same, with full citations of cases.

belong? When I mail a letter, in the eyes of the Post Office Department it is within my control until it is delivered, but once in the addressee's hand, the letter belongs to the receiver as far as its physical ownership is concerned. But what about the text itself? Has the recipient a right to publish it? Or to whom does that right belong? The courts have decided that it is vested in the author. The right to publish is his property. This being established, do rights of publication descend to the author's heirs and if so, through how many generations? In considering these rights how shall 'publication' be defined? These are queries of a practical importance to many people.

In 1904, I published for the author, A. E. Gallatin, *Whistler's Art Dicta and other Essays*. The edition was small, two hundred and fifty copies I believe, of which one-half were assigned to me and the rest to Elkin Mathews for the London market. For one illustration of his book Mr. Gallatin had supplied an autograph letter of Whistler. It concerned the varnishing of his painting, 'Blue and Violet — Amongst the Rollers,' and was not printed in the text, but, neatly reproduced, was tipped in before the beginning of the first essay.

After the book was published and partly distributed, I received a letter of the following import from the law firm of Brandeis, Dunbar & Nutter. They had been instructed by a client, Miss Birnie Philip, executrix of Whistler's estate, to call my attention to the letter which I have just described. I was told that the publication of this letter was unauthorized by her and therefore illegal. Four demands followed: (1) that I should surrender to Miss Philip all unsold copies of the book; (2) that I should apologize for its publication; (3) I must pay for the expenses of publishing the apology; (4) it was further demanded that I should sign an agreement not to publish any Whistler letters which might come into my possession in the future.

Some of these demands seemed a bit high-handed, but as the book was not mine, I submitted them to Mr. Gallatin for instructions. He directed me to remove the reproduction of Whistler's letter from the unsold copies of the book and make no further reply to the lawyers' letter. This I did and heard no more of the matter. I have understood, however, that Elkin Mathews surrendered the copies sent to him.

Six years afterwards a similar case arose and this reached the courts. Fourteen letters of Mrs. Mary Baker Eddy were offered for sale at auction by C. F. Libbie and Company the year after Mrs. Eddy's death. In the auctioneer's catalogue the letters were described separately and extracts from nine were printed. Shortly after the catalogue had been distributed and before the sale took place, the executor of Mrs. Eddy's will filed a bill in equity against the auctioneers in the Supreme Court of Massachusetts, praying for an injunction to restrain the vendors 'from further publishing, selling, circulating, or in any manner making public or showing such letters' and 'from further circulating . . . said catalogue.'

In its answer to this petition the court followed the precedents, so far as the publication of the letters was concerned, but the decision, written by the Chief Justice, limited its definition of 'publication' to 'the sense of making public through printing or the multiplication thereof.'

On the question of ownership of the paper and ink which constitute the physical properties of a letter, the court stated that 'so far as they were aware, the exact question had never been presented for adjudication.' The court found, however, that 'the right in the receiver of an ordinary letter is one of unqualified title in the material on which it is written. He can deal with it as an absolute owner subject only to the proprietary right retained by the author for himself and his representatives to the publication or non-publication of idea in its particular verbal expression.' There are, however, some cautionary words preceding this language which would seem to indicate that the 'right' of the receiver, although 'absolute' in ordinary cases, might be regarded differently in others where there was something unusual in the contents of the letter or where some confidential relation between writer and recipient existed.

Apart from proprietary rights in their contents, several interesting questions have arisen concerning the ownership of autographs. Some of these questions are concerned with docu-

ments of more or less official nature. In the *Acts and Laws* of
the State of Massachusetts, there is a statute passed in 1897
which reads:

> Whoever unlawfully keeps in his possession any public
> record or removes it from the room where it is usually kept,
> or alters, defaces, mutilates or destroys any public record or
> violates any provision of this chapter shall be punished by a
> fine of not less than ten or more than five hundred dollars....

I came in contact with this law a long time ago. I had
catalogued a document in the autograph of Nathaniel Morton.
Morton was a Pilgrim father of Plymouth Colony. As an office-
holder he was a man of importance. Besides being Secretary to
the Colony, he was keeper of its records, writer of the colonial
laws and copyist of the same, assessor and tax-collector of
Plymouth, and member of many town committees. He was
also clerk of the town, secretary of the council of war in the
campaigns against King Philip, secretary of the Pilgrim Church,
and compiler of its records. With all of the labor attendant on
these positions he found time for history-writing, and in his
New England's Memoriall we find the only list of signers of the
Mayflower Compact. He was an active man.

Among these varied duties was the charge of probate records
and Morton's autograph which I had bought at auction was
his signed notation on the back of a will. Unacquainted with
the statute quoted above, I described the piece in the usual way.
The catalogue attracted the notice of an antiquarian who came
into the shop, examined the piece, and went out. Almost immediately the State Record Commissioner walked in and asked
to see it. Did I not know that wills belonged to the public
records and that I was violating a state law in holding this
ancient document? He read the statute to me, but questions
arose in my mind. Was there a public depository for wills at
that early date? If not, could the Legislature of Massachusetts
penalize me in 1897 for the possession of what had been lawfully
held by its previous owners for two hundred years?

With these doubts I hesitated and asked to be allowed to

take counsel in the matter, which was agreed to, but on a later consideration of the fact that violation of the law was made a criminal matter and that I was probably wrong anyway, I decided to drop the matter without further investigation and, after holding the document awhile, sent it back to Plymouth.

The distinction between public and private property in autographs has brought up other questions, sometimes not easily solved, particularly in regard to correspondence received by individuals as public officers. Taking a specific case, what of letters addressed to the chairman of a special committee of the Legislature of the Province of Massachusetts Bay? This committee was a temporary body and presumably had no permanent office. Are the letters addressed to its officers now rightfully in private ownership, or do they belong to the Commonwealth of Massachusetts? What about great collections like those which Mr. Clements bought in London — the Gage and Clinton papers? How does it happen that in England, where the property rights in manuscripts have been so carefully protected, no provision seems to have been made until recently for the public control of documents so clearly official in their nature?

In the past the line between public and private papers seems not to have been drawn; it was of no one's particular concern. Many public officers also had no depository for their correspondence outside of their own houses. These facts partly explain situations like one which arose a few years since when letters which had descended to their holders through inheritance from the Reverend Joseph Willard were catalogued for sale at auction in Boston. They were addressed to Willard during his term of office as President of Harvard College which began in 1781 and concerned college affairs. Some of them referred to the conferring of honorary degrees, and one was from Alexander Hamilton accepting the proffered honor of a doctorate of laws. Upon representation of the rights of the college to the manuscripts they were withdrawn from sale and are now in the college archives.

Other questions of autograph ownership are easily settled. Loot of public documents, like that in the South during the

Civil War, and thefts from private collections today are no different in principle. Stealing is stealing and stolen property should be restored to its owners when discovered. Autograph-dealers ought to subscribe to this sentiment if only for prudential reasons, for they are by no means infrequent sufferers from pilferers. I once owned a fine letter written by Edgar Allan Poe to Horace Greeley. Here is a part of it:

> In the printed matter, I have underscored two passages. As regards the first: — it alone would have sufficed to assure me that *you* did not write the article. I owe you money — I have been ill, unfortunate, no doubt weak, and as yet unable to refund the money — but on this ground you, Mr. Greeley, could *never* have accused me of being habitually 'unscrupulous in the fulfillment of my pecuniary engagements.' The charge is *horribly false* — I have a hundred times left myself destitute of bread for myself and family that I might discharge debts which the very writer of this infamous accusation (Fuller) would have left undischarged to the day of his death.
>
> 'The second passage underscored embodies a falsehood — and *therefore you* did not write it. I did *not* 'throw away the quill.' I arose from a sick-bed (although scarcely able to stand or see) and wrote a reply which was published in the Phil. 'Sp. of the Times,' and a copy of which reply I enclose you. The 'columns of the Mirror' were tendered to me — with a proviso that I should forego a suit and omit this passage and that passage, to suit the purposes of Mr. Fuller.

I thought this letter of such importance that I had a line-plate made reproducing for a forthcoming catalogue the quotation given above. A few days before the catalogue was published, Mr. Manning of Albany, famous at the time as a collector of autographs, called at the Park Street shop and asked me what I had to offer him. 'I have something you will like,' I replied, turning to the two modest-sized boxes holding at the time my stock of autographs when, 'suddenly as rare things will, it vanished.' Poe's letter was gone, but where, I never learned; it may have been taken by a stranger or the thief may have been one of my own assistants. I never traced the guilty man nor do I know the present possessor of the letter.

Many autographs which the owners have intended to destroy
are brought to market by scouts. If people carelessly consign
the discards of their correspondence to the wastebasket without
mutilation, only to find them offered for sale later, the primary
fault is their own. Book-scouts have a keen scent. Junk-shops,
or even waste-barrels, are to them a legitimate field for search,
and great finds have been made in such places. Mr. Z. T.
Hollingsworth once profited handsomely from such a source.

Besides having a magnificent collection of engraved portraits
of Washington (which, I am glad to say, his sons still own), Mr.
Hollingsworth had a fine set of autographs of the signers of the
Declaration of Independence. One document in this set has
an interesting history. It is in the hand of Elbridge Gerry and,
besides his own signature, bears the autographs of the four other
'signers' from Massachusetts, John Hancock, Samuel Adams,
John Adams, and Robert Treat Paine. The date is also important — only five days after the Declaration was signed. It
went through a number of hands before it was given to Mr.
Hollingsworth by a friend, and the story runs that it was
originally retrieved from an ash-barrel in Charlestown where
it caught the eye of a passer-by who took it for its antiquarian
interest, not knowing its value. When Mr. Hollingsworth's
autographs were sold at auction in 1927, this remarkable document was knocked down to me for eighteen hundred and fifty
dollars.

In the past dealers and collectors have sometimes profited
from the discards of Government archives. I once received
a letter from a woman living in Washington saying that she had
found amongst the papers of her husband, who had been
employed in the State Department, a collection of documents
signed by several of the Presidents which she would like to sell.
She gave a general description of them and her price for the lot
of some forty or fifty pieces by various Presidents of the United
States from Tyler down to Lincoln. Each autograph was signed
to a lithographed form which read as follows: 'I hereby authorize
and direct the Secretary of State to affix the seal of the United
States to (..........) dated this day, and signed by me and

for so doing this shall be his warrant. . . .' The date, following the President's signature, was at the end of a description of the document to which the authorization referred.

I had no sooner bought these autographs than doubts arose in my mind. Might it not be that they had been unlawfully taken from the Government files? Troubled in mind, I wrote to the seller asking her not to consider the transaction closed until I had assurance of her right to them. To decide this I would, with her permission, write to the Secretary of State. On her assent I made inquiry. Secretary Root replied that he had investigated the matter and had found that these documents were part of a lot which, being regarded as of no further value, had been removed from the Government archives to be destroyed during the second Cleveland administration. He added that, although the Department did not think it necessary to take any action then concerning them, any transaction of the kind in the future would be severely punished.

Apart from the value of the presidential signatures themselves the interest in these papers was, of course, in ratio to the importance of the proclamations to which they referred. One of those signed by Lincoln, for example, authorized the fixing of the seal of the United States to 'My proclamation appointing a day of humiliation, prayer and fasting (12th August 1861'.' Another, signed by Polk, referred to his 'Proclamation of War with the Republic of Mexico.'

Considering these matters, it is evident that dealers have to exercise discretion in dealing with autographic material. The danger of giving offence to someone having the right to prohibit the publication of a letter is sufficient to warn against carelessness on that point, but even when such restraint does not appear, questions of delicacy or propriety may be involved. Where property rights are not involved in the sale of letters, there may yet be something in the contents of the letters which, made public, would injure others and in these cases, decency requires that they be destroyed. I have had letters of such a nature that I could not even return them to the writers for the mortification it would cause them.

Where letters are of historical importance but contain material which might bring embarrassment to someone now living, a fitting way of disposing of them would be by gift to a library or historical society under seal for a specified time. An instance of this sort occurred when I found in the papers of the historian James Ford Rhodes certain letters from Charles Francis Adams which had to do with personal relations within the Massachusetts Historical Society of which Rhodes and Adams were prominent members. These letters I sent to the Society sealed and under certain restrictions.

Boston has always been a prolific source of supply for autographs and literary property generally, but the local material offered to us has been mostly the product of American writers. Our stock of foreign celebrities comes chiefly from London purchases or, in the case of French autographs, from Paris. When I first went abroad only a few of the English booksellers dealt in autographs, although some of the larger establishments had a limited stock of particularly valuable letters and manuscripts. Dobell in Charing Cross Road was one of the smaller dealers who specialized in this line. On my memorable first London visit he sold to me for seventeen pounds an album which contained, besides miscellaneous documents, letters, and signatures, two valuable manuscripts — a poem by David Garrick and two stanzas of verse by Byron. Byron's lines which showed some textual alterations, were of the album type:

> I saw thee weep, the big bright tear
>   Came o'er that eye of blue,
> And then methought it did appear
>   A violet dropping dew;
> I saw thee smile, the sapphire's blaze
>   Beside thee ceased to shine —
> It could not boast the living rays
>   That filled those eyes of thine.
>
> As clouds from yonder sun receive
>   A deep and mellow dye,
> Which scarce the shade of coming eve
>   Can banish from the sky;

> Those smiles into the moodiest mind
> Their own pure joy impart,
> Their sunshine leaves a beam behind
> That lightens o'er the heart.

Garrick's were so characteristic that they scarcely needed his initials to identify them:

Upon D. G.'s reception at Wynnstay's. Extempore.

> The representing Kings hath bred
> Such whimsies in the Actor's head,
> So swelled the Pigmy's empty pride,
> He's half a King in Every Stride!
> I who have strutted many an hour
> In royal Robes with royal Power;
> Whene'er I laid my Sceptre down
> Gave up my pomp and tyrant frown
> For tho' to vanity inclined
> It swell'd not so to taint my mind:
> But now, tho' I have left the stage
> And should be (?) for my age
> Yet tasting ev'ry social sweet
> At Wynnstay's hospitable seat;
> Where Beauty smiles, and pleasures reign,
> The Circe cup has reach'd my brain:
> So honour'd, flatter'd and carres'd
> Such kindness in Each Act express'd;
> No wonder Vanity takes wing —
> That NOW I feel myself a KING.
>   D. G.

In accord with the low prices (seventy-five dollars each) at which these pieces were sold, I find in the same catalogue a letter from William Godwin with a six-line poem in Shelley's autograph and signed by him on the reverse of the sheet which could have been bought for fifty dollars. Even that low price failed to bring a purchaser; in fact this Godwin-Shelley combination was catalogued four times before it was sold.

Most of my autograph buying in London was done at Sotheby's famous auction rooms where books, manuscripts, and prints have been sold for nearly two hundred years. Sotheby's business, established by Samuel Baker in 1744, is the oldest of its kind now in existence. Much of the autographic material sold there in lots allowed a handsome profit to the purchaser when he retailed them separately.

Certain names in good demand could always be bought cheaply. Autographs of Henry IV, Louis XIV, Louis XVI, and Napoleon of France, the two Charleses, the last two Georges, and Queen Victoria, of England, all in good demand, were then obtainable for very moderate amounts. Of nineteenth-century English statesmen, lawyers, and generals, the list of names which brought low prices at auction would include Canning, Croker, Peel, Palmerston, Melbourne, Salisbury, Bright, Cobden, Gladstone, Brougham, Wellington, *et al*. These were obtainable in bundles for a few shillings each or less. Many of the minor Victorian authors — if one may be allowed to include Moore, Southey, Jeffrey, Rogers, Macaulay, Proctor, Lingard, Mill, Arnold, Lockhart, James, Lever, Trollope, Lang, Mrs. Hemans, Joanna Baillie, Miss Mitford, Mrs. Oliphant, and Mrs. Jameson in this category — brought little more, while philanthropists and clergymen excepting a few names of especial appeal were a drug on the London market. I found a better demand for them in Boston. It was a day when many buyers were making general collections, and in the fortnight which followed the mailing of my current autograph catalogue, it was not uncommon to receive orders which filled several sheets of paper and which took the greater part of the day to fill. Today more interest is shown in the contents of letters or documents. Promiscuous buying of autographs is now diminished and the lesser names are quite neglected; it is an era of specialization. Postage-stamp collecting has now more separate lines of interest than autograph-collecting ever had; the buyer of antiques today covers his walls with clocks, fills his shelves with pressed glass, and the specimens of furniture on his floors are the work of individual craftsmen, while the attention of bookshop print-buyers who, a decade ago, became wildly enthusiastic over colored costume plates extracted from the *Godey's Magazine* of our great-grandmothers' reading, now seems firmly fixed, for the time, on colored prints which came from the lithographic presses of Currier and Ives in the Godey period.

During one visit to London I inserted an advertisement for autographs in the 'personal' column of the London *Times*. It was worded something like this: 'American visiting London wishes to purchase collections of autographs or single specimens of desirable names. Address.........., Times Office.' Two insertions of this card brought one hundred and forty-three replies. One letter which seemed to have good possibilities took me to Cornwall. The writer, who owned a collection of between one and two thousand pieces, stated that they had been acquired before 1850. Unfortunately these letters were chiefly of persons famous in their day but long since forgotten. The lot contained, however, two long interesting letters written by Darwin while on the famous voyage of the *Beagle* which had such far-reaching results to him and to the world. These, I wished to buy, but could not, apart from the others.

Replies to my card in the *Times* came from all over England and from all sorts of people. One letter was written by a lady of the highest social rank; the lot she offered was worth less than ten shillings. Although my total purchases on this occasion, with the exception of one manuscript, amounted to less than one hundred pounds, the result was, on the whole, satisfactory. The manuscript I refer to was written by Charles Dickens and was of a curious nature.

In 1854 Dickens was associated with the charitably minded Baroness Burdett-Coutts in a scheme for building an institution to care for outcast girls of the London streets. Dickens's manuscript was a prospectus of that undertaking. A part of it was written on the back of a letter addressed to Dickens by one of the unfortunates whose misery had moved his compassion. I gave a hundred and twenty-five guineas for the piece and sold it after my return to the Bibliophile Society of Boston by whom it was printed as one of their publications. After the book was printed, the manuscript was sold at auction for twenty-nine hundred dollars, nearly three times the amount it brought me!

An amusing incident followed the publication of one of our autograph catalogues a good many years ago. I have searched for the catalogue entry without success, but according to my recollection, it was something as follows. Mark Sullivan, then, if I mistake not, the editor of *Collier's Weekly*, printed in that journal at the head of the first page column the following line without comment:

> From Goodspeed's October autograph catalogue.
> Norton, Charles Eliot, Professor. Autograph letter signed. $.50
> Sullivan, John L., Pugilist. Autograph letter, signed. $1.50

That issue of *Collier's* was barely on the news-stands when a reporter from the *Boston American* hurried in and demanded (I use the word in the newspaper sense) sight of these autographs. He bought them. He then looked up John L. Sullivan and asked what he thought of the relative value of his autograph and Norton's. John L. rose grandly to the occasion. 'Sure!' he said. 'If Goodspeed's says my autograph is worth a dollar and a half and Professor Norton's is only worth fifty cents, Goodspeed's is probably right; they would find it a good deal harder to get my autograph than Norton's.' This interview, with reproductions of both letters, appeared in the *American* and was reprinted in various parts of the country as far as Texas.

In the eyes of some, all collectors are more or less crazy. Against this rampant philistinism it is hardly necessary to protest, yet one must admit that examples of eccentricities bordering on, or within the limits of, insanity are not infrequent in the bookseller's experience.

Twenty-five years ago a quietly dressed woman of middle age came into the shop inquiring for an autograph of Oliver Cromwell which she had seen in the window. Was it unsold? It was. I pointed to Cromwell's signature with a mezzotint portrait and a quarto broadside announcement of his appointment as "Captain-General of all the Forces of this Commonwealth," hanging against the chimney-piece above our old fireplace mantel. She asked if it could be reserved a few days for her. As she talked, her interrogations were followed by a voluble narrative delivered in crescendo. She was an inventor. Her marvellous discovery would revolutionize industry. Unlimited power was at her control. Money was needed to market the invention. Her wealthy friends had not responded. Only that morning was their neglect explained. 'Why do you suppose they have not written me before?' Her voice, as she answered herself, dropped — '*Because they have only just now heard how badly I need the money and have decided to give me double the amount !*'

From this point, her delusions appeared rapidly. She was related to Anne Hathaway. How did she know it? 'Because Shakespeare told me so himself.' 'What, have you met Shakespeare?' 'Oh yes! He visits me very often; he went to church with me last Sunday.' Growing more eager in speech, she named autographs which she lacked. Had I an autograph of Sir Humphrey Gilbert? I had not. Did I know just what happened when the ship of that navigator was lost on her voyage from Newfoundland to England in the fall of 1583? Well, she did — 'The Historical Society would give a great deal to know what Gilbert has told me about it!'

Not long after the interview the autograph collection which this woman made came into the market. The letter from Washington's mother to her son mentioned previously came from it.

I do not know the precise nature of the mental disease from which this woman suffered; hers may have been a 'manic-depressive' case. 'Manic-depressive' cases are defined by the medical writer as 'characterized by extreme affect fluctuations which may at one time be of the deepest depression and at another by extreme exhilaration and excitement: (1) flight of ideas — that is, ideas of grandeur, etc., (2) extreme psychomotor activity, and (3) emotional exaltation.'

I have a striking remembrance of these symptoms as they were shown by three persons who were customers at various times. Two of them, at least, were not regular customers, but as their mental disturbances arose, more frequent visits and an increased familiarity or friendliness followed. I had no idea at the time that these men were abnormal and it is only within the last few years, as I look back over my relations with them, that I have come to realize the manic-depressive conditions which controlled their actions. The manifestations that I speak of were always followed by a disappearance due to an enforced retirement. Later, perhaps after several years, the patient would turn up — happy, smiling, and apparently in health. One man had been for several years a regular and profitable customer. His excitation, following the usual course, showed itself in extraordinary activities in outings or collecting jaunts to which I was invited and I was not conscious of the connection between these holiday seasons and the depressive period which followed until long afterwards.

I do not profess to interpret character from handwriting; neither do I question the ability of others to do so. When we look at Washington's gracefully flowing handwriting — easy, regular, and as lovely as the rolling surf in its curves — can anyone fail to recognize that it has firmness and beauty?

Washington's penmanship is, in my estimation, the handsomest of any I have seen. Lincoln's hand is as homely and as convincing of sincerity as the man himself. Nevertheless, the usual

character interpretations of experts more often appear to illustrate minor traits of the writer. Opinions on this point, however, differ. Examining some autograph specimens to see what they might suggest, I was about to observe that Washington Irving's writing shows something of the elegance of his style, when I suddenly discovered that Poe, in his 'Chapter on Autographs' written for the *Southern Literary Messenger* in 1838, comes to an opposite conclusion. He calls both the composition and the handwriting of Irving 'slovenly'! One skeptical autograph-buyer tells me that he thinks phrenology offers a more rational basis for interpreting character than handwriting does!

Whatever significance handwriting may or may not have, of this there can be no doubt: letters show in their contents not only the character of the writer but also, to a considerable degree, his mind. His powers of penetration and analysis, his learning, and the fluency of his thought are often shown in a manner not revealed by his speech.

There is one more characteristic which autographs very clearly display — the nationality of the writer. Some people doubt this. When I saw the film of *David Copperfield*, it surprised me to notice that, with all of the care given to the production, there was one small detail in which it failed. David's letters to his aunt were shown on the screen, not in the handwriting of an English youth of a century ago, but in atrocious Spencerian script which was certainly not in use in 1848 either here or in England. Yet one man declared to me his belief that this style of penmanship might have been used in England in 1848 and that nationality did not figure in penmanship at all! I once happened upon the following anonymous paragraph on this subject, to the general truth of which I can testify:

It is a remarkable fact that no man can ever get rid of the style of handwriting peculiar to his country. If he be English, he always writes in English style; if French, in French style; if German, Italian, or Spanish, in the style peculiar to his nation. Professor B—— states: I am acquainted with a Frenchman who has passed all his life in England, who speaks English like one of our own countrymen, and writes it with ten times the correctness of ninety-nine in a hundred of us, but yet who cannot, for the life of him, imitate our mode of writing. I knew a Scotch youth, who was educated entirely in France, and resided eighteen years in that country, mixed exclusively with French people — but who, although he had a French writing-master, and perhaps never saw anything but French writing in his life, yet wrote exactly in the English style; it was really national instinct. In Paris, all the writing-masters profess to teach the English style of writing, but with all their professions and all their exertions, they can never get their

pupils to adopt any but the cramped hand of the French.
Some pretend to be able to tell the characteristics of individuals
from their handwritings. I know not how this may be, but
certainly the nation to which an individual belongs can instantly be determined by his handwriting. The difference between the American or English and the French hand-writing
is immense — a schoolboy would distinguish it at a glance.
Mix together a hundred sheets of manuscript written by a
hundred Frenchmen, and another hundred written by English-
men or Americans, and no one could fail to distinguish every
one of them, though all should be written in the same language
and with the same pens and paper. The difference between
Italian, Spanish and German hand-writings is equally decided.
In fact, there is about as great a difference between the hand-
writings of different nations as in their languages. And it
is a singular truth, that though a man may become identified
with another nation, and speak its language as well, perhaps
better than his own, yet never can he succeed in changing his
handwriting to a foreign style.

It is a pity that the fine art of letter-writing is almost lost. Since
the days of Chesterfield, Walpole, Gray, and Cowper, the
practice has so deteriorated that now with the employment of
the shorthand writer, and the general use of typewriter, dicta-
phone, and other mechanical aids, all letter-writing has become
afflicted with a terseness admirable in business but lamentable
in private communications. We no longer look to our friends'
letters for those glimpses of life, manners, and customs which
distinguished the correspondence of a more leisurely day, although some profess to think lightly of the loss we have suffered. Even a century ago Sydney Smith wrote: 'I quite agree
with you as to the horrors of correspondence. Correspondences
are like small-clothes before the invention of suspenders; it is
impossible to keep them up.' But this opinion may have been
merely a convenient sentence from which to hang another
witticism, and I think that most people will agree with me that
the decay of letter-writing is a misfortune — one it is now too
late to mend. Regard it as we may, there are few who today
can say with Eugénie de Guérin of their dependence on friendly

correspondence — 'I live between the folds of a sheet of paper.'

Autographs written in answer to requests of hunters who play upon the good-nature or the vanity of others are seldom of much interest, but there are exceptions. One such from the pen of that prince of American essayists and friend of the auto-graph-begging fraternity — Oliver Wendell Holmes — may serve as a tail-piece to this chapter.

> I am very sorry to say that
> so numerous have been the applications
> like your own, the supply has utterly
> failed to meet the demand.
> — ODES gave out six weeks ago.
> — 'Lines' and 'Stanzas' ran dry about
> six weeks since.
> — The last EPIGRAM was squeezed out
> about the middle of this month.
> — I should have to come to ACROSTICS
> and THAT I can NOT stoop to.
> Nothing respectable is left but an
> autograph, which I here annex.

XI. CAVEAT EMPTOR

THERE are three kinds of rogues who plague the book trade: shoplifters, sellers of stolen goods, and fabricators. The sneak-thief is the least dangerous of them, for a stolen book means only a loss of money, but the purchase of stolen articles or of fraudulent merchandise may bring unfortunate results to an innocent tradesman. The sneak-thief might be compared to the crow in the cornfield, but with this difference — the farmer is protected in a measure by shot-gun and scarecrow. When a marauder defies these, he risks the hanging of his carcass as a warning to others; no cases against the crow are filed nor is he given probation.

It is more difficult to protect a bookshop from thieves. If you invite visitors to undisturbed browsing and then spy on them, you are risking their notice of that unfavorable attention. Yet a degree of watchfulness is necessary, although even when such care is taken, some thief may escape your notice. Here is a recent happening.

One morning on opening the rare-book vault in our Ashburton Place shop, a vacancy like that of a missing tooth appeared on the second shelf. Walter de la Mare's *Songs of Childhood*, a first edition enclosed in a morocco case, was gone from our best-protected books. The loss was a mystery and, as such, perplexing in its implications, for one of the curses of book-thievery is the suspicion it throws on innocent people.

Who could this thief be? The place was carefully guarded and access by a stranger seemed unlikely. It was several weeks later that we recovered the book from a friendly dealer and then his account of it was only a partial solution of the enigma. The book was sent to him by a buyer of antiques who lived in a small Maine town two hundred miles from Boston and who got it from a stranger whom he met in a railway train. We paid the Boston dealer thirty-seven dollars, the amount he gave for it. The profit to the thief was small, for the book passed through several hands before we got it again. Who he was, we never discovered.

Troublesome though the pilferer be, it is when he becomes a seller that he is most dangerous. When a book is offered for sale, the vendor's honesty must be appraised, furtively or openly as the circumstances prompt; if your judgment of human nature is poor, you may acquire stolen property — a situation sure to result in embarrassment and peril. The value of a lost book is usually no great matter, but the buyer of stolen property may have a criminal action laid against him. Prudence dictates, therefore, that at all times great caution must be observed in dealing with unknown persons. Volumes offered must be examined for erasures of ownership marks — removal of bookplates, eradication of rubber stamps, or smoothing out of embossed markings. Crooks are clever, and despoilers of public libraries are skilful in the art of removing protective devices.

Even as I write, a letter which illustrates this comes from a valued customer. He has found the stamp of a public library on a page in a set of books bought from us six years ago. We shall now have to refund him the amount he paid and return the book to the library from which it was taken unless the library be willing to accept its replacement value. In either case we are in for a loss, since the dealer from whom we bought the book is, unfortunately, one of the less responsible members of the trade and not likely to recompense us. It must be said here, with regret, that some dealers have been known to buy books, either with the knowledge that they have been stolen, or at least with such neglect to assure themselves that this is not the case as amounts to the same thing. Fortunately there are few men who degrade themselves in this way and these have little standing in the trade.

A case of book-larceny, exasperating in its conclusion, happened a few years ago. We were offered a very fine copy of John B. Wyeth's *Oregon, or a Short History of a Long Journey from the Atlantic to the Region of the Pacific*, Cambridge, 1833. Something in the seller's manner aroused the suspicion of the buyer in our Americana department who on that account gave extra care to his examination of the book. Surely enough, evidence of crookedness, although very slight, appeared in the faint remains of an embossed library stamp which, although so effectively ironed out as to make identification impossible, was not wholly obliterated. On some pretext the vendor was induced to leave the book and asked to come back later. In the intervening time inquiry of local libraries showed that a copy of this same work was missing from the Boston Public Library. An employee in the order department of the library left his duties immediately and came to see the one which had been left with us. After examining it he said: 'Although I know positively that this is our book, I am afraid it would be useless to claim it. All the marks have been so skilfully removed that I could not prove that it was ours were I called on to do so in court. The mere fact that our copy is missing and that you have had this one offered to you would not, I believe, be sufficient evidence to bring a conviction.'

Failing in the attempted identification, it became necessary for us to return the pamphlet, but when doing so we plainly told the would-be seller our reason for refusing to buy it — that we believed it to have been stolen; a warning which failed of its intention to scare the thief, for he was sentenced to the House of Correction not long after for stealing from another library.

Again, in buying one must not only be on guard against the dangers mentioned; discretion must also be exercised when dealing with unknown people, for even where the good faith of the seller is unquestioned, other conditions that may cause trouble are likely to exist. Quite recently an engraving was offered to us under unusual circumstances. The owner's story was told with a frankness that disarmed any possible suspicion of dishonesty, yet the circumstances which attended her acquisition of it made us hesitate.

This was her account: While on a visit to a friend at a certain school she was shown a miscellaneous lot of pictures, chiefly rubbish left there by former students as not worth taking away. Invited to help herself to any she might like, she chose the one now brought to us for valuation and an offer. It proved to be worth a thousand dollars. When asked to buy it we felt obliged to decline the opportunity. The woman's title may have been good and would never, I suppose, be questioned. Yet the one who had ignorantly abandoned an article of value might possibly discover his loss and seek to repossess himself of the engraving. Even if such an effort proved unavailing, the situation was one to be avoided.

As these pages will show, our own business has not wholly avoided these pitfalls. Everyone in the trade is likely to stumble into them at some time; nor can we claim to have escaped loss from the devices of the fabricator, he who forges everything likely to be found in a bookseller's stock. What kind of merchandise have these rascals not imitated?

There is before me a life-size bas-relief in terra-cotta, a portrait in profile purporting to be of Paul Revere, signed on the back 'Giuseppe Cerrachi fec 1795.' It was left for sale more than two years ago by a stranger who gave what seems to have been a fictitious address, for letters sent him fail of delivery. He has never come back to claim his property on the merits of which I am not justified in offering an opinion, for, were the subject not of local historical interest, it would be outside of our field.

Sculptor's work is not, of course, sold in bookstores. Book-dealers are conservative folk; to gain recognition of their occupation as a profession rather than a trade, they should resist the temptation to go far afield, or to add to their stock more profitable articles of general utility not related to their regular merchandise. It is proper for a bookseller to run a circulating library, a magazine counter or a news-stand; possibly it may be allowable for him to sell writing paper, but not even in trade reprisal are cosmetics, electrical gadgets, whisky, canary-birds, bathing-suits, or mouth-washes admissible. He holds himself above such things.

Facsimiles and Forgeries is the title to a pamphlet descriptive of 'A Timely Exhibition' in the William L. Clements Library published in 1934. Fifty specimens of forgeries, ranging from a pictorial clay tablet of supposedly American aboriginal origin to modern brochures described by Carter and Pollard in their recent *Enquiry into the Nature of Certain Nineteenth Century Pamphlets*, were shown at the time. Matter descriptive of literary and historical forgeries has also been published in the monthly bulletins of the New York Public Library, and there are likewise monographs on individual examples such as R. G. Vail's study of the Washington memorial number of the *Ulster County Gazette*. Also useful to the public is a pamphlet written by Mr. Gavit of the New York State Library listing numerous other reprints or facsimiles of particular newspaper issues. These reproductions of old newspapers were not issued to deceive the buyers, but having come into general circulation, they are now sometimes used for that purpose, although their owners are usually innocent believers in their genuineness. Simon Gratz in *A Book about Autographs* has compiled more extensive material on this subject than these pages will admit, and he also gives references which will allow the reader to make further studies if he wishes to do so. All of these expositions should be read by collectors.

In the broad field of collecting there is need for a general work covering all kinds of spurious articles — silver, china, furniture, and paintings, as well as books and autographs. We once bought in London a small painting of a brig. It was a genuine specimen of Robert Salmon's work, interesting to local collectors of ship pictures, not only for the reason that Salmon was a good painter, but because he lived in Boston for some years in the early nineteenth century. The brig carried an American flag at her stern and the name *Boston* was on her bow, but on examination the flag and the name were found to be spurious, for when this part of the canvas was examined under a magnifying-glass, it was seen that the fine cracks which covered the rest of the surface were here painted on! The flag and the name were modern additions designed to increase the value of the picture. Shortly after we had made this discovery and returned the painting to London, we learned that the canvas had been in the United States once before, consigned to a local collector who also returned it. Not many months afterwards, it turned up again, this time in the hands of a New York dealer. It was discovered there by the collector to whom it was first sent in Boston and who was highly amused at its appearance for the third time on this side of the Atlantic. When the history of the ship and the reconditioning which she had received was told to the last purchaser, another voyage to London followed, making her sixth trip over the Atlantic, possibly a record.

During recent years there have been notorious sales of other kinds of spurious merchandise in or around Boston. With some articles, like silver, the pieces themselves were genuine; the fraud lay in the recent addition of an early craftsman's name. A well-known collector of Paul Revere silver once told me of her experience with faked examples of that silversmith's art. According to her account, she had been buying what she supposed to be Revere silver from one dealer before a museum authority told her that the maker's stamp on her pieces was not genuine. On this information she wrote a letter to the party who had sold the silver to her telling him, in effect, that he knew that her collection had been made for ultimate museum use and, as she now found that the pieces were not suitable for that purpose, she was returning them to him and would thank him for a check to the amount of her purchases. The remittance is said to have followed without argument.

In his own proper vocation the bookseller will meet with forgeries of everything he sells. Books themselves, in whole or part, book-bindings, title-pages, illustrations, *ex-libris*, autographs, old newspapers — even the contents of books — all these have been counterfeited at some time to his loss.

Of all these things, antique tooled book-bindings might seem to promise the least return to a faker. It requires unusual craftsmanship to copy the decorations of old bindings convincingly, and before such imitations can be produced, it is necessary for the forger to obtain appropriate books upon which to apply his skill.

It happened many years ago, in 1923 to be exact, that a small lot of forged bindings came into my possession through an ill-considered purchase. Young, dark, and smartly dressed, the arguments of a less aggressive saleswoman might not have been convincing, for, on most of the group of calf and morocco-bound volumes she offered, the application of the decoration was inferior to the kind of work we look for on the books of royalty or people otherwise distinguished. Not having learned to decide the genuineness of a questioned article on a hundred per cent correct basis nor to give greater weight to one definitely wrong feature than to any number of favorable ones, I foolishly allowed the proffered bargain to deceive my wavering judgment. The fact that these books bore bindings contemporary with the sixteenth and seventeenth centuries in which they were printed should not have influenced me when their provenance and decoration were of doubtful origin.

A few weeks after this purchase, not having come to a decision concerning their genuineness, I decided to resolve my doubts by referring these bindings to a proper authority, A. W. Pollard of the British Museum. Mr. Pollard's report, courteously given, was illuminating and mostly adverse. Of one volume, which the rough memorandum of the vendor described as having been bound for Jean Grolier and on which a valuation of six hundred and fifty dollars was given with the notation that the book came from the library of 'Prince Alex. Cardinal Estensis,' Mr. Pollard wrote:

> L. Julius Florus. Res a Romanis gestae. Coloniae Agrippinae. 1592.
> Probably a Cologne binding with ornamented back small corner pieces, centre piece and gold rules. Inscription Io. Grolierii et amicorum, and strap work and dots, all added. Grolier died in 1565, twenty-seven years before the book was printed.

Books of which several editions are published without textual change in the same year as the first often attract the forger on account of the ease with which a 'second-edition' title-page may be replaced by a reproduction of the one belonging to the first edition. This fraud may usually be detected by a careful examination of the first signature of the book. If a new title has been inserted, it is easy to see where it has been tipped in unless the volume has been rebound. It is for this reason that books of this class when not in their original covers are avoided by the judicious collector. Dickens's *Great Expectations* is an example.

Reproductions of text do not come in the category of frauds unless their presence is concealed. The imperfections of Shakespeare folios and other valuable books are often supplied by facsimile work. When these necessary reproductions are made, a memorandum of them ought to be made in the volume where they appear. A sermon by Cotton Mather was once sent by us to Rivière in London for the facsimile replacement of a missing leaf. Having carelessly neglected to record the number of the missing page and the binder being equally negligent, the most careful scrutiny failed to identify the restored leaf, so admirably were both paper and typography matched to the original.

It is with autographs that we find the forger most active. In this field his fraudulent productions remain for years unsuspected. Too often, and often too late, some collector is shocked to learn that a highly prized specimen has no better place of origin than the chamber of an impecunious penman whose skill might have been more gainfully employed in an honest occupation. The number of these undetected frauds in private ownership is appallingly large.

In a few cases forgers have entertained the world by publishing their confessions. William Henry Ireland, the forger of Shakespeare autographs, is perhaps the most notable.

It seems incredible now that the fabrications of this nineteen-year-old lad should have deceived eminent pundits a century and a half ago, but such is the fact. After Ireland's forgeries were exposed, his own father died in firm belief that his son had really discovered authentic manuscripts of Shakespeare and books containing Shakespeare's signature. The high priests of Shakespeare's shrine accepted these offerings as genuine. James Boswell, Esquire, was also taken in. Poor Bozzy, his judgment confirmed by a glass of toddy, knelt and kissed them.[1]

My specimen of the Ireland-Shakespeare forgeries came from a famous collection — that of Richard Heber. 'William Shakespeare' is written on the title-page of a volume on my angling shelves. The title of the book reads:

Fishermen Fishers of Men. A Sermon Preached at Mercers Chapell on Mid-Lent Sunday the 26. of March, 1609. By John Rawlinson Doctour of Divinitie. London ... 1609.

There is nothing of angling in this book save by way of analogy, but it contains such a preview of Walton [2] as this:

And lastly, as fishes when they are wounded, have recourse to the *Tench*, the *Physitia of fishes*, whom if they do but touch, they are healed: So must wee when wee are *wounded with sin*, repaire to our Savior Christ the true *tench*, the *Physitian of Kings*, and *King of Physitians*, whom if we due but touch *Tactu fidei*, with the touch of true faith, we shall bee *whole*.

The reverend doctor also anticipates Walton's use of the Master's promise, 'I will make you fishers of men,' a text of which he says:

Not a *Metaphor* thorowout the whole volume of Gods booke, that more willingly dilates and spreads it selfe into an *allegory*.

[1] On second thought, it seems unfair to the reader to omit the full picture. 'At length, finding himself rather thirsty, he requested a tumbler of warm brandy and water; which having nearly finished, he then redoubled his praises of the manuscripts; and at length arising from his chair, he made use of the following expression: "Well; I shall now die contented, since I have lived to witness the present day." Mr. Boswell then kneeling down before the volume containing a portion of the papers, continued, "I now kiss the invaluable relics of our bard: and thanks to God that I have lived to see them!" Having kissed the volume with every token of reverence, Mr. Boswell shortly after quitted Mr. Ireland's house.' (*The Confessions of William Henry Ireland*, 1805.)

[2] '... and shall tell you next, for I hope I may be so bold, that the Tench is the physician of fishes; for the Pike especially, and that the Pike, being either sick or hurt, is cured by the touch of the Tench.' (*The Compleat Angler*.)

From these and some other passages, I suspect the writer of this book to have been a fisherman himself despite his reference to the apostles as 'silly fishermen,' for if the adjective 'silly' should savor of detraction it was appropriate in his day to the calling of a fisherman, signifying no more than that they were of a harmless and innocent occupation, which fishing truly is.

When we come to explore Elizabethan tracts, we discover metal that we have not suspected and, as with this old sermon, find ourselves astray from the subject on which we started. For its slight allusion to another sport, I shall quote the closing paragraphs of Rawlinson's homily:

> And (for conclusion) I will ad this corollary of comfort to my bretheren *fellow-fishermen, fellow laboreres* in this heavenly function; that as *Aulico paru resert quomodo a cateris destimetur, dummodo principi se probet*: Little cares the Courtier how others esteeme of him, so that he approove himselfe to his Prince, who is able to exalt and bring him to honour: so they need not much respect how little men respect them (eclipsing, extenuating, maligning their calling) so that they approove themselves unto God, who both can, and will heereafter highly advance them.
>
> That bright, glorious and capacious globe of the Sun, is (to see to) but *Instar pilae pedalis*, No bigger than a foot-ball: yet is it no lesse than *Luxmundi*, The light of the world: So they, albeit in the eies of men they are no better than a foot-ball, a very play-game fit to kickt and spurnd at; yet are they in Gods eies (who seeth not as man seeth) Luxmundi, Matth. 5. glorious and beautifull as is the Sun in the firmament, farre above which they shall one day be exalted in the highest heavens, there for ever to shine in glory with him who is Sol Iustitiae Mat. 4. even the *true sonne of righteousnesse Christ Jesus*.

Returning from this digression, the Ireland forgeries created a tremendous sensation on their appearance and for a year they were the chief topic of discussion in London literary circles. Ireland is said to have used for copy the facsimile of Shakespeare's signature which had been reproduced by George Steevens. The six known autographs of Shakespeare vary

FISHERMEN
Fishers of Men.
A
SERMON PREA
CHED AT MERCERS
Chapell on Mid-Lent
Sunday the 26. of
March 1609.

By

IOHN RAVVLINSON Doctour
of Diuinitie.

Bernard. ad Henricum Senonensem Archie-
piscop. Ep. 42.
Non vos ergo fœlicem, quia præestis : sed
si non prodestis, infœlicem putate.

LONDON,
Printed by *Arnold Hatfield* for *Edward Blount*
and *William Barret.*
1609.

FORGED SHAKESPEARE AUTOGRAPH

considerably. Of these the two which Ireland's forgery resembles most are found, one on a deposition, and the other as the main signature to his will.

Professor Carl F. Schreiber's paper on the Schiller forgeries of Georg Heinrich Karl Jacob Victor von Gerstenbergk, written for *The Colophon,* is the best account I have seen of the forgeries of one author's manuscripts. It appears in the eighth number of that publication. Anyone who wishes to know more of this subject will be well repaid for a reading of Professor Schreiber's article.

During the last century several men produced forgeries in England. Spurious letters or manuscripts of Burns, Shelley, Keats, Wordsworth, Scott, and other authors of prominence, and of Queen Elizabeth, Mary of Scotland, and statesmen from the Elizabethan to the Cromwellian periods, deceived booksellers and collectors some eighty or ninety years ago.

In recent times the autograph forger has increased the scope of his productions to accord with changing values and the demands for other kinds of documents. Robert Spring of Philadelphia was the most notorious of old-time forgers in the United States. Washington documents were his specialty and although he died in 1876, his fabrications are still in circulation. One of them, reproduced here, may be compared with the genuine signature given on another page.

It was many years ago that, as I walked up Bromfield Street

at noon, I saw in the window of Leonard's auction room articles for sale that day. Amongst them was a small document framed with a portrait of Washington. In the afternoon a customer came into the shop bringing this with him. 'Why didn't you tell me you were going to buy this?" I said. 'I would have steered you away from it.' 'What's the matter with it?' he demanded. 'It's a fake,' I replied. 'Washington never wrote it.' The thought that he had been deceived by a spurious autograph annoyed my cautious customer and he hurried back to the auction room to demand the return of his money. Leonard, the auctioneer, tried to bluff him. 'Here is the owner Mr. L——, whom you must know by reputation,' he said, introducing the two men. 'He will guarantee that this is Washington's autograph.' 'Certainly I will,' said L——, 'and I will tell you where it came from. I bought it a long time ago out in Ohio from an old man in whose family it had been for years.' The buyer was unsatisfied. Addressing Leonard, he said, 'I have no doubt this gentleman is honest and I don't question his opinion that the autograph is all right, but I have no knowledge of his experience with autographs and Mr. Goodspeed says it is wrong.' 'Goodspeed!' Leonard exclaimed, 'what does he know about it? How much experience has he had? Suppose that I get Libbie's opinion or Mr. Lichtenstein's, of Burnham's Book Store, what would you think of their judgment?' 'I should think very highly of the opinion of either of these gentlemen.' 'Very well,' Leonard answered, 'we will see what they have to say about it.'

The outcome of this reference was unfavorable to my position, for, while Lichtenstein cautiously declined to give an opinion, Mrs. Fogg, Libbie's autograph expert, declared that, although the writing differed in some particulars from any of Washington's which she had seen, she thought it was genuine.

When Mrs. Fogg's opinion was brought to me, I asked to have the document left with me for a few days. That afternoon I went to Philadelphia to attend a print sale. Stopping in New York I called on W. R. Benjamin. 'Mr. Benjamin,' I said, 'here is something I would like you to look at. Please write me a note stating just what this document is.' He glanced at it, sat down and wrote: 'The document purporting to be a pass written by George Washington, and dated —— is one of the well-known forgeries executed by Robert Spring in Philadelphia about the year 1870. Walter R. Benjamin, Autograph expert.'

I thanked him and left. The next day at Henkels's auction rooms in Philadelphia, I ran across Joseph Sabin. As I showed him the same document, I said, 'Mr. Sabin, you handle a good many Washington autographs' — 'I have sold more Washington letters than any man living' — he interjected — 'tell me then, what you think of this.' Lifting his bushy eyebrows, he gave it a look and returned it with the short comment — 'Pure fake. One of the Spring forgeries.' Back in Boston I made a report which my customer showed to Leonard who then returned the money to him.

Soon after this happened another customer, O'Donnell by name, a retired wood-engraver formerly employed on John Stetson's *Police Gazette*, called on me. O'Donnell was an agreeable old fellow who liked to gossip concerning his hobby and especially to chuckle over the responses which his crafty solicitations of autographs from celebrities brought. When I told him the story I have just related, he exclaimed, 'Why, you knew about that Washington forgery. Don't you remember that I told you about it two years ago?' Thus recalled, I vaguely remembered the story which I asked him to repeat.

It seems that one day when walking through Merchants' Row, O'Donnell saw a document in a watch-repairer's window, a pass, written, as it appeared, by Washington. The price, fifteen dollars, seemed a bargain. He bought it, but in a few days he came upon an article on Robert Spring and his forgeries which convinced him that he had bought one of Spring's productions. The next morning the watchmaker was surprised to have the document presented to him for refund. 'It is a forgery!' O'Donnell declared, 'and I want my money.' 'Oh! You do! You collect autographs and know something about them?' the watch-maker queried. O'Donnell admitted the case. 'Look here, I don't pretend to know anything about such matters. This document was brought here for me to sell. You bought it on your own judgment; I paid for it, less a commission. I don't know the man who left it with me, I don't know his name, and I don't know where he lives. If there is a loss, it's yours.'

O'Donnell left the shop and started homeward by the elevated railway. In the car he chanced to meet a man whom he knew, the same man who afterwards sold the alleged Washington document at Leonard's. Being asked by him what he had in his hand, O'Donnell showed his purchase and told him how he got it. The other man declared his belief that it was genuine. 'I'll give you fifteen dollars for it!' O'Donnell quickly accepted the offer. The buyer, after holding it for a time, sent it to the auction house for sale with the result previously told.

Many of my trade contemporaries will remember a rascal who for years has victimized libraries, individuals, and dealers in a number of ways. At a time when book-plates and rare engravings of Washington were much sought, he purloined such prints from library stacks, especially in the older and less-guarded institutions. Much of his ill-gotten merchandise was sold to collectors through correspondence. Finding it was easy to sell these engravings, he went from stealing to forging and made successful counterfeits by mechanical processes. One example, a copy of Revere's engraving of King Philip, is reproduced here. It is a better piece of work than would appear from its crudeness, for the original print is almost as badly executed. This man's peculations also extended to whole volumes and a story is current that he once spent some days in a certain library in Canada posing as an American scholar engaged in research. The tale goes that before leaving he had looted the library of most of its valuable Americana, shipping it, under various aliases, to rare-book buyers in the United States.

When I last heard of this man he was offering for sale autograph letters, whether his own productions or another's I do not know. Samples of these have never come my way, but stories are told which show his cunning in disposing of them. Selecting the name of a well-known buyer, he would write to him in this fashion.

I have just come into possession of some property from the estate of an uncle who lived in London for some years. Amongst

PHILIP *KING* of Mount Hope

P. Revere fc

FORGED REVERE ENGRAVING

his effects there are some autograph letters which look valuable.
Being told that you collect such things, I enclose four letters,
two of George Washington, one of Benjamin Franklin, and
another of Abraham Lincoln. If you are interested in buying
them, please send me a check for what they are worth to you.
I leave the amount to your judgment as I have no knowledge
of such matters.

The tall, spare frame of this man, his nervous manner and high-
pitched voice were well known to the bookshops of New York,
Boston, and Philadelphia, as also to public libraries from Canada
to South Carolina thirty years ago. Now, down at the heel and
innocuous, his appearance occasions only such mild curiosity as
Charles Ponzi might excite on the streets of Boston today.

Unlike this individual, who hailed from Philadelphia, the
bookseller's public rascal number two was an Englishman. His
cockney accent was unmistakable. He also appealed to the
cupidity of buyers by protesting his ignorance of values. That
attitude effective years ago is not without potency today. Its
victims are not confined to dealers; they include people who,
as in my case, in the experience of years ago which I am now to
relate, are tempted by the chance of profit from another's supposed ignorance, and lacking knowledge of the things offered
them, become an easy prey.

The only time I saw this fellow was about twenty-five years
ago when he brought me some old manuscripts and a few relics
which he said had been sent to him from Canada. Thinking
that there might be a good market for historical material in the
United States, the friend who owned them had sent them here
for sale. My visitor continued that he had offered them to a
professor at Harvard College who referred him to the Bostonian
Society. From there he had been sent to Charles H. Taylor, Jr.,
of the *Boston Globe* who, in turn, told him to see me.

Of course I should have been warned by the absurdly low
price — sixty-five dollars — placed on the lot. The improbabil-
ity that all these people would have passed along such a bargain
would not have gone unnoticed had I not been blinded by the
importance of the material offered.

The principal value of the collection was in a number of pen-and-ink plans of American forts and one of New York City. Several of them bore the name of 'Jno. André.' The New York plan had not only André's signature, but also the initials of Sir Henry Clinton, dated October 2, 1780. The numbers on some of the margins suggested cipher references.

With these plans were a few miscellaneous articles — an old metal inkwell, the initials 'J.A.' crudely scratched on its side, a parchment tobacco pouch with 'Jno. André, 23rd Foot, Hounslow' written around the neck, and a delicate cameo turquoise-set locket, pendent from a fine gold chain. The lot also included a small copy of Churchill's poems in which figures resembling those on the manuscript plans were written on a blank page. These figures and the underlining of words and letters in the text of the book suggestive of a cipher gave an element of mystery to the collection.

As may be guessed, the vendor was not long in making a sale. I thought it a wonderful find and plates in reproduction of several of the plans were speedily made for use in our next catalogue. Before preparing the catalogue descriptions, however, I took the precaution of sending the New York map to a certain institution for comparison with specimens of André's handwriting. The reply, although given unofficially, was favorable.

Having then not the slightest suspicion of the material, I was about to proceed with the catalogue when Frank Coburn, a bookseller with whom I dealt, came in to see me. 'I wish you would come down to my store,' he said, 'and look at two curious Revolutionary caricatures. I haven't bought them. The owner has left them with me for an offer. I can't quite make them out and I would like to know what you think of them.' This was sufficient to arouse my interest, so I put on my hat and went down to Cornhill with him.

To make clear what follows, I must explain that about two years before this a woman brought to the shop two water-color drawings said to be the work of Rowlandson. Not then handling drawings and having no familiarity with Rowlandson's original work, I made no offer for them. They had no titles or other lettering.

When we arrived at Coburn's place, my feelings at seeing the 'Rowlandson' drawings that had been offered me two years before, now converted by suitable inscriptions into Revolutionary cartoons, may be imagined. I will describe one of them. The picture contained several figures. A man, one hand thrust into his trousers pocket, was perusing the long sheet of reckoning held before him by a companion whose right hand was represented as chucking the chin of the compliant, buxom innkeeper. A porter laden with baggage was leaving the room. When I first saw this drawing there was nothing to show that it was more than a common inn scene. Since then, however, a political turn had been given to the drawing by the addition of these words:

The British leave Boston after a short sojourn.
Madame Boston presents her bill for accommodation. 1776

A satire on the evacuation of Boston.

Upon my explaining to Coburn the questionable status of these drawings, he asked, 'What makes you think that they aren't genuine?' 'I am satisfied that the *pictures* are genuine; but the titles give them a different meaning and thereby make them fraudulent,' was my answer. 'Do you mean to say that the inscriptions are not old? See how brown the ink is,' replied Coburn. To this I returned, 'The ink is brown and, as you say, it looks old, but the writing is modern for all that, for I saw the drawings without anything on them two years ago!'

The reader may wonder what the faked 'Rowlandson' drawings had to do with the so-called 'André' lot then in my possession. The relationship was in the handwriting on them which was identical. It was evident that I had been the dupe of a faker. If I had any doubt of this, the appearance of more forgeries in the same general style of handwriting about the same time would have convinced me. These other forgeries are worth a description if only for their variety. None of them, it should be said, were copies of originals; they were all conceived and executed by the forger.

The knave whose cleverness is responsible for this transformation may well have been inspired by the forger of Shakespeare's autograph. In his *Confessions*, Master Ireland records his guilt of a similar imposture:

> As I one day chanced to pass through Butcher Row, I saw a curious old drawing hanging up for sale. It was framed, and placed between two glasses, in order to display the back and front of the paper; on one side of which was the representation of an aged figure in the habit of a Dutchman, while on the reverse appeared a young man gaily attired in an English dress of the period of James the First. As it suddenly struck me that the limning might be of utility to me in my Shaksperian employment, I made a purchase of it, and took it with me to chambers; where, taking out one of the glasses, I turned my purchase to the following account.
>
> On the side bearing the representation of the old Dutchman I painted a pair of scales and a knife, in order that it might pass for the representation of Shylock in the Merchant of Venice; and on the reverse, whereon appeared the gaily dressed youth, I delineated, in one corner, the arms of Shakespeare; on the shield of which I from thoughtlessness reversed the spear, making the point directed to the right hand, whereas it really ought to have pointed to the left corner. On the opposite side I introduced the initials W S, with the titles of a few of Shakspeare's plays: and having before me a copy of Droeshout's print, I altered the lineaments of the face of the figure represented, giving it as much as possible a resemblance to the print before me. Having made these alterations, I replaced the drawing in the frame, and after fastening down the glass, presented it to Mr. Ireland.
>
> The drawing of the old Dutchman **was** instantly construed to represent Shylock the Jew, although it was deemed rather extraordinary that the character should have been arrayed in the *costume* of a North-Hollander, which was really the case. The figure on the reverse (having the coat-of-arms of Shakspeare, the initial letters of his name, with the titles of some of his dramas, and bearing the faint resemblance which the altered physiognomy held to the print of Droeshout) was soon conceived to represent our bard in the character of Bassanio

'MADAME BOSTON PRESENTS HER BILL FOR ACCOMMODATION'

From the drawing, before the forged title was added

in the Merchant of Venice: and so far did conjecture go on
this head, that it was gravely stated the drawing had in all
probability graced the green-room of the Globe theatre.

While making final mention of Ireland, his account of the
way he, a lad of seventeen, overcame a minor difficulty in
preparing his Shakespearean forgeries for acceptance may be
found interesting. It shows what attention Ireland gave to the
details of his fabrications.

As old papers containing trivial accounts are usually bound
together, it was deemed extraordinary that the numerous play-
house receipts, which were written on small slips of paper,
should be brought forward without being tied up. I was for
some time anxious to obviate this objection, yet dreaded a
discovery, by producing a thread or string of the present day,
the texture and weaving of which I conceived might betray
me: in consequence of this a considerable period elapsed ere
I was able to compass my point, which was at length effected
in the following manner.

As Mr. S. Ireland very frequently made it a point to go to
the house of lords in order to hear his majesty's speech and be
present when he was robed, I happened to be in company
with him on one of those occasions; when, having to pass
through some adjoining apartments, where many persons were
waiting, and wherein we were also detained for a short time,
I observed that the walls of the chambers were hung with very
old and mutilated tapestry; when the idea suddenly struck
me, that, by procuring a small remnant (knowing its antiquity),
I might unravel the worsted and turn it to my immediate
purposes. In consequence of this conjecture, I took up a loose
piece (being about half the size of my hand) which was worn
by time from the hangings of an apartment; and on returning
to my Shakspearian occupation I drew out the worsted thread,
which afterwards served me whensoever I had occasion to
attach any of the receipts or other papers together.

It is often through the observance of care in seemingly unimportant features or in their neglect that the literary forger
succeeds or fails, for it is precisely to these small points that

256 YANKEE BOOKSELLER

the expert examiner first looks for the disproof or confirmation
of a questioned document.

Of the other forgeries which I have referred to as having been
produced by the party who made the 'André' plans the one
I shall mention first was offered for sale at Libbie's auction
room. It was a silhouette, reproduced in facsimile as a frontispiece to the sale catalogue. Below the silhouette were the words:

George Walton
George Walton. A Token from his Friend
Button Gwinnett, June, 1776.

followed by the cataloguer's comment: 'Silhouette portrait
cut by Button Gwinnett of George Walton, both Signers of the
Declaration of Independence from Georgia. An unique historical relic' — which it would have been indeed, had it been
genuine! Fortunately evidence of the fraud was discovered in
time and the auctioneers bid the thing in for withdrawal from
the market.

Another fabrication which had appeared not long before
this was in the form of a presentation inscription by Oliver
Goldsmith. It was written on the fly-leaf of Tooke's *The
Pantheon* (London, 1767). The inscription is reproduced here
in facsimile.

P. K. Foley was the forger's victim in this transaction. He did not know of the fraud until W. H. Arnold, the well-known collector of association books, to whom he sold it, returned the volume to him. In 1932 Mr. Foley turned the book over to the New York Public Library, where it now is on the shelves containing a collection of forgeries. I quote from the bulletin of that institution [1] which comments on its history:

> The Reverend Thomas Contarine seemed a most happy choice for a Goldsmith inscription. This uncle was the only member of Goldsmith's family who ever evidenced interest or pride in him, and it was he who bore much of the expense of Oliver's schooling.
>
> This Goldsmith fraud was brought to a Boston bookdealer in 1902 by a little English girl. In a most innocent way she told of her family's recent departure from its home in Cambridge, Massachusetts. In moving, a barrel had been filled with discarded books and papers which fell in the way of a Harvard professor. Several of the books seemed valuable to him and he suggested they be taken to certain booksellers in Boston. So, the story goes, this book came to Boston. The bookseller questioned the girl for documentary evidence about it or some information regarding its provenance, but she made no answer.
>
> The book was purchased by a prominent New Jersey collector who sent it for examination to Austin Dobson, the English poet who had published his authoritative *Life of Oliver Goldsmith* some years before. Dobson reported that the assumed beneficiary of Goldsmith's inscription, the Reverend Thomas Contarine, had been an 'incurable imbecile' at the date of publication of the volume and had remained so until his death.

In both this and the example which precedes it here, the handwriting, apart from the counterfeited signatures, was of so close a resemblance to that on my 'André' plans that there is scarcely a doubt that one man wrote them. The example which follows also points to an origin common to all three.

[1] Vol. 37, No. 3.

A piece of engraved sheet music was the medium of this forgery. Its title was, 'Be mine, tender Passion,' and on it was written, 'Martha D. Custis G. W. Oct. 1758.' The piece was folded, enclosed in an envelope, and endorsed (in a modern hand): 'Harpsichord music formerly belonging to "Martha D. Custis," afterwards the wife of Genl. Geo. Washington, 1st. Pres. of the United States of America." '

This sheet was brought to me by a dealer in this city who asked my opinion of the inscription. This being soon after my experience with the 'André' lot and as the writing agreed with that on the other documents, I gave him a prompt answer. As usually happens on such occasions, reasons were demanded. Instead of reasons, I offered a suggestion. 'Why don't you look up the man who wrote the music and see how his date fits in?' That test was conclusive. The forger had dated the inscription 1758; Stephen Storace, the composer of the music, was born in 1763.

Having now decided from internal and concurrent evidence that my 'André' manuscripts were spurious, I gave the gold trinket (this and the inkwell being the only genuine things in the 'André' lot) to my daughter, who still has it. The rest of the collection — forged plans and pseudo-relics — I kept by me for a while, finally exchanging them for a trifle, as curiosities, but before I let them go one of the plans was published. William Loring Andrews, a famous New York bibliophile, was in the shop one day, and looking this material over he questioned my judgment in condemning it. After hearing the long account, the substance of which I have given, he admitted that I was probably right. 'But,' he added, 'I never saw an original of that New York plan; and I should like to reproduce it in a book I am writing on New York at the close of the Revolution.' 'Very well,' I replied, 'you are welcome to use it, but knowing what it is I shall charge you nothing. However, my opinion must be clearly understood. The map is a fake.'

Satisfied, nevertheless, Mr. Andrews took the plan to Sidney L. Smith to engrave and in due time returned it. The plate will be found (minus the signature of André) in Mr. Andrews's

FORGED ANDRÉ PLAN OF NEW YORK

book, which was published for him under the title of *New York as Washington knew it at the close of the Revolution.*[1]

After the 'André' manuscripts had gone from my possession, I regretted that I had been so indiscreet as to part with them. Gossip said that the New York plan had found its way to the bookshops. It was reported that George H. Richmond had given a New York view valued at fifteen hundred dollars for it. Where it is, or by whom it may now be treasured, I do not know.

As I have said, I had but one transaction with this forger. During a visit to London in the year after his call on me, I saw products of his industrious pen in an auction room and in one bookshop. His work also continued to appear in this country for a number of years, although, judging by the low prices he asked, he must have lived from hand to mouth.

What I have written on the foregoing subjects will give an idea of some dangers attending the purchase and sale of books and manuscripts, either privately or by the trade. The best protection to the collector is a resolution to buy only from those who have a reputation for honesty and intelligence. Honesty, brains, good judgment, and a dash of skepticism in dealing with strangers, are the best defences of the dealer.

[1] In the original drawing André's name was at the lower right-hand corner. Space limits caused its omission on the catalogue plate from which reproduction here given has been made.

Some works are great for what they accomplish, others for what they suggest. At present Mr. Ruskin's fame stands on his achievements as a writer. Twenty years hence it is conceivable that he may be best remembered for his experiments as a social reformer. COOK (1890).

XII. THE SPELL OF RUSKIN

I BEGAN to collect first editions of Ruskin fifty years ago; my latest purchase — the revised proof-sheets of *Sesame and Lilies* — was in 1935. I started with Wiley and Putnam's 1847 reprint of the first volume of *Modern Painters* picked from the sidewalk box outside Bartlett's shop in Cornhill, reasoning that if the English edition of this book was valuable, the American reprint must have some importance. The idea was right in principle, for undoubtedly many American reprints of famous books are sought, but this was not one of them. Had I been lucky enough to pick up, as a local scout once did, the first American Bunyan, it would have been a real find, for this, one of the two copies of the Boston 1681 edition of *The Pilgrim's Progress* which have come into the market, brought thirteen hundred and sixty dollars nineteen years ago. If I had even discovered the first American *Pickwick* amongst the discards from Bartlett's stock, the purchase would have been worth while. As it happened, I paid fifteen cents for — a fifteen-cent book!

Notwithstanding this false start, a beginning had been made and, with the knowledge which comes from mistakes when once recognized, I assembled a Ruskin collection of modest size which, as I have told elsewhere, I parted with when I began my career of bookselling. I regretted the necessity of parting with these books the less for having discovered my mistake in getting them rebound. The blue half-morocco bindings in which they were reclothed by Sanford, our local workman, were well enough in their way, but I learned that their value was thereby diminished. The primary rule that pamphlet issues of all kinds, if intended for sale to collectors, must be preserved in their original form was one of the first of the lessons learned in the school of book-merchandising.

Fortunately for me I found my Ruskin enthusiasm was shared by at least one kindred spirit. Caleb B. Tillinghast, then State Librarian, was, like myself, an earnest Ruskin collector. Tillinghast was a placid, smiling, broad-faced man with flowing hair. These features, surmounted by a wide-brimmed hat, gave him a marked resemblance to certain portraits of Benjamin Franklin, whom I like to picture as sauntering, in the spirit world, down the once steep slopes of Beacon Hill pausing to look in Goodspeed's window on the way, as did his modern double a hundred and fifty years later.

It may be that the influence of Professor Norton, one of Ruskin's most intimate friends (and perhaps also the most critical of them), was responsible for a mild local interest in Ruskin then prevalent; possibly my own earnestness, less discriminating, may have helped in a small way to keep alive the fading Ruskin tradition. Anyway, I found little difficulty in disposing of a constantly renewed stock of Ruskin firsts. I believe that I bought more of these books abroad than any other American dealer, building up my own collection while replenishing the stock on the shop shelves. It is true that the nine-volume set comprising *Modern Painters*, *The Seven Lamps of Architecture*, and *The Stones of Venice*, was always on the shelves of the larger booksellers, the price not varying much from a hundred and fifty dollars. These sets were made up of the first editions, excepting (as the dealers were obliged to explain) the first two volumes of *Modern Painters*. The later issues of these were chosen, it was said, to make the set uniform in size, the first volume of *Modern Painters* having been printed in duodecimo while the others were large octavo. Buyers were also reminded that the first editions in this set included all of the illustrated volumes. Uniformity in size of volumes, however, has never been considered of importance by collectors; and the real, though unmentioned, reason for this inclusion of later issues in a set of first editions was the rarity of the first edition

of the first and second volumes of *Modern Painters*, especially
volume one. If all of the Ruskin nine-volume sets were made
up of first editions only, they would have been seen less commonly in the shops.

Outside of these three books and the *Poems* of 1850, booksellers generally ignored Ruskin in making their London
purchases and I found no competition in this field.

Ruskin's books have some features which ought to make
them of interest to book-collectors today. In the first place they
occupy, if not the highest, at least high rank in modern English
literature. Although his style is criticised, Ruskin is conceded
to be a great prose writer. Even in his earlier, florid manner,
no one can escape the charm of his descriptive writing and at
his best he wins general admiration. Take for example one of
many famous passages, his picture of the Rhone at Geneva, once
selected by Professor Charles Waldstein as 'the most perfect
instance of Ruskin's style':

> For all other rivers there is a surface, and an underneath,
> and a vaguely displeasing idea of the bottom. But the Rhone
> flows like one lambent jewel; its surface is nowhere, its ethereal
> self is everywhere, the iridescent rush and translucent strength
> of it blue to the shore, and radiant to the depth.
> Fifteen feet thick, of not flowing, but flying water; not water,
> neither, — welled glacier, rather, one should call it; the force
> of the ice is with it, and the wreathing of the clouds, the glad-
> ness of the sky, and the continuance of Time.
> Waves of clear sea are, indeed, lovely to watch, but they are
> always coming or gone, never in any taken shape to be seen
> for a second. But here was one mighty wave that was always
> itself, and every fluted swirl of it, constant as the wreathing
> of a shell. No wasting away of the fallen foam, no pause for
> gathering of power, no helpless ebb of discouraged recoil;
> but alike through bright day and lulling night, the never-fading
> flash, and never-hushing whisper, and, while the sun was up,
> the ever-answering glow of unearthly aquamarine, ultramarine,
> violet-blue, gentian-blue, peacock blue, river-of-paradise blue,
> glass of a painted window melted in the sun, and the witch of
> the Alps flinging the spun tresses of it forever from her snow.

There is much more — and even more picturesque writing — in this passage, which Waldstein characterizes as 'a masterpiece of observation, analysis, selection, and rhythm,' but the extract I have made is enough to establish the point made concerning Ruskin's style.

Again, Ruskin's books are worthy of a book-collector's attention for their quality as examples of book-making. His major art works, comprising the nine volumes of *Modern Painters*, *The Seven Lamps of Architecture*, and *The Stones of Venice*, were printed in royal octavo; type, paper, and bindings show that the publishers were instructed to do their best, but it is principally in illustration that they excel, and it would be hard to find other books of the day of like excellence both in the drawings, chiefly by the author, and the engravings after them. When the time came for Ruskin to publish his own books, he gave minute attention to all of these features. *Præterita, Deucalion, Proserpina*, and the other books issued in parts are models of book-making.

As for the rarity of Ruskin's works, it is true that most of his writings have never been considered as particularly scarce, yet since the disposal of the accumulations of Ruskin first editions so common on English booksellers' shelves thirty years ago, I do not find them replaced there to any extent with other copies. A buyer will not find them as obtainable today as I did in the past, and the real rarities are at least no more common now than they were thirty years ago. Ruskin's juvenile poems collected by his father and privately printed in 1850, *The King of the Golden River*, illustrated by Doyle, published in 1851, the private editions of *War* (1870), and some minor pamphlets are all still difficult to find, while if the searcher for rarities should discover a copy of Wedderburn's collection of Ruskiniana (1891–92), he will be luckier than I have been, for I have never seen one of the ten copies printed. Tillinghast seldom came into the shop without reminding me that I hadn't found a copy of *Ruskiniana* for him.

Another Ruskin collector besides Tillinghast, a later customer and one whose idealism in public life I fancy has been influenced by Ruskin, is my friend John G. Winant. I sold to him my extra-illustrated copy of *Præterita* which contains, besides the assemblage of rare prints and autograph letters collected for that book, Ruskin's self-portrait in water-colors of which a reproduction may be seen in Collingwood's *Life of John Ruskin*. R. B. Adam of Buffalo was, I am told, a Ruskin enthusiast. He was not my customer, but he made a fine Ruskin collection, now in Yale University Library.

With the encouragement which came from association with those like-minded, the Ruskin collection on my home shelves increased to a respectable size. As its scope was enlarged to include all the authorized editions of Ruskin and his biographies, it grew from moderate proportions to include more than five hundred volumes, which crowded the rest of my books unduly. Partly on that account, but principally in consideration of Ruskin's interest in the education of girls and from the fact that both of my daughters were graduated from Wellesley College a few years ago, I thought it proper to send the collection to that institution. From that time I have made occasional additions to the Wellesley collection, now and then picking up a Ruskin item of interest for myself. Opportunities of self-indulgence in this direction have come at various times in the past. Through the disposal in Boston of the effects of Miss Francesca Alexander after her death in Florence in 1917, I came into possession of the copy of *Ethics of the Dust* which contains Ruskin's inscription to Miss La Touche — to me a precious memento of Ruskin's tragic love affair. This book was given by Ruskin to Miss Alexander after Miss La Touche's death. Another presentation copy of the same book, given to Professor Norton, was bought in London when Norton's son's books were sold. The personal inscriptions in the different copies of this book are identical in form — '... with the old lecturer's love, 1866.'

Frankly, these details concerning the works of an author strangely neglected today, while told especially for their relation to myself, are given partly in the hope that they will arouse a new interest in Ruskin, at least with collectors. As literature,

Ruskin's work will care for itself. G. Bernard Shaw, in a small volume published a few years ago, has given striking testimony to Ruskin's influence on modern social questions while other modern writers have paid tribute to the charm of his personality, the striking beauty of his style, and the fructifying influence of his thought. Does it not, therefore, seem reasonable that at a time when third-rate authors are competed for at extravagant figures, collectors should renew their interest in Ruskin? He was a Victorian, but his critics have never accused him of having a part in the shams and pretensions which have obscured the valuable features of Victorian times. Whatever Ruskin was, or said, he was neither a Pharisee nor insincere.

The last event, or series of events, overshadowing all of my experiences in Ruskin-collecting, happened between the years 1930 and 1932. When Ruskin died in 1900, his cousin Mrs. Arthur Severn and her husband, who had lived with him at Brantwood, his home in the lakeland village of Coniston for many years, owned the Brantwood estate. Ruskin had originally bequeathed the place to the Severns and in his will (made inoperative as it regards Brantwood by a deed of gift before his death), he expressed himself concerning the future of the place in these words:

> I leave all my estate of Brantwood aforesaid and all other real estate of which I may die possessed to Joseph Arthur Palliser Severn, and Joanna Ruskin Severn his wife, and to the survivor of them and their heirs for their very own, earnestly praying them never to sell the estate of Brantwood or any part thereof, nor to let upon building lease any part thereof, but to maintain the said estate and the buildings thereon in decent order and in good repair in like manner as I have done, and praying them further to accord during thirty consecutive days in every year such permission to strangers to see the house and pictures as I have done in my lifetime.

While it may be that Ruskin's wishes regarding the estate altered before he died, I know of no evidence of such change, and it was with much surprise that I received in the early part of July, 1930, a catalogue from Sotheby and Company, offering

RUSKIN AND MRS. SEVERN AT BRANTWOOD
From a photographic negative owned by Messrs. B. F. Stevens and Brown

for sale 'The manuscripts and remaining library of John Ruskin removed from his residence, Brantwood, Coniston, and sold with the consent of Arthur Severn, Esq., and of his trustees,' indicating an entire disregard for the implicit injunctions of Ruskin's will as originally made.

This sale was of one hundred and twenty-two lots. Sixty of them were of books, drawings, or letters of Kate Greenaway; the letters were written by her to Ruskin, and the books and drawings were given by her to him. About fifty of the other lots were of books from Ruskin's library, and the eleven numbers which concluded the sale were of Ruskin's own manuscripts. From these eleven lots I bought manuscripts of *The King of the Golden River*, a portion of *Fors Clavigera*, and *Præterita*. *Præterita* I kept myself; the others I sold.

A second sale of Ruskin books and autographs ('the final portion') was held at Sotheby's on the eighteenth of May in the following year. On this occasion I bought various manuscripts including two examples of early writings in prose and verse that are of special interest. One, a birthday address to his father, was written when Ruskin was eight years old; the other, a manuscript entitled 'Essay on the relative dignity of the studies of painting and music and on the advantages to be derived from their pursuit,' he wrote to interest a girl friend visiting the Ruskin family at Herne Hill when he was nineteen years old. Ruskin writes of this particular episode in *Præterita*:

> We got to like each other in a mildly confidential way in the course of a week. We disputed on the relative dignities of music and painting; and I wrote an essay nine foolscap pages long, proposing the entire establishment of my own opinions, and the total discomfiture and overthrow of hers, according to my usual manner of paying court to my mistresses. Charlotte Withers, however, thought I did her great honour, and carried away the essay as if it had been a school prize.

Also in the same lot was an extraordinary composition lettered on the back of its modern binding 'Early Geology.' Considering that the author was twelve years old when he wrote it, the sustained effort required for a manuscript of over one hundred thousand words on one subject is evidence of an unusual industry and power of concentration. It contains a curious shorthand alphabet referred to by its author in late life — '. . . and [I] invented a shorthand symbolism for crystalline forms before I was fourteen.'

Closely following the final sale of Ruskin's books and manuscripts, in fact only two days later, came the third catalogue in the dispersal of the dismantled house at Brantwood. This time the pictures were sold. There were sketches by Gainsborough and Romney, a number of Turners, a Botticelli, a Tintoretto, two Reynolds, and Ruskin's father by Raeburn; of works by modern artists, the water-colors of Burne-Jones were the most noteworthy.

My interest was not in these, however, but in Ruskin's own drawings. There were several hundred of them. Acting under cabled instructions to buy up to seven hundred pounds in amount, my agents, B. F. Stevens and Brown, secured what they described as the cream of the sale. George Richmond's two portraits of Ruskin, the full-length water-color of 1842, and the 1847 drawing in colored chalk, fell to me at moderate figures, with a large number of all sorts of drawings by Ruskin — water-colors, pencil sketches, topographical scenes in pen and ink (made at the age of fourteen when travelling with his parents on their first Continental tour), drawings made for his books (including architectural sketches for *The Stones of Venice*) — and, of superlative interest, the pencil sketch of Miss Rose La Touche (of whom I also secured another portrait, a colored photograph on porcelain, at a sale of the contents of Arthur Severn's town house in the same month of July, 1931).

I had in mind to give here the story of Ruskin and Rose La Touche, prefaced by an account of Ruskin's marriage with Euphemia Gray, but not having found myself able to condense it into a proper narrative of reasonable limits, and also discovering that the subject would not relate itself to the rest of this book, I shall reserve an account of these episodes for another place.

Anything more comic, in the externals
of it — anything more tragic in the
essence of it — could not have been
invented by the skilfullest inventor
in acter line.

In my social behaviour and mind
I was a curious combination, crystallized like granite — out of the
three elements of Mr Traddles,
Mr Toots, and Mr Winkle.
I had the fidelity and single-mind
edness of Traddles, the readiness
grace — and conversational abilities
of Mr Toots — the ambition of
Mr Winkle — and all these
illumined by the _imagination_ feelings of
Mr Copperfield at his first
Norwood dinner — But the shyness
and unpresentableness of all this
~~was partly~~ _as it was_
was stiffened and, ~~rend~~ by
a patriotic and protestant conceit

MANUSCRIPT PAGE FROM RUSKIN'S *Praeterita*

Interesting as the drawings by Ruskin are, the three manuscripts secured at the sale in 1930 call for more special mention. *The King of the Golden River* is not only the manuscript of a children's story which had a wide sale in its published form, but is also of biographical interest, as Ruskin wrote it for the distantly related cousin whom he married seven years after its composition. The manuscript of *Fors Clavigera* (although only a fragment of the work, the greater part being now probably non-existent) is important as it contains the beginning of *Præterita*, there first published, and the first draft of the *Creed of St. George*. This, as well as *The King of the Golden River* manuscript, is now in the library of Yale University.

It is for the manuscript of *Præterita*, however, that I have most regard. I had bought it when published in periodical form, looking forward to each succeeding number with a keener interest than the modern reader would have for the weekly installment of a story by Agatha Christie in the *Saturday Evening Post*. I hope that some of my older readers may have a similar memory of the book,[1] which, of all Ruskin's writings, has been most widely approved for the serenity of its temper and the perfection of its style. I cannot imagine a temptation sufficient to make me part with Ruskin's portrait of Rose La Touche and his manuscript of *Præterita*.

The last Ruskin sale[2] took place at Brantwood also in July, 1931. All movable contents of the house were included in the seven hundred and ninety-one lots described in the sale catalogue. One item excited me greatly, for it revived my early interest in mineralogical specimens, never entirely lost. The catalogue description read:

> Exceptionally well-made mahogany section bookcase by Snell, of London, 9 feet 6 inch by 8 feet 6 inch by 2 feet deep, 6 glazed doors enclosing innumerable specimen drawers containing a large quantity of varied minerals, also catalogues with full descriptions of such minerals.

[1] Ellery Sedgwick, editor of the *Atlantic Monthly*, tells me that he was one of these.
[2] In 1932 the freehold of Brantwood was offered at auction. It has now passed from private hands and is preserved as a Ruskin memorial.

This lot was of great promise, for, although Ruskin had given selections from his mineralogical collection to various schools at different times, there might well be a residue of value. As, however, I had already invested several thousand dollars in Ruskin books and manuscripts, and as this lot was a speculation and there being no time for inquiry and report, I reluctantly decided to let it pass; yet as I thought it over again on the Sunday before the Tuesday of the sale my imagination tempted me. Supposing (I thought) there are a lot of the fine gem minerals there, silicates in all their beautiful crystal forms, lovely violet fluorites, rare agate formations, chalcedonies, richly colored amethysts, tourmalines, unusual crystallized specimens of copper, silver, or even of gold; it would be a pity if I should miss the chance of their going for a small amount, which indeed I thought possible at a place so far from London.

I knew that Ruskin's cabinet contained at one time specimens of exceeding beauty and was of large value to the mineralogist. What should I do? Nothing, it would seem, was possible, for, as I pondered the matter on my way to town Monday morning, I realized that by the time I reached my shop it would be noon in London and too late for the cable to be serviceable, the Brant-wood sale being advertised for 11.30 the next day. Yet there was a chance of getting information and I took it. Immediately on arrival at my office, I called my London agents on the telephone. Yes, they had been at Brantwood to look things over. The minerals? Ah! they had been sold privately in advance of the auction — to a Hungarian, they thought — 'and won't there be a merry row when the bidders at the sale are told of it!'

As I look at the catalogue of this three-day concluding sale of Ruskin's effects, it is a melancholy document. It starts with contents of the butler's pantry, principally of wine-glasses for port, sherry, champagne, etc.; continues through the dining-room ('six mahogany chairs in green cloth with carved backs,' mahogany sideboard, liquorstand, Copeland ware dessert service, fire screens, coal scuttle, vases, tables, etc.) to the study (where the mineral shelves were) with its miscellaneous furnishings, antique inlaid French brass inkstand, solid ivory goldbeater's hammer, bedside watchstand, a 'capital oak knee-hole writing-table with inlaid leather top and — [these must have belonged to Arthur Severn] — 3 fishing tackle boxes.' Following the study came the contents of the drawing-room, of the boudoir and entrance hall, the silver and plated goods, contents of the billiard-room, bedrooms, two staff rooms (soiled linen baskets besides bedding), caretakers' bedrooms, nursery, schoolroom, kitchen and scullery, books, workshop contents, carriage house, potting shed, and (tell it not in Gath!)

Ferns, aspidistras, begonias, Indian azaleas, hydranges [*sic*], Nile lilies, African lilies, primulas, orchids, chrysanthemums, carnations, dahlias, geraniums, and others —

in fine, the contents of the garden, offered to bedraggled bidders in a dreary rain; and so,

End of Sale.

I am, sir, a Brother of the Angle.   WALTON.

XIII. A BOOKSELLER'S RECREATIONS

SOMEONE has said, 'When we have to explain our pleasures they are pleasures no longer.' A somewhat similar thought is expressed by H. M. Tomlinson in these words: 'What is it we find in Beethoven or Christobal? Nothing that can be quoted on the Stock Exchange; nothing which can be stated explicitly without arousing mirth in our enemies and indignation in our friends; for it would involve the whole mystery of the arts and the philosophic reduction of beauty to its elements.' Just so; yet may we not occasionally exhibit our pleasures for their glorification while reserving their inward and private attractions for our own spiritual refreshment?

I did not get a chance to do any real fishing until I was nearly fifty. Before then I had to stick closely to business, but even as a boy there were tokens of what my future recreations might be. The love of gardening appeared before I left the grammar school. I remember my enjoyment of an abandoned group of narcissi which had become naturalized in a far corner of the grass, and I also recall some disheartening attempts to conquer a particularly tough quitch-grass sod when trying to make a garden. Earlier still the boyish instinct for fishing cropped out as, equipped with a birch pole, cotton string, and bent-pin hook, baited by pellets of dough from the kitchen, I angled for shiners from the banks of a near-by pond. Golf was reserved for later years, for, although I was a member of the Wollaston Golf Club more than forty years ago, I resigned membership on removal to New York and did not join any club when I came back to Boston three years later, finding that golf and business were bad companions to one whose way in life had not been established.

These three pastimes — fishing, golf, and gardening — have been my recreations supplementing book-collecting and the pleasant vocation of rare-book buying and selling.

As between fishing and golf, fishing, I suppose, interests the greater number of men. Fishermen, however, have fewer opportunities than golfers for gratifying their passion. Deforestation of head-waters, harmful industries along rivers and streams, increase of population, and the automobile have curtailed the weekend sport of the angler, and fishing journeys to remote lakes and streams necessitate the employment of guides and board at camps where city comforts are furnished. These things cost money and the days of inexpensive fishing are gone, though sport is still to be had by those who wish to just 'go-a-fishin'.' Fishermen are of many kinds: the night-fisher for horn-pout and the dry-fly specialist are so far apart in their ideas of sport that it is difficult to reconcile their extremes; yet whatever one's own practice may be, I think that all anglers ought to be catholic enough to admit still-fishers and trollers to their fellowship, at least in name. Personally, much as I dislike the methods which some men use in fishing, I would not exclude any user of rod, line, and single hook.

Yet to me the greatest enjoyment of fishing is found in the use of the fly. Fly-casting is such a delicate exercise of skill that it is a pleasure in itself. Fishing a wet-fly one afternoon on Moosehead Lake, I made some three-hundred-odd casts between two rises. Although my wrist was a little tired and I took no fish, I returned contented to camp. The mere taking of fish is not essential to one's enjoyment of his rod; the 'feel' of it as sixty or more feet of tapered line shoots ahead and falls gently on the water is a joy to be experienced, not described.

Mountain-stream fishing is of another sort. The thought of fishing in the woods tempts one to rhapsodize. The sheer beauty of it all — the tiny brook tumbling to music of its own making over mossy stones, flowing clear and cold through the parent forest, around granite boulders, or resting in miniature

THE AUTHOR IN 1921
From a pencil drawing by E. Pollak-Ottendorf

pools where, under the foam, trout may hide; the solitary flower, bird, or animal habitant that surprises the angler on his way, and the flaming cardinal-flowers which greet him from the gravelly shallows in the open — these are sights which it is hard to write about soberly. It is true that the fish taken in such streams will be small, mostly to be returned unharmed to the brook, but an occasional half-pounder will settle the inquiries of friends concerning one's afternoon employment. What, besides the trout, you profited by the outing, is your own affair.

'But is fishing not the pleasure of the lazy man?' someone asks. I should be sorry to think so, for the idea of loafing and inviting one's soul to loaf also is distasteful.[1] Any soul of New England stock would scorn the invitation. Fishing is an exercise which awakens dormant faculties; it inspires reflection. Read *The Tarn and the Lake* [2] and find what significant thoughts have been suggested to one angler by his recreation: meditations on the vicissitudes of the dictator pike, intelligentsia trout, and proletarian perch in their mutual relations and the parallel with the changing conditions of human society during the Renaissance which they offer.

In my early fishing experiences, at the suggestion of friends I spent many precious days in early May on the larger Maine lakes trolling for trout and landlocked salmon. The weather was cold and wet, the mushy ice barely gone down the outlets, and the amount of clothing required for morning and evening comfort almost unbelievable, but being younger than I am now and a novice, I found pleasure in that kind of fishing and did not mind the drawbacks. The guides, although skilled sportsmen and friendly comrades, were expensive companions, for as the fishing season was short their wages were accordingly

---

[1] Theologians of different schools agree on certain points, as on this, for Isaac Watts wrote:

> 'For Satan finds some mischief still
> For idle hands to do —'

and Swedenborg, in sterner mood, declared that not even in hell is idleness tolerated.

[2] *The Tarn and the Lake. Thoughts on Life in the Italian Renaissance.* By C. J. Holmes. London: Philip Lee Warner, 1913.

high and I also thought they spent too much time getting the dinner. I often wished that a pocket of sandwiches or a bit of broiled fish with a pot of coffee, which would have satisfied me, would have been acceptable to them also. Their culinary skill, however, was a matter of pride. My wife, who went with me on one of these fishing trips and who has a woman's memory for such details, declares that Jack Sullivan's pot demanded a full pound of coffee. For the noon meal the johnny-cake, bacon, eggs, and butter, the sirloin steak or chicken, the pie and cake (with such fish as the morning's efforts afforded) were supplied in too generous quantities for fishermen; and the hour spent in preparing this food seemed lamentably wasteful. To my mind the virtues of a lunch alfresco are moderation and simplicity, although, judged from the collations usually served at picnics of all sorts, this opinion is not generally shared by others.

I have never had good opportunity to use the dry-fly. It is a mode which has able advocates, and being, without doubt, the most sportsmanlike method of fishing, it seems likely to be generally adopted by the best anglers. It also requires considerable practice to fish properly with the dry-fly, which should be in its favor. The unsuitability of this method to conditions surrounding many of our American streams is obvious, yet if my own fishing days were not so nearly over, I should use the dry-fly wherever I found it workable.

Angling has been celebrated many times in verse. The poet Thomson appears to have enjoyed the sport — at least he writes well on it. His famous descriptive lines in *The Seasons*, found in the chapter on *Spring*, do not appear in the first edition of the book, a fact singularly unnoticed by angling bibliographers. The passage I refer to, beginning —

> Now when the first foul Torrent of the Brooks,
> Swell'd by the vernal Rains, is ebb'd away;
> And, whitening, down their mossy-tinctur'd Stream
> Ascends the billowy Foam: now is the Time,
> While yet the dark-brown Water aids the Guile,
> To tempt the Trout. The well-dissembled Fly,
> The Rod fine-tapering with elastic Spring,
> Snatch'd from the hoary Steed the floating Line,
> And all thy slender watry Stores prepare —

was not included by Thomson until the publication of the fourth edition in 1744. Daniel Fearing bought the first edition, 1730, for his angling collection, ignorant of the fact that there was not a line on fishing in it.

The fisherman who is also a book-collector can extend his joys to cover the whole year. When he is not fishing or pottering with his tackle, he can look over booksellers' catalogues or rummage their shops for editions of Walton or any other fishing books which he may fancy. The number of books on the subject is so very large that, if he is wise, he will restrict his collection to one branch of the subject, otherwise his interest may become dissipated through weariness. If he limits himself to the various editions of *The Compleat Angler*, he will set a high mark for himself; the first two are not only high-priced; [1] they are also difficult to get. Even some of the cheap modern editions of Walton will be found elusive. My angling collection falls a little short of one hundred and fifty copies of this book (which is scarcely more than half the number of known issues), but, unfortunately, it begins with the third edition, 1661. I shall never own the first two Waltons, for the sufficient reasons indicated in the figures, but I have others in which I can find a modest satisfaction. There is, for instance, the pretty Chiswick Press edition of 1824, a beautiful piece of miniature book-making, with 'Jno. Farmer. Presented by Rev. R. W. Emerson' written on the fly-leaf, followed by 'John Farmer, Esq. from his friend R. W. E.' on the half-title. Another inscribed copy is one edited by James Russell Lowell and presented by him to his friend Charles Eliot Norton. Still another of my *Compleat Anglers* was autographed by that famous fisherman and story-writer, Lord Tweedsmuir, when, as John Buchan, he was a plain Scotsman.

But the most interesting association copies on my shelves are two thin volumes from Edmund Gosse's library. Austin Dobson sent Walton's *Lives* and *The Compleat Angler* to Gosse with in-

---

[1] Here are the figures which frown on the poor man's pocket:

The Compleat Angler.	First edition.	1653.	£925
Idem	Second edition.	1655.	$875

These are the latest auction records for good copies.

scriptions in the front which make these inconspicuous editions by Dent delightful possessions. To this copy of the *Angler* Dobson has added his lines about Walton, a better reading (as it seems to me) than the earlier printed version where the first line reads — 'I care not much how folk prefer.' The reader, however, may decide this point for himself. The autograph verses, quoted through courtesy of Mr. A. T. A. Dobson and the Oxford University Press, read —

> I care no whit how men prefer
> To dress your chub or chavender;
> I care no whit for line or hook
> But still I love old IZAAK's book,
> Wherein a man may read at ease
> Of gandergrass and culverkeys,
> Or with half-pitying wonder note
> What TOPSELL, what DU BARTAS wrote,
> Or list the song, by *Maudlin* sung,
> That MARLOWE made when he was young:
> These things, in truth, they like me more
> Than all old IZAAK's angling lore.

In the other book Dobson wrote an inscription to Gosse even more felicitous than his praise of Walton. It is given in his own hand on the opposite page.

Gosse's *Donne* was published three years afterwards, fulfilling the prophecy of the first stanza.

To show what an expensive pastime any collecting may become when its limits are not rigorously held, I mention a copy of Donne's *Poems* in my fishing collection. Although *The Baite* is a poem quoted in *The Compleat Angler*, this edition of Donne, printed in 1635, is not the one in which it was published first, and I did not buy the book, therefore, because *The Baite* was in it. The justification for including a book of fifty pounds' value in my collection is found in Donne's portrait, finely engraved by Marshall, with lines by Walton in eulogy of his friend which appear here for the first time. Also, in further apology for the extravagance, the impression of the portrait is brilliant and the book itself is a crisp copy, unwashed.

One of the loveliest of all the beautiful books that Charles

To I. G.

You write your life of Donne. I will be
A masterpiece of sympathy.
Exact, I know, in fact and date,
And skilled to read, to stimulate,
To show, as you would have him seen,
That morbid, mystic, mighty-Dean.

But will you catch old Izaak's phrase
That glows with so easy of praise?
Old Izaak's ambling unpretence
That flames with untaught eloquence.
Will you? I pause for a reply,
And you must answer, friend, not I.

Austin Dobson

Ealing
Oct. iv, 96.

Whittingham printed for William Pickering is *The River Dove*, the Dove being the classic river of (for the once) *Cotton and Walton*. It was written in dialogue in imitation of the style of *The Compleat Angler* by J. L. Anderdon and was published in 1847. Westwood and Satchell list it as the first book in their *Bibliotheca Piscatoria* and whet the reader's appetite for rarities by saying that an edition under a slightly different title, limited to six copies in quarto and twenty-five in duodecimo, was printed in 1845.

Not long ago, I ordered from the catalogue of a London bookseller this 1845 edition of *The River Dove*. It was one of the smaller size, priced at three pounds. The cataloguer in his

280YANKEE BOOKSELLER

description took occasion to correct what he called an error of
the bibliographers in placing the date of the book (it being
published without imprint or date), citing as his authority
a note dated 1835 in the copy he offered. When the book came
to hand, a bibliographical problem arose, for it contained a
note in manuscript that only six copies were printed in 1835 and
that this one for some unexplained reason was thought to be
'the only perfect copy now remaining.'

Taking my duodecimo volume I went to the Treasure Room
of the Harvard College Library to compare it with the copy
in the Fearing collection. To my surprise I saw that the two
were not the same. Fearing's was of the edition correctly described by Westwood and Satchell as published in 1845, but the
text showed it to be a different book from mine. The mystery
was solved. I had bought an earlier, and apparently unknown,
edition, one which may indeed be unique.

Shortly after this I got the 1845 edition from another dealer,
thus completing my set of the issues of this book.

The contents of this *River Dove* book of Anderdon's have received little comment from writers on angling literature, but
it is worthy of note that they were written as a pious tribute to
one whom all fishermen delight to call their master — Izaak
Walton.

As I come to the subject of gardening, I ought to explain that
I am not a real horticulturalist. I cultivate a garden because
I love flowers and like to work about them. When I dig and
hoe I am doing something that gives me pleasure just as I enjoy
watching plants and trees grow. Nearly every day this summer
I have stopped to look at the broad unfolding leaves of a white
birch seedling, transplanted from the gravelled edge of the
driveway when it was only two inches high, in the autumn of
last year. Now it measures over a foot, a year from now it will
top a yardstick, and in ten years its chocolate-brown bark will
turn to a pearly white. Sometime, years hence, my sapling will
be a sturdy tree like its parent, which was taken from the woods
thirty-two years ago and now measures twenty-two inches
through the butt.

Akin to pleasures like these is the encouragement and care of shrubs and flowers found in woodland and pasture. Before speaking on this subject I shall have to describe the place I live in.

It is now thirty-five years since I first spent a summer in this hill-town of central Massachusetts. Finding the elevated white-pine region favorable to the health of my family, my wife and I decided to make it our permanent summer home. Shirley Center, an hour's motor ride west of Boston, is a village of some forty houses grouped around or radiating from the middle of an undulating plateau about three miles in extent. Viewed from one side, the tower of Groton School chapel six miles away rises against the eastern hills, and farther to the south long lines of barracks at Camp Devens are visible. This little community is located two miles from railroad or main highway, and its old buildings — church, town-hall, and simple country houses — are, with few exceptions, standing yet. Our cottage, at the westerly part of the village, overlooks a forest mostly of pine with some hardwoods, which conceals the towns intervening between it and Mount Wachusett twenty miles away.

It would be a pleasant task to take my readers for a ramble about Shirley Center or to delve into its history as recorded by the annalists. Town histories always contain interesting material. One might comment on the general similarity of their contents, their sociological importance, and their value as material for the historian, or on the fact that New England is more extensively town-historied than any other area of its size on the globe, but these themes, tempting as they are, lead far afield from the subject of gardening which is before us for the moment. The kind of gardening that I now have in mind, however, does not concern the cultivation of flowers in enclosures. What I am thinking of is generally called wild-flower gardening, although it is really little more than the guidance and care of Nature.

During the many continuous seasons we have spent in summer residence at Shirley, striking changes have taken place in the aspect of the land. Being gradual, they have passed almost unnoticed from year to year, yet as I look in memory at the original three-acre lot on which we built, and the adjacent fields acquired afterwards, they are strangely barren, for, before we came to occupy this pasture-land, the cows kept it clean of all growth save the ground junipers which were too tough for their digestion. When the cows went, the transformation began.

What took place reminds me of a passage in a book which I heartily recommend to my readers — *The Adventure of Old Age* by Francis Bardwell.[1] An old woman is speaking to him. He has been trying to get her to leave her lonely, decaying house, with its sagging roof and broken attic-windows, scarcely habitable, for the security which the town provides for the aged and helpless. Listen to her sturdy soul, old in years, but young in spirit:

I was born here and lived here most a hundred years.... My winter's wood is in the shed. I've canned a lot, I have my hens, my dog, my cat. Will they take my family at the Poor Farm? ...

You don't understand; no one understands. Can't you see I am fighting a fight, a battle against the fingers of the wilderness; — they are always extended, always sowing seeds, always clutching, and I am all there is left to fight the fight....

I have seen forty acres of good farm-land fade into forest. It doesn't go overnight, you know. But the minute you stop fighting, it creeps upon you. First the hill pastures — you see a little sheep laurel, a little sweet fern, a little ground juniper, a savin or two — next year a few birches in the fence corners; they are the forest's spies. Then the pines, pasture pines at first, then white pines — and so your pasture becomes a woodlot. Then in natural order your mowing becomes pasture, your ploughed land mowing, and always the wilderness is advancing. I know! Winter nights, when the wind blows, it plays on the great trees as one plays an organ. But it is always triumphant music, the music of victory, the wilderness claiming its kingdom. I have heard it, I know. No, I'll stay! You noticed no sprouts or saplings, no juniper or fern in the home-close about the house. No! That is *my* kingdom, my battlefield. I'm ninety-six, but I'll not desert!

Rugged individualism!

[1] Houghton Mifflin Company, 1926.

This is what has happened to hillsides all over New England. It is what is happening on my place. Beyond my flower-garden and the row of grapevines which borders it to the west, two acres of land drop steeply to a hemlock-gully, with traces of an old town road, leading no one now knows where, carved along its lower slope. This land was not a part of my first purchase, and when I bought it ten years ago it was a smooth hillside pasture. Now it is a riot of wildness. Where, ten years ago, cows grazed and there were no shrubs other than juniper, steeple-bush, or patches of sweet-fern, now a great variety of sprouting trees — white maple, ash, birch — white and gray — poplar, elm, hemlock, white and pitch pine, oak, hickory, and red cedar — have appeared. All these, sown by birds or by seeds borne on the wind, have come ready to battle for the land. It is the old woman's story repeated.

In this case, Nature must lose; the sunset view must be preserved, the lot must be cleared, but what is to replace the growing trees, I do not know. Possibly the heather, purple and white, now growing in the north pasture will furnish seedlings for the slope, or the decision may rest with some future tenant. What force within us is it which urges us to carry on with tasks undertaken too late in life?

Across the narrow gully which carries a streamlet of surface water in the spring, relic perhaps of a torrent which cut its way in ancient times, there are sister groves separated by an old cart-path. One of these on dry ground is almost entirely of pine. In the other grove there are springs, and the pines are mixed with deciduous trees, elm and maple principally, and a promising growth of young hemlock. These woods, particularly in the damp places, are now sanctuaries for those flowers and ferns which find soil and shade there of their liking. Intruding blackberry vines and other shrubs have been destroyed at the cost of much labor, but for the most part the native flowers take care of themselves and they do it surprisingly well, rewarding the slight care given them by generous growth. Where not long ago one might look in vain for the trailing arbutus, there are now many flourishing colonies. Sizable patches of other

low-growing flowers — anemone, partridge-berry, Canada mayflower, wintergreen, and fringed polygala — cover large spaces,
the last crowding close about the maple trunks. In one retired
spot there is a wide space concealed from predatory trespassers
which is covered with club mosses of two varieties. The ferns,
too, ten or more kinds, give a good account of themselves in the
mossy springy places. Maidenhair, royal, sensitive, Christmas,
rattlesnake, interrupted and cinnamon ferns, with others whose
names do not come to me just now, make a perfect covert for
the partridges which rear their annual brood in this safe hiding.
It is marvellous to see how quickly the partridge chicks dis-
appear before one's eyes as, once surprised outside of their
bounds, they fade into the protective colors of leaf and stone
while the parent bird struts enticingly away.

Of other native flowers found here in the grove those most
conspicuous are the columbines, the blood-root, the common
lady's-slippers, bellwort, false and true solomon's-seal, clintonia,
cardinal-flowers, clematis, and bluets. Bottle-gentian, snake-
root, pink turtle-head, showy lady's-slipper, and various kinds
of trilliums are introductions from other localities. I must not
omit mention of the Jack-in-the-Pulpit, *Arum triphyllum* akin
to the *Arum maculatum* of Robert Bridges's *The Idle Flowers* —

> And in the shady lanes
> Bold Arum's hood of green
> Herb Robert, Violet,
> Starwort and Celandine —

The old botanists represent both the *Arum* and the greater
celandine to be poison when eaten. Nevertheless, in the *Herball*
of Gerard we learn that 'Beares after they have lien in their
dens forty daies without any manner of sustenance, but what
they get with licking and sucking their owne feet, doe as
soone as they come forth eat the herb Cuckow-pint, through
the windie nature thereof the hungry gut is opened and made
fit again to receive sustenance: for by abstaining from food so
long a time, the gut is shrunke or drawne so close together, that
in a manner it is quite shut up, as *Aristotle, Ælianus, Plutarch,
Pliny,* and others do write.'

THE WILD-GARDEN IN APRIL

As it happens, all the bears that were ever in Shirley migrated over the border to the forests of New Hampshire or farther north many years ago. The deer, which still make some claim of tenantry to our woods at certain seasons, not hibernating, have no similar use for this herb, although they occasionally nip the tops of other plants. The reference made by Gerard either concerns the habits of bears on the Continent or is a bit of ancient folklore, for the bear appears to have been extinct in Great Britain after the eleventh century.

In collecting the literature of gardens, Bacon's *Essays*, 1597, comes first for its famous treatise on gardens, although Hill's *The Profitable Art of Gardening* was published four years earlier. Hill, like most of the old garden writers, was strong on mazes, a form of landscaping now out of favor. Lyte's translation of Dodoen's *A Niewe herball or historie of plantes*, 1578, and the first editions of Gerard and Parkinson are excellent complementary works to Hill and Bacon. Gerard's was published first, in the same year as Bacon's *Essays;* Parkinson's not until the year 1629. If the collector of herbals chooses to go abroad for other authors, he will find Mattioli's *Commentarii in libros sex Pedacii Dioscorides* (1554), Clusius's *Rariorum plantarum historia*, 1601, and Bauhin's *Pinax theatri botanici*, 1623, books he should own if he can get them. Both English and Continental literature of the sixteenth and seventeenth centuries abound in herbals which, though compiled for their medicinal value, are today among the most fascinating of nature books.

The observations of one John Josselyn of Maine, made about the middle of the seventeenth century and recorded in a small volume entitled *New-Englands Rarities Discovered...*, are to be desired by every collector of American botanical works. The first edition of Josselyn, published in 1672, brings a good price, but there are modern editions not expensive nor difficult to obtain. Assuming (which is likely) that his bookseller cannot find for him Doctor Jacobus Cornuti's *Canadensium Plantarum*, which was printed in Paris thirty-seven years before Josselyn's book, the collector will do well to get a copy of the latter for the foundation stone of his American botanical collection. If he can afford the first edition of Josselyn he will, of course, buy it, but even so he ought to have the Veazie edition of 1865 for the valuable notes by Professor Edward Tuckerman which are in it. Josselyn's book is important for the account it gives of both the fauna and the flora of New England.

I find a few of the later American botanists in early editions among my own books. I have a mint copy of Gray's *Manual* of 1848, and two early books of medical botany, both published in 1817 and especially interesting for their colored plates. One of them is Barton's *Vegetable Materia Medica*, and the other, Doctor Jacob Bigelow's *American Medical Botany*. The latter shows what I think is the earliest attempt at color printing from copper plates in this country. Books of this kind, although they have no large interest by themselves, might form the nucleus of a collection, and if their value seems too small to make them worthy of mention, it must be remembered that the larger number of collectors are not rich, and the wise bookseller is no less attentive to their needs than to the buyers of rarer items.

As I write the reddening swamp maples show that autumn is here. The flowers are gone, the falling leaves will soon make a protective covering in the woods, and the fisherman will be putting his tackle away, but golfing is at its prime, for a sunny October day on the golf-links in New England is a foretaste of heaven.

Golf was once looked upon as an exclusive, almost a snobbish, sport. That time has gone. Golf courses have multiplied, club dues are lower than ever, tax-supported links are available, and the transient player is no longer looked on as a vagrant — in fact most clubs now welcome him. Yet, with all this increase of public interest in the game, collectors of books on golf are rare, probably for the reason that there are few books on the subject worth a collector's attention. A few early English books make short references to golf, but 'An heroi-comical poem' ... *The Goff* 'in three cantos,' by one Thomas Mathison, published first in Edinburgh in 1743, is, as far as I know, the earliest book of especial interest to golfers. Mathison appears to have been the first of a line of humorists who have found golf a profitable theme, and various bits of pleasantry, in fiction or *pseudo-classical* dialogue (Andrew Lang wrote such), may be dug out of the mass of modern golf literature. Time has revenged the ladies by giving a humorous slant to the words of a writer on golf in the ninth edition of the *Encyclopædia Britannica* (1879) which soberly inform us that 'there is some evidence that ... the unhappy Mary Stuart was, *in some sort of a feminine way* [my italics], a golfer.'

Research in the history of golf in the United States has yielded results which may be interesting to golfing readers. While investigating titles to the lands of the Unicorn Golf Club in Middlesex County, Massachusetts, Richard W. Hale of this city dug from official sources the following information. After premising that there is some evidence that Governor William Burnet of Massachusetts, who died in 1729, was the first American golfer, Mr. Hale quotes from the inventory of Burnet's estate:

Nine Gouff clubs & One Iron Ditto @ 4/p....£2....
Seven Dossen balls @ 1/p..................4.4....

Mr. Hale also remarks concerning American golf:

It is unlikely that there was anything resembling a modern golf course hereabouts in those early days. But it should be remembered that golf in the eighteenth century was seldom played upon courses set off and reserved for the game. Indeed, there still survives in many of the Scottish rules a provision that when a player finds his ball resting upon washing spread over the ground, he may pick it up without penalty.

Some have believed golf to be a sport of more ancient record than the early eighteenth century in this country. When it was introduced in 1892 by members of The Country Club of Brookline, golf was thought to be a new sport in New England. The evidence just adduced from the will of Governor Burnet shows that this was a mistake.

As for the antiquity of the sport in the United States, the *Laws and Ordinances of New Netherlands* [1] has been elsewhere quoted [2] to show that the game was played in Albany at the time the following vote was passed:

> The W. Commissary and Commissaries of *Fort Orange* and Village of *Beverwyck*, having heard divers complaints from the Burghers of this place, against playing at Golf along the Streets; which causes great damage to the windows of the Houses, and exposes people to the danger of being wounded, and is contrary to the freedom of the Public Streets: Therefore their Worships, wishing to prevent the same, forbid all persons playing Golf in the streets, on pain of forfeiting fl. 25 for each person who shall be found doing so.

On its face, this passage would seem to indicate that golf had been introduced in this country at a very early date, for the Ordinance was made in 1659, yet it seems quite certain that the translation of the word 'kolpen' in the Dutch original to the English 'golf' is misleading, for however correct the etymology may be, the game there referred to had no resemblance to golf as played today.

In the South, from the fact that a golf club is known to have existed in Savannah before 1800, it may be reasonably inferred that Scottish settlers brought the game to Georgia when they came over to that province about 1736. I believe that the first American description of golf is found in the edition of Hoyle's *Games* printed in Boston in 1814, where two pages are given to 'The Game of Goff, or Golf.' Six kinds of clubs are described as in use — 'the common club, used when the ball lies on the ground, the scraper and half scraper when in long grass; the spoon when in a hollow; the heavy iron club when it lies deep among stones or mud; and the light iron ditto, when on the surface of shingle or sandy ground.' The balls were made of horse leather stuffed with feathers and boiled. Light balls were used when playing with the wind and heavy ones against it.

For practical use there is one modern book on golf which,

---

[1] *Laws and Ordinances of New Netherlands, 1638–1674.* Compiled and translated ... By E. B. O'Callaghan. Albany, 1868.

[2] *The Country Club* [of Brookline, Mass.], privately printed, 1932, p. 63.

when read with proper attention, is to my mind of more value than any of the manuals of instruction which yearly afflict thousands of golfers to the ruin of their game. Probably books which tell the golfer the 'what' and the 'how' of the sport fail in their purpose, not because they give wrong information, but because the average player is not able to apply the instruction. There is no book on the technique of golf which will replace the lessons of a competent professional. If, however, the novice is serious, as all golfers should be and most golfers are, and if he wishes to build his game on the sure foundation of right principles — even to the sinking of a substructure to the hard bottom — let him read *The Mystery of Golf.*

Here is a book which tells of things to which most golfers give scant heed — facts which concern their mental, moral, and physical endowment, and the relation it bears to their game. Without going into an account of Mr. Haultain's essay, it may be well to remind the reader of one truth which is the heart of the book — golf calls for the sum total of a man; success does not depend on the condition of his muscles only, or the state of his eyes, his nerves, his joints or arteries, nor even the alertness of his brain or the resolution of his soul. None of these alone will make a golfer — it is only through their coördination that supremacy is attained. This is why golf is more than a game; this is why it is hard.

As a golfer, I belong to the inglorious company of those who receive the largest handicap allowed by the rules, but who, nevertheless, occasionally play such a game that they start out the next time confidently believing that they are finally on the road to success when secretly they know better; I am one of those numberless victims of self-delusion who persistently refuse to believe themselves as bad players as, in their heart, they know they really are.

> *Who, passing through the valley ... make it a place of springs.*

XIV. SPRINGS

BELIEVING that people generally are curious of what others read, I had thought to finish this book with some account of my own small library. I had in mind to speak in more detail of my fishing collection, of my books by Doctor Thomas William Parsons, and also to describe a few single volumes that I have selected at various times for some feature which particularly interested me. I find, however, that the space which remains will not admit of this undertaking and I therefore choose the topic of favorite books for leave-taking.

Before entering on this theme, however, I wish to speak briefly on a different subject, one having some bibliographical interest and possibly suggesting a new field for collecting — new, that is, for collectors today, although it has been cultivated in the past. I am thinking about hymns and hymnology.

Let us begin with *America*.

When I was a boy, my father took me one day on a drive of four miles to Newton Centre in quest of a minister to supply the pulpit of a pastorless church in Needham where we lived. Returning, as we jogged along the country road in the fresh spring air of the Sabbath morning, I looked on the slight figure of the Reverend Samuel Francis Smith seated beside me. Sixty years have passed since then, but I can still see his bright eyes, gentle smile, ruddy cheeks, and whisker-aureoled face; I recall the thin, piping voice in which he delivered a long and prosy sermon. As I grew older, I saw him occasionally in his home, and I remember that his cordial reception of visitors did not exclude the tribe of autograph-seekers. I doubt if Smith ever denied an application for a copy of *America* in his autograph. I have before me his reply to one of those numerous petitions, in which he writes:

> I take pleasure in fulfilling herewith your request. I send the copy for your friend to your address, supposing that you may wish to write with it a word of explanation, inasmuch as it might appear unseemly that it sh. go to her baldly, from a stranger. But I am glad that she sh. have it. We ought to gratify as many as we can, & as much as we can in this short life of our pilgrimage.

Doctor Smith had a mellow wit. Others may remember, as I do, that clergymen of the older school were wont to greet a stranger, especially if a youth, with the inquiry, 'Are you saved?' — a salutation slightly formal though less so than a secular 'How do you do' would be. It is said of Doctor Smith that a young man who bore the Biblical names of *Moses Paul* — his friends spoke of him as belonging to both the old and new dispensations — was presented to him one day. Taking his hand with a cordial grasp, the venerable preacher remarked, '*I hope, brother Paul, you have had a Damascus experience.*'

It is odd that we should have three national songs. *The Star-Spangled Banner* is carelessly spoken of as our national 'anthem.' Not even the Congress of the United States can, in correct usage of the word, make an anthem out of it.[1] It is, in fact, a martial ode to the flag. Smith's *America* and *America the Beautiful* by Katharine Lee Bates are hymns, each appropriate to its occasion; *America* is suited for gatherings where patriotism is combined with religious and ancestral feeling, while Miss Bates's beautiful lines, more modern in sentiment, are expressive of a national spiritual unity. *The Star-Spangled Banner* is formal, official, war-inspired.

Samuel Francis Smith wrote his *America* for no particular occasion and the manuscript remained unused in his portfolio until Lowell Mason caused it to be sung at a Sunday School

[1] By an Act of the Seventy-First Congress, approved March 3, 1931, *The Star-Spangled Banner*, comprising both words and music, was designated 'the national anthem of the United States of America.'

CELEBRATION

OF

AMERICAN INDEPENDENCE,

BY THE

BOSTON SABBATH SCHOOL UNION,

AT PARK STREET CHURCH, JULY 4, 1831.

ORDER OF EXERCISES.

1. SINGING.
[By the Juvenile Choir.]

This is the youthful choir that comes,
  All dressed so neat and gay ;
As bright as birds that soar and sing,
  And warble all the day.

This is the youthful choir that loves
  The teacher to obey ;
That meets to sing, and pray, and learn,
  On every Sabbath day.

This is the youthful choir that goes
  Through wind and storm away,
From peaceful home to Sabbath school,
  To learn salvation's way.

This is the youthful choir that sings,
  When all the town is gay ;
That praises God with gratitude
  On Independent day.

2. READING THE SCRIPTURES.

3. SINGING.
[By the Choir.]

With joy we meet,
With smiles we greet
  Our schoolmates bright and gay :
Be dry each tear
Of sorrow here—
  'Tis Independent day.

'Tis freedom's sound
That rings around,
  And brightens every ray,
On banner floats,
And trumpet-notes :
  On Independent day.

O who from home
Would fail to come
  And join the children's lay—
When praise we bring
To God our king,
  On Independent day.

For liberty,
Great God, to thee
  Our grateful thanks we pay ;
For thanks, we know,
To thee, we owe,
  On Independent day.

While thunder breaks,
And music wakes
  Its patriotic lay,
At temple-gate
Our feet shall wait,
  On Independent day.

O Saviour, shine,
With beams divine,
  And take our sins away ;
And give us grace
To seek thy face,
  On Independent day.

4. PRAYER.

5. SINGING.
[By the Choir.]

My country ! 'tis of thee,
Sweet land of liberty—
  Of thee I sing :
Land, where my fathers died ;
Land of the pilgrim's pride ;
From every mountain-side,
  Let freedom ring.

My native country ! thee—
Land of the noble free—
  Thy name I love ,
I love thy rocks and rills,
Thy woods and templed hills ;
My heart with rapture thrills,
  Like that above.

No more shall tyrants here
With haughty steps appear,
  And soldier-bands ;
No more shall tyrants tread
Above the patriot dead—
No more our blood be shed
  By alien hands.

Let music swell the breeze,
And ring from all the trees
  Sweet freedom's song :
Let mortal tongues awake—
Let all that breathes partake—
Let rocks their silence break—
  The sound prolong.

Our fathers' God ! to thee—
Author of liberty !
  To thee we sing ;
Long may our land be bright
With freedom's holy light—
Protect us by thy might,
  Great God, our King !

6. ADDRESS TO THE CHILDREN.
BY REV. DR. WISNER.

7. SINGING.
[By the Choir.]
Hosanna, Hosanna, Hosanna in the highest.

[By the Congregation.]
Tune—DUKE STREET.

What are those soul reviving strains
That echo thus from Salem's plains ?
What anthems loud, and louder still,
So sweetly sound from Zion's hill ?

[By the Choir.]
Hosanna, Hosanna, Hosanna in the highest.

[By the Congregation.]
Behold a youthful chorus sings
Hosanna to the King of kings,
The Saviour comes—and they proclaim
Salvation sent in Jesus' name.

[By the Choir.]
Blessed is he who cometh in the name of the Lord.

[By the Congregation.]
Proclaim hosannas loud and clear,
See David's Son and Lord appear,
All praise on earth to him be given,
And glory shout through highest heaven.

[By the Choir.]
Hosanna, Hosanna, Hosanna in the highest.

8. CONCLUDING PRAYER AND BENE-DICTION.

FIRST PRINTING OF *America*

celebration in the Park Street Church in Boston. The exercises
of that event were on the Fourth of July, 1831, and the words of
Smith's poem which included a fifth stanza (the third in order)
were first printed on a sheet for use at the meeting. The third
stanza, wisely omitted later, read:

> No more shall tyrants here
> With haughty steps appear
> And soldier-bands;
> No more shall tyrants tread
> Above the patriot dead —
> No more our blood be shed
> By alien hands.

I reproduce here one of the six known copies of this, the first
printing of *America*. In book form the verses came out first in
Lowell Mason's church hymn-book, *The Choir* (1832).

As for Francis Scott Key's *The Star-Spangled Banner*, the poem
was printed in various newspapers after the bombardment of
Fort McHenry in Baltimore during the War of 1812 which it
celebrates, but *The Analectic Magazine*, published in Philadelphia
in November, 1814, has the honor of containing the first appearance of it within covers.[1] There it bore the title *Defence of
Fort M'Henry* and was introduced by an account of the successful defence of the fort watched by Key on the night of September
13–14. The ode, set to music with the new title *The Star-Spangled
Banner*, was first published by Joseph Carr in Baltimore, un-
dated, but sometime in 1814. A copy of this issue was recently
sold by us to the New York Public Library.

America the Beautiful by Professor Katharine Lee Bates came
out first in *The Congregationalist* and, like Smith's *America*, was
used in celebration of the Fourth of July. Its date in *The
Congregationalist* is July 4, 1895. The Baker and Taylor Company published it first in book form in a collection of *Famous
Songs*, New York, 1895.

Miss Bates's poem was inspired by the magnificent view un-

[1] The song also appears in the *National Songster*, Hagerstown, 1814, but as
The Analectic Magazine was issued less than two months after the attack on the fort,
it seems more likely to have been printed there first.

folded from the summit of Pike's Peak, Colorado. The author wrote of the occasion, 'It was then and there, as I was looking out over the sea-like expanse of fertile country spreading away so far under those ample skies, that the opening lines of the hymn floated into my mind.' The poem as first written by Miss Bates differed very much from her revision of it which was first printed in the *Boston Evening Transcript* for November 19, 1904.

Many of our American authors have also written notable church hymns. Francis Scott Key wrote in 1826 one still in use — *Lord, with glowing heart I'd praise thee;* and Oliver Wendell Holmes (who in the early days of the Civil War contributed two additional verses to *The Star-Spangled Banner*) published in his *Professor at the Breakfast-Table*, 1860, the felicitous verses:

> Lord of all being, throned afar,
> Thy glory flames from sun and star —

no less esteemed now than when first written. Samuel Francis Smith wrote one or two notable missionary hymns, but beyond these and *America* his contributions to literature are unimportant. Of the compositions of others of our early clergy, Congregationalist Timothy Dwight's *I love thy kingdom, Lord,* Unitarian Edmund H. Sears's *It came upon the midnight clear*, and Episcopal Bishop A. C. Coxe's *Oh, where are kings and empires now*, to mention but a few of them, are living hymns today.

Three of our best American hymns were given us by 'our own Whittier,' as the poet has been affectionately called. The poem (*The Eternal Goodness*) which contains the stanza — *I know not what the future hath of marvel or surprise* — and that entitled *Our Master* (*Immortal love, forever full*) both had their first book publication in *The Tent on the Beach* (1867) and the even greater favorite, *Dear Lord and Father of mankind*, was printed as a part of another poem, *The Brewing of Soma*, to which it is little more than a supplement.

There is a slight, but interesting, variant in this last hymn between the author's version of the second line — *Forgive our foolish ways!* — and that of the hymn books, where 'feverish' is substituted for 'foolish.' The change has often been commented upon and the explanation, though not generally known, is simple. If one refers to page 93 of *The Pennsylvania Pilgrim* (1872) he will find that the six verses (the fourth omitted) which have been reprinted as a hymn can be used appropriately as a poem apart from their original setting. Considered as such, 'feverish' seems a more fitting word than 'foolish' and it scans better; but when we examine the relation of these stanzas to the whole poem, the text of the poem shows Whittier's reason for writing 'foolish.' In the first part the poet traces the painful development of worship from the barbaric rites of Soma in 'the morning twilight of the race' through 'sensual transports, wild as vain,' in the endeavor to 'lift men up to heaven.' Used in this connection, in the lines which continue almost abruptly —

> Dear Lord and Father of mankind,
> Forgive our foolish ways —

'feverish' would not be the more suitable word, yet in the hymn it is the better one.

First editions of *The Tent on the Beach* and *The Pennsylvania Pilgrim* are good books to own and may be secured for small amounts. To collect these books with others containing the first appearance of famous hymns ought to be enjoyable to any book-lover. He might find it pleasant to continue for hymnology what Carroll A. Wilson has done for that subject, in part, in his book on the first appearance of familiar quotations; that is, to investigate and describe the books in which all of the best-known hymns have first appeared. Addison's hymn, *The Spacious Firmament on high*, for example, was contributed to what may have been thought at the time an ephemeral publication, *The Spectator*, a flimsy, two-page, daily sheet. That hymn, splendid in imagination, appeared in the number for August 23, 1712. Pope's hardly less famous *Rise, crown'd with light, Imperial Salem rise!* appeared in *The Spectator* for May 14 of the same year.

I imagine that few young people know how much influence the old hymns have had on the lives of their elders. Not even the familiar Bible passages ordinarily memorized in childhood were so easily learned or as long retained, for rhythm and music are great aids to the memory. To my generation hymns were buttresses of faith voicing aspiration and fostering spiritual life.

When one considers the quality of the old hymns as, winnowed of trash, they now appear in the standard hymnals with the worthy additions of modern composers, it speaks ill of the taste of masses of people that they accept so much of the rubbish which is printed for chapel use. Pieces like *There's a church in the valley by the wildwood*, with its tum-tum-tum refrain, or incongruous compositions like *On a hill, far away stood an old rugged cross* (compare this production with Watts's *When I survey the wondrous cross* and Bowring's *In the cross of Christ I glory*) show that the popular taste in sacred song, while not so low as that in dance music, has fallen from the high standards of the past.

At the conclusion of the morning celebration of Harvard's Tercentenary many who stood there in the rain must have been moved as I was to hear the vast gathering, representative of forty countries of the world, sing that impressive paraphrase of the ninetieth psalm —

O God, our help in ages past [1] . . .

Think what one may about Watts's theology, he wrote some good hymns.

But the whole subject of hymnology is so involved with emotion, association, and sentiment, even more than with musical and literary taste, that there is danger in expressing personal opinions dogmatically.

Coming now to the topic of favorite books, I offer a list of my own in which many, seemingly indispensable, have been omitted because they are on every bookshelf. *The Odyssey*, Dante's *Divine Comedy*, Shakespeare, Milton, and some others, are the hardy perennials of our reading, or, to change the figure, they are the necessary food for intellectual and spiritual growth. But the books I choose to name belong to the class of personal preference, where each picks his own favorites and no two persons entirely agree. Such lists often include (as in this case) books differing very much in value. They may or may not have

[1] Watts wrote *Our* God; the word was changed by Wesley in 1738.

high rank in literature. There are even some, like olives, of little food value — mere ticklers of the palate. I hope that with this explanation and the profession of a catholic taste, no one will criticise me for putting *The Dolly Dialogues* and *Religio Medici* in close association.

Here is the list I offer.

I begin with a small book which I find excellent reading — Cavendish's *Life of Cardinal Wolsey*. This sample is for any unacquainted with it:

> The court being thus furnished and ordered, the judges commanded the crier to proclaim silence; then was the judges' commission, which they had of the pope, published and read openly before all the audience there assembled. That done, the crier called the king, by name of 'King Henry of England, come into the court etc.' With that the king answered and said, 'Here, my lords!' Then he called also the queen, by the name of 'Katherine Queen of England, come into the court, etc.'; who made no answer to the same, but rose up incontinent out of her chair, where as she sat, and because she could not come directly to the king for the distance which severed them, she took pain to go about unto the King, kneeling down at his feet in the sight of all the court and assembly, to whom she said in effect, in broken English, as followeth. . . .

My copy of the great Cardinal's portrait as drawn by his gentleman usher is of the lovely Chiswick Press edition by Singer. The collector must have the first edition of 1641, although of small value for reading as it is abridged and garbled.

Robert Bridges's *Poetical Works*. Lovely craftsmanship in poetry —

> There is a hill beside the silver Thames,
> Shady with birch and beech and odorous pine —

is beautiful verse. The solemn music of *Elegy on a lady* —

> Cloke her in ermine, for the night is cold,
> And wrap her warmly, for the night is long —

recalling Bishop King's *Exequy*, is beyond praise of mine.

Clio (afterwards published under the title *The Recreations of an Historian*) by George Macaulay Trevelyan, I like especially for the essay on *Walking*, but all of the papers in the book are good reading.

Pride and Prejudice. The Bennets, Mrs., Elizabeth, Kitty, Lydia, and the whole family, also Mr. Collins, the perfect ass, are immortal. Darcy, in Miss Austen's day, was not impossible.

Butler's *Analogy of Religion Natural and Revealed, to the Constitution and Course of Nature*, may look odd in a list of favorite books, but there are times when no other will take its place. My copy is in tree-calf without even a crease at the joints, bound by some unknown craftsman when calf was a leather fit for use on good books.

Stevenson's *An Inland Voyage.* 'The Oise in Flood' is a wonderful chapter — its air... clear and sweet among all these green fields; its shivering reeds... this lively and beautiful river... the old ashen rogue death and the neat homily following, on page 106... My copy of *An Inland Voyage* is of the second edition, quite satisfactory to read from, and much cheaper than the first! (Though a bad business suggestion for a bookseller to make, a good deal might be said for collecting *second* editions.)

Wordsworth's *Poems.* My *Wordsworth* is the pretty six-volume Moxon edition of 1841 in fresh, but slightly faded, plum-colored cloth; although why I or anyone not a scholar or a student should wish a complete Wordsworth, I do not know. Poems like *The Solitary Reaper*, the *Character of the Happy Warrior*, and *Laodameia* are a pure delight, but the merits of others — *The Fountain*, for example — puzzle me. I should like to page Matthew Arnold for their elucidation, although it is quite possible that the absurdities which disfigure *The Fountain*, as I read that poem, do not really exist.

Hudson's *A Traveller in Little Things.* W. H. Hudson is the author whose books have given me the greatest pleasure in recent years. Hudson attracts me by the harmony between his style and the things he writes about. Sympathy and insight might also be expected from one who could say of himself —

> Sky and cloud and wind and rain, and rock and soil and
> water, and flocks and herds and all wild things, with trees and

flowers — everywhere grass and everlasting verdure — it is all part of men, and is me, as I sometimes feel in a mystic mood, even as a religious man in a like mood feels that he is in a heavenly place and is a native there, one with it.

The only book of Hudson's that I have read and cannot speak of enthusiastically is *Green Mansions* (described by a friend as 'pure emotionalism').

Emily Dickinson's *Poems*. Miss Dickinson found the secret art of crystallizing carbon into diamonds; sound bookish sense, too, crops out of her verse —

> A precious, mouldering pleasure 'tis
>   To meet an antique book,
> In just the dress his century wore —

Moby Dick. If Herman Melville had not happened to be a mystic, I might not have cared for *Moby Dick* — but what would *Moby Dick* have been with the mysticism left out? My copy of this great book is of the edition fittingly and lavishly illustrated by Rockwell Kent.

Tuckwell's *Reminiscences of Oxford*, Dean Hole's *Memories*, and Le Fanu's *Seventy Years of Irish Life* — three books of amusing reminiscences and gossip. Tuckwell gives the full text of *The Masque of Balliol* — eighteen stanzas — the first of which is the well-known

> First I come: my name is *Jowett:*
> Whatever can be known I know it.
> I am the Master of the College:
> What I know not is not knowledge.

These are books which make dons and big-wigs human and supply the humor needed for intellectual salvation. Le Fanu's story of Archbishop Whately, his curates, and the mushrooms, is a good one.

Guy Mannering. It is hard to say which one of the Waverley Novels I like the best, for *The Heart of Midlothian*, *The Antiquary*, and *Redgauntlet* follow so close to *Guy Mannering* that I am at a loss in choosing. *Kenilworth*, for all its dramatic scenes, I place below those named. I find Scott most enjoyable in the old two- or

three-volume form; my *Guy Mannering* is that kind, though of
the fourth edition. It is badly printed, for Ballantine was not
even an indifferent typographer; yet the Abbotsford edition of
the Waverley Novels, for all its fine paper and grand illustrations, fails to give one the sense of nearness to the author which
we get from the original, cheaply made, octavo volumes.

Matthew Arnold's *Poems*. *The Forsaken Merman* and *The
Scholar-gypsy* (with its 'Dark bluebells drench'd with dews of
summer eves') are in the anthologies; is *Rugby Chapel* no longer
read? — or *Bacchanalia*, picturing *The New Age* of seventy-five
years ago —

> Carolling and shouting
> Over tombs, amid graves —
> See! on the cumber'd plain
> Clearing a stage,
> Scattering the past about,
> Comes the new age.
> Bards make new poems,
> Thinkers new schools,
> Statesmen new systems,
> Critics new rules....

Handley Cross. This, and the four other entertaining books [1] by
Surtees which should go with it, ought to be better known. The
characters are inimitably drawn, the robust, British humor is
delightful and wholesome. The plots, although slight, are
sufficient to keep one's interest, while Leech's woodcuts and
colored etchings are the finest illustrations in nineteenth-century
fiction.

Keats's *Poems*. I have half a dozen editions of Keats, each
desirable for some reason, but the little Moxon of 1851 is the
only one which is at all rare. My first reading of *Endymion* fifty-
two years ago *was* an experience!

Two Years in the French West Indies. To read a book written by
that curious man Lafcadio Hearn is like coming on a dark
muddy pool covered with fragrant lilies. What the writer of

---

[1] *Mr. Sponge's Sporting Tour, Mr. Facey Romford's Hounds, Ask Mamma*, and *'Plain
or Ringlets?'* All illustrated by John Leech.

Two Years was made of is an enigma, but it must have been something delicate and fine to produce such a treasure. I search for some half-dozen lines which will give a hint of the book's magic.

> *Les Porteuses* (unloading) —
> — And they mostly make answer, '*Toutt douce, chè, — et ou?*' (All sweetly, dear, — and thou?) But some, overweary, cry to him, '*Ah! déchâgé moin vite, chè! moin lasse, lasse!*' (Unload me quickly, dear; for I am very, very weary.) Then he takes off their burdens, and fetches bread for them, and says foolish little things to make them laugh. And they are pleased, and laugh, just like children, as they sit right down on the road there to munch their dry bread.

The Dolly Dialogues. Good for the t.b.m. As the book is small, add *The Old Flame* for good measure and a dash of sophistication.

De Quincey's *Confessions of an English Opium-Eater.* This I put high on my list particularly for episodes like that of the entertainment of the wandering student by the household of ingenuous young Welsh people; the pathos of Ann of Oxford Street, and the melancholy of De Quincey's early years. My copy is of the first edition, uncut, and with the advertising leaf, but, alas, rebound. (Mr. Brussel reminds us [1] that the edition published in Boston by Ticknor & Fields in 1850 is the first to contain the complete text of this book.)

Sir Thomas Browne's *Religio Medici.* To this add, of course, *Urn Burial.* The *Religio Medici,* when taken on my first trip abroad years ago, I found unreadable, yet the identical volume has since been my companion for thousands of miles — to London, Chicago, Moosehead Lake, and Florida. At home it is kept on my bedside stand.

Margaret Ogilvy. Sir J. M. Barrie's perfect tribute in the vein of true Barrie humor.

Meredith. *The Egoist.*

Borrow's *Wild Wales.* Most people would rate *Lavengro* and

[1] *Anglo-American First Editions, 1826–1900, East to West,* London and New York, 1935.

Romany Rye, or possibly *The Bible in Spain,* before this. I like them all, but *Wild Wales* is my first choice.

News from the Duchy by Sir Arthur T. Quiller-Couch. A collection of charming Cornish tales of which *Our Lady of Gwithian* is especially delightful.

Selections from Clarendon. Bits of a noble book; one really should have the whole *True Historical Narrative of the Rebellion.* Clarendon's characterization of Cromwell illustrates both the prejudice and the fine — almost paradoxical — discrimination of the author:

> He was one of those men, *quos vituperare ne inimici quidem possunt, nisi ut simul laudent;* for he never could have done half that mischief without great parts of courage, industry, and judgment. He must have had a wonderful understanding in the natures and humours of men, and as great a dexterity in applying them; who, from a private and obscure birth, (though of a good family,) without interest or estate, alliance or friendship, could raise himself to such a height, and compound and knead such opposite and contradictory tempers, humours, and interests into a consistence, that contributed to his designs, and to their own destruction; whilst himself grew insensibly powerful enough to cut off those by whom he had climbed, in the instant that they projected to demolish their own building. . . .
>
> Without doubt, no man with more wickedness ever attempted any thing, or brought to pass what he desired more wickedly, more in the face and contempt of religion, and moral honesty; yet wickedness as great as his could never have accomplished those trophies, without the assistance of a great spirit, an admirable circumspection and sagacity, and a magnanimous resolution.

The volume from which I quote has the autograph of Robert C. Winthrop, 1889, on the half-title; a most fitting association, for Winthrop was in his earlier years a Speaker of the national House of Representatives and long given to public affairs; he might well be called a gentleman of the old school, if gentility were of any period.

The Compleat Angler. No one aspires to all editions of one author without loving his book. Yet the satisfaction I find in meeting seven *thats* in one sentence after myself battling *which* through three hundred pages of manuscript would be keener if they were found in any other book than Walton's!

Whittier's *Poems* I like because I am a New Englander and find Whittier, in sentiment and description, the most New England of the New England poets —

> O gems of Sapphire, granite set!
> O hills that charmed horizons fret!
> I know how fair your morns can break,
> In rosy light on isle and lake;
> How over wooded slopes can run
> The noonday play of cloud and sun,
> And evening droop her oriflamme
> Of gold and red in still Asquam...

A Summer Pilgrimage is not great in either imagination or reflection, but it pictures the New England hill country as perfectly as the old daguerreotype did the dress of our grandmothers.

Grace Abounding to the Chief of Sinners by John Bunyan. My copy of *Grace Abounding* is a shabby, miserably printed Glasgow edition, doubtless one which brought spiritual comfort to the poorer Scottish folk nearly a century and a half ago. Few persons today who might have picked it up from a lot of book junk, as I did, would have thought it worth taking away. I have reserved it for special comment, as probably not one person out of five hundred has ever heard of the book and perhaps not one of a hundred thousand has read it. Yet it had great influence in its day and place, and for this reason, and also because of its literary value, I venture on a few short quotations.

(Bunyan's Vision)

... But the same day as I was in the midst of a game at cat, and having struck it one blow from the hole; Just as I was about to strike it the second time, a voice did suddenly dart from Heaven into my soul, which said, *Wilt thou leave thy sins and go to Heaven? or have thy sins and go to Hell?* At this I was put to an exceeding maze; wherefore, leaving my cat upon the ground, I looked up to Heaven and was as if I had with the eyes of my understanding, seen the Lord Jesus looking down upon me, as being very hotly displeased with me...

(People of God)

But upon a day, the good providence of God did cast me to Bedford, to work on my calling and in one of the streets of that town I came where there were three or four poor women sitting at a door in the sun, talking about the things of God. ...

(Meditates on Persecution)

But notwithstanding these helps, I found myself a man, and compassed with infirmities; the parting with my wife and poor children, hath often been to me in this place as the pulling the flesh from my bones; and that not only because I am somewhat too fond of these great mercies but also because I should have often brought to mind, the many hardships, miseries and wants, that my poor family was like to meet with should I be taken from them, *especially my poor blind child*, who lay nearer to my heart than all I had besides: O the thoughts of the hardship I thought this child might go under, would break my heart to pieces.

Poor child! thought I, what sorrow art thou like to have for thy portion in this world? Thou must be beaten, must beg, suffer hunger, cold, nakedness, and a thousand calamities, tho' I cannot now endure the wind should blow upon thee: but yet recalling myself, thought I, I must venture you all with God though it goeth to the quick to leave you ...

I do not know how this writing may strike others, but to me, the artless sincerity of Bunyan's narrative entitles it to a high place in religious biography. Bunyan's spiritual experience was of a different kind from that met with today, but it was vital, and out of it came *The Pilgrim's Progress*. *Grace Abounding* has its place in the hierarchy of spiritual autobiography whereof Augustine, Saint Theresa, Madame Guyon, George Fox, John Wesley, and John Woolman are bright stars.

Considering that piety is not a characteristic of our time, the output of religious literature, or perhaps it is more correct to say of the literature of religion, of our day has a singular vitality; yet a great part of it seems to me futile. However others may interpret this, the gist of my belief in the matter is found in a sentence which Sir Arthur Helps wrote many years ago.

You cannot hope for anything like contentment so long as you continue to attach that ridiculous degree of importance to the events of this life which so many people are inclined to do.

I would go even further. That the social aspects of the Gospel teachings have been too long neglected is generally admitted. But, while agreeing that efforts to carry out these principles are proper objectives, I believe that the Protestant Church will lose an essential principle of religion if it follows its present trend of preoccupation with man's material well-being. I think that there are many who, whatever philosophical or theological views they may hold, will agree that we might infer from the attitude of not a few influential church oracles of the day that human personality dies with the body.

This is not my conception of the future. Having reached the age of seventy, and being conscious that it is impossible for reason to decide the momentous question of immortality, I view the prospect of life after physical death with confidence. With the image which appalls us in Marvell's haunting lines —

> But at my back I always hear
> Time's wingèd chariot hurrying near,
> And yonder all before us lie
> Deserts of vast eternity —

I contrast Arnold's call from *Rugby Chapel* —

> On, to the bound of the waste,
> On, to the City of God.

THE END

INDEX

Hoe Library, 103
Hoffses, Miss, 3
Holden, Edwin B., 39
Hole, Dean Samuel R., 299
Holinshead's *Chronicles*, 33
Hollingsworth, Amor L., 22
Hollingsworth, Sumner R., 22
Hollingsworth, Zachary T., 22, 39, 43, 44, 224
Hollis Street Church, Boston, 178
Hollis Street Theatre, Boston, 7
Holman, Louis A., 126, 160; *Graphic Processes*, 160
Holmes, Sir Charles J., 275 *n.*
Holmes, Oliver Wendell, 27, 139, 235, 294; bibliography by Ives, 174; hymn, 294; *Professor at the Breakfast Table*, 294
Holmes, Justice Oliver Wendell, 172; collection in Library of Congress, 82
Holy Bible in Verse, The (Harris), 68–70, 102
Homer, Louise, 137
Hooper family, 11
Hope, Sir Anthony, 297, 301
Hopson, W. F., 118
Hornby, Lester G., 136
Houdini, Harry, 137; collection in Library of Congress, 82
Houghton Mifflin Co., 141, 282 *n.*
Housman, A. E., 94
Howard family, 2
Howe, Gen. Sir William, 187, 188, 190, 191 *n.*
Howells, W. D., 91, 134
Hoyle, Edmond, 288
Hudson, W. H., 298–299
Human Tragedy, The (Austin), 96
Hunnewell, James F., 22
Hunt, Dr. David, 22
Hunt, Leigh, 67 *n.*
Huntington, Henry E., 103, 199; library and art gallery, 83 *n.*, 148
Huntington, Samuel, 189
Hurst, Bishop John F., 28, 55, 56
Hutchinson, Gov. Thomas, 103, 188
Hyannis, Mass., 9
Hymnology, 291–296

I know not what the future hath … (Whittier), 294

I love thy kingdom, Lord (Dwight), 294
Iconography of Manhattan Island, The (Stokes), 120
Idle Flowers, The (Bridges), 284
Immortal love, forever full (Whittier), 294
Impartial History of the War in America, An, 164–165
In the cross of Christ I glory (Bowring), 296
In the Dawn of the World (Burne-Jones), 159
Inland Voyage, An (Stevenson), 298
Innocents Abroad (Clemens), 96
Insanity, 230–232
Iolaüs (Carpenter), 158
Ireland, William Henry, 244–245, 246, 254–255; *Confessions*, 245 *n.*, 254
Irving, Washington, 232
It came upon the midnight clear (Sears), 294
Ives, George B., 135; *Holmes*, 174

Jackson, Herbert I., 124
Jacob, 44
James, G. P. R., 228
Jameson, Anna B., 228
Jeeves, 57
Jeffers, Robinson, 94
Jeffrey, Lord Francis, 228
Jenkins, Lawrence W., 99–100
Jewett, Sarah Orne, 133
Joan of Arc (Shaw), 66
Johnson, Esther, 'Stella,' 181
Johnson, Samuel, 24, 28, 116, 150, 151; *Dictionary*, 24; *Life* by Boswell, 116
Johnson, Gen. Sir William, 113, 188
Johnston, Thomas, 39; *View of Yale College*, 122
Joline, Adrian H., 215
Jones, Herschel V., 204
Josephus, 37
Josselyn, John, 285–286
Jungle Book, The (Kipling), 91, 92

Kalbfleish, Charles H., 103
Kane, Dr. E. K., 179
Kane, Grenville, 39
Keats, John, 13, 86, 138, 300; *Endymion*, 13, 86, 171, 300; *Ode to Autumn*, 138; autograph forged, 247; *Poems*, 300
Kellogg, Rev. Elijah, 12, 13 *n.*

INDEX

McCance, Andrew, 22, 29–30, 59–60, 175–177
McGill University, 146
McGuffey's schoolbooks, 179
McKee, Thomas J., 199
Melbourne, Lord, 228
Mellon, Andrew W., collection in Library of Congress, 82
Melville, Herman, 299
Memorial R. G. S., 89
Memories (Hole), 299
Men, Women, and Books (Hunt), 67 *n.*
Mendoza, Isaac, 17, 18
Mere Literature (Wilson), 90
Meredith, George, 301
Meredith, Owen, 98
Merritt, E. P., 151–152
Merritt, E. P., Mrs., 152
Merrymount, Quincy, Mass., 76
Merrymount Press, 141, 159, 160, 161
Metropolitan Museum of Art, 117
Mikado, The (Gilbert & Sullivan), 7
Miles, Maj.-Gen. Nelson A., 133
Mill, John Stuart, 57, 228; *Autobiography*, 57
Miller, J. DeWitt, 28
Miller, Joaquin, 91, 166; *Pacific Tales*, 166
Milton, John, 296; poem on by Blake, 148, 149
Mineral collections, 12, 269–270
Mitchell, E. P., 97
Mitchell, James T., 39, 40; sale, 164
Mitford, Mary Russell, 228
Moby-Dick (Melville), 299
Modern Painters (Ruskin), 26, 261, 262–263, 264
Monaghan, Ireland, 53
Moore, George, 94, 159
Moore, Julia A., 95, 97
Moore, T. M., 111–112
Moore, Thomas, 167, 228
Moosehead Lake, Maine, 274
Morgan, J. P., 140, 178, 204; library, 204, 216
Morley, Christopher, 134
Morris, Clara, 91
Morse family, 11
Morse, George D., 31, 32

Morton, Nathaniel, 221
Morton, Thomas, 76
Morton, Dr. William T., 79, 145
Mount Wachusett, 115, 281
Moxon, Edward, 298, 300
Mr. Facey Romford's Hounds (Surtees), 300 *n.*
Mr. Sponge's Sporting Tour (Surtees), 300 *n.*
Muir, P. H., 174
Mulliken, Jonathan, 108
Murders in the Rue Morgue, The (Poe), 197
Murdock, Harold, 150–151
Murphy, Michael, 29–30
Museum of Fine Arts, Boston, 38
Mystery of Golf, The (Haultain), 289

Napoleon Bonaparte, 228
'Napoleonic Memoirs,' 26, 183
Narrative of the Expedition of an American Squadron to the China Seas and Japan (Perry), 153
Nash, Nathaniel C., 143
National Reader, The (Pierpont, ed.), 178
National Songster, 293 *n.*
Nature (Emerson), 80
Nauvoo, Ill., Mormon Temple at, 129
Needham, Mass., 3
Newell, W. W., 176
New England Historic-Genealogical Society, 35; *Register*, 32
New England Primer, 55, 69, 70, 71
New England's Memoriall (Morton), 221
New-Englands Rarities Discovered (Josselyn), 1672, 285; 1865, 286
New English Canaan, The (Morton), 76–77
New System of Husbandry, A (Varlo), 78
Newton Centre, Mass., 5
New York [Burgis view of], 114, 115
New York as Washington knew it . . . (Andrews), 259
New York Mirror, 223
New York Public Library, 81, 83 *n.*, 103, 115, 257, 293; *Bulletin*, 241, 257
News from the Duchy (Quiller-Couch), 302
Newton, A. E., 161
Niewe herball or historie of plantes, A (Dodoen), 285
Norman, John, 39, 42, 123; portraits of

Rittenhouse, David [engraving of], 116
River Dove, The (Anderdon), 279–280
Rivière, Robert & Son, 26, 244
Rivington, James, 191
Robinson, A. Mary Frances, 79–80
Robinson, Beverley, 191
Robinson Crusoe (Defoe), 24
Rochambeau, Comte de, 188, 190
Rockhill, W. W., collection in Library
of Congress, 82
Roden, R. F., 102
Rogers, Bruce, 134, 141, 158, 161
Rogers, Col. Robert, 188
Rogers, Samuel, 228
Romans, Bernard, 39, 112, 114; *Battle
of Bunker Hill*, 112, 114, 115
Romany Rye (Borrow), 302
Romeo and Juliet (Shakespeare), 7
Romney, George, 268
Roosevelt, F. D., 138
Roosevelt, Theodore [engraving by
Smith], 122
Root, Elihu, 225
Rosenbach, A. S. W., 110
Rowlandson, Thomas, 252–253
Ruddigore (Gilbert & Sullivan), 7
Rugby Chapel (Arnold), 300, 305
Rush, Dr. Benjamin [engraving of], 116
Ruskin, John, 13, 14, 19, 20, 26, 77, 141,
260, 261–271; *Seven Lamps of Architec-
ture*, 14, 26, 262, 264; *Modern Painters*,
261, 262–263, 264; *Sesame and Lilies*,
261; *Stones of Venice*, 262, 264, 268;
Deucalion, 264; *King of the Golden River*,
264, 267, 269; *Poems*, 263, 264; *Præ-
terita*, 264, 265, 267, 269; *Proserpina*,
264; *War*, 264; *Ethics of the Dust*, 265;
'Early Geology,' 267; 'Essay on
painting and music,' 267; *Fors
Clavigera*, 267, 269; *Creed of St. George*,
269
Ruskiniana (Wedderburn), 264

Sabin, Joseph, 108 *n.*
Sabin, Joseph F., 40, 192, 249
Sadleir, Michael, 174
Sage, Dean, 142
Saint Charles College, 20
Saint-Gaudens, Augustus, 89 *n.*

Saint-Mémin, C. B. J. F. de, 130
Saint Peter's Church, Salem, Mass.,
100
Salaman, Malcolm, quoted, 106
Salisbury, Earl of, 228
Sally Brass, 13
Salmagundi quoted, 156
Salmon, Robert, 241
Sanborn, Frank B., 81, 139–141, 154;
Personality of Thoreau, 141
Sand, George, 47
Sanford, P. B., 261
Sangorski [bookbinder], 214
Sartor Resartus (Carlyle), 29
Saturday Evening Post, The, 201, 269
Savage, Edward, 39 *n.*, 115–116
Savannah, Ga., 288
Schiff, Jacob H., collection in Library
of Congress, 82
Schiller forgeries, 247
Scholar-gypsy, The (Arnold), 300
School books, 177–179
Schreiber, Carl F., 247; collection in
Library of Congress, 82
Scott, Sir Walter, 13, 26, 60, 167, 299;
Waverley Novels, 13, 299, 300; *Marmion*,
167; autograph forged, 247; *Anti-
quary*, 299; *Heart of Midlothian*, 299;
Kenilworth, 299; *Redgauntlet*, 299; *Guy
Mannering*, 299–300
Sears, Rev. Edmund H., 294
Seasons, The (Thomson), 276
Sedgwick, Ellery, 269 *n.*
*Sentimental Journey through France and
Italy, A* (Sterne), 24
Sesame and Lilies (Ruskin), 261
Seven Lamps of Architecture, The (Ruskin),
14, 26, 262, 264
Seventy Years of Irish Life (Le Fanu), 299
Severn, J. Arthur P., 266, 267, 268, 271
Severn, J. Arthur P., Mrs., 141, 266
Sewell, Alfred L., 113
Shady Hill, Cambridge, Mass., 142
Shakespeare, William, 20, 231, 296:
Hamlet quoted, xiv; folios, 2, 244;
Romeo & Juliet, 7; *Twelfth Night*
quoted, 212; autographs forged, 244–
247, 254, 255
Shattuck, Dr. F. C., 145